AVOIDING
CRITICAL MARKETING
ERRORS

HOW TO GO
FROM DUMB
TO
SMART
MARKETING

RICHARD D. CZERNIAWSKI

CO-AUTHOR OF CREATING BRAND LOYALTY AND COMPETITIVE POSITIONING

Library of Congress Cataloging-in-Publication Data

Czerniawski, Richard D.
    AVOIDING CRITICAL MARKETING ERRORS: How to Go from Dumb to Smart Marketing/ Richard D. Czerniawski

Includes index.

Library of Congress Control Number:2019910961

ISBN: 978-1-7332608-0-0 Paperback
ISBN: 978-1-7332608-1-7 Hardcover
ISBN: 978-1-7332608-2-4 E-book

Brand Development Network *International*

PRAISE FOR AVOIDING CRITICAL MARKETING ERRORS:

HOW TO GO FROM DUMB TO SMART MARKETING

Richard is at the very top of the list when it comes to people who can help someone understand how to be a great marketer. He has the best insights of anyone I have ever met on what it takes to prepare your brand or business to be highly competitive. Pay attention to what he says, and challenge yourself to follow through on it, and your business will perform. So, be smart and study what he has to say. You will be all the better for it—I know it has helped me tremendously!

Kurt Kane,
EVP Chief Concept & Marketing Officer, The Wendy's Company

Richard is the godfather of marketing excellence. Having worked alongside him for clients like Bristol-Myers Squibb and J&J, I have seen firsthand how he can transform a room, contest an undifferentiated brand strategy, or super-charge a mediocre creative campaign. In AVOIDING CRITICAL MARKETING ERRORS: How to Go from Dumb to Smart Marketing, Richard courageously exposes the unfettered truth about ill-advised strategies, missed targeting and mundane creative campaigns, among other marketing errors. Yet, he does so with the irresistible charm and wit of a generous mentor. This book will make you laugh at outrageous gaffes, wince in recognition of your own mistakes, learn how to avoid marketing traps, and most importantly, put your brand on a bullet train headed straight for brand loyalty.

Robin Shapiro,
Global President, TBWA/WORLDHEALTH

Every business needs smarter businesspeople if it is to drive growth profitably in the absolute and versus competition. Marketers need to acknowledge and accept responsibility for the competitive and economic implications of their performance on the ultimate success of the company and their brand. Richard Czerniawski's book AVOIDING CRITICAL MARKETING ERRORS: How to Go from Dumb to Smart Marketing is the de facto tool for all marketers to get smart(er) so they may elevate their business impact! This book contains extremely practical guidance from a master practitioner in the field of marketing excellence.

Ben Cook,
President, Acumen Learning

There are good books, better ones and delighters. In this delighter, Richard reminds us vividly that marketing, now more than ever, has a critical role to play to generate impact and lasting results. From covering the fundamentals, to challenging our views and evolving our thinking, it sheds laser light on the marketing reality we face every day. Avoiding those critical mistakes is not only about gaining an edge; it is about the survival and growth of marketing, which you will experience by reading further!

Didier Devaud,
Vice President Global Marketing and Education iTero, Align Technology

Richard Czerniawski continues to challenge our way of thinking and address common misperceptions about marketing and the value marketers can add to organizations in this smart book. Smart marketing is smart business. Richard pushes us to take a much more disciplined approach in terms of how we practice marketing. He identifies those all-too-frequently-committed critical marketing errors. Importantly, he shares universal principles and best practices that all organizations should adopt and implement to make their marketing activities link directly to business objectives and results. Now, everyone can do smart marketing.

Rafael Chan,
Chief Commercial Officer, New World Medical, Inc.

Richard Czerniawski's book is a must-read for marketers and senior leaders alike. He sagely makes the case that marketing is underutilized as a revenue growth driver due to narrow thinking and critical marketing errors of omission and commission. As a senior leader, who has driven several major marketing-centric business transformations, I can attest that Richard's focus on genuine marketing excellence delivers the incremental sales impact, ROI and accountability that everyone in the organization should demand. Now you can demand and achieve more from your marketing with this smart book.

Peter Valenti,
Division President, Hologic, Inc.

Businesses face extreme pressures for growth today due to fierce competition and extra-ordinary focus on the short-term. Sadly, marketing, which has the potential to make a crucial difference, is not fully appreciated. At times, marketing is driven by unenlightened leadership, poorly trained marketers, or tactical thinking. Marketers can err in not doing the right things; or in doing the right things but not in the most effective way to drive sales. Richard Czerniawski shares practical advice on avoiding critical marketing errors. And, importantly, he identifies what marketers should do and how to do it correctly to actually grow brands, even in the face of today's intense competition.

Bill Weintraub,
Professor at the University of Colorado, previously Chief Marketing Officer at
Kellogg Company, Tropicana, Coors Brewing Company

Richard Czerniawski surgically cuts to the bone in his diagnosis of why and where your marketing is failing to stay relevant today. While we are inundated with more data and tools, marketers overlook doing critically important things and/or do them incorrectly. Warren Buffet, 3G Capital and zero-based budgeting demand more accountability, and we need to rise to that challenge to remain relevant. Richard shows you how to restore marketing relevance by 'avoiding critical marketing errors' and adopting smart marketing.

David M. Bryla,
Chief Executive Officer, WasteZone

Richard Czerniawski challenges marketing mindsets and practices to reveal critical marketing errors that snatch defeat from the jaws of victory in creating winning brands. This is a no-nonsense book with practical advice and plenty of examples on doing smart marketing from a successful, veteran marketer. Richard reveals proven principles, best practices and quality processes that will benefit all marketers, regardless of experience level or sector, on making your marketing matter more.

Santosh Chaturvedi,
VP, New Products Planning & Portfolio Strategy, Global Oncology, EMD Serono

A century and a half ago, John Wanamaker, founder of the department store in Philadelphia bearing his name, famously said, "Half the money I spend on advertising is wasted; the trouble is, I don't know which half." This wasted half is dumb marketing, and it goes beyond advertising. Richard Czerniawski identifies what is dumb and why, and he shares insights into how we can avoid or fix these mistakes and, importantly, how to embrace "smart," regardless of business sector or category. AVOIDING CRITICAL MARKETING ERRORS is a must-read for any professional responsible for getting the most out of their marketing budget and delivering line-of-sight sales to strategies and initiatives essential to accelerating growth in today's competitive marketplace.

Tom Hayden,
Lecturer, Department of Integrated Marketing Communications, Northwestern
University, formerly Executive Vice President and Director, Bozell Worldwide

In this matchless book, Richard Czerniawski draws on his nearly 50 years of experience transforming marketing for leading global brands, and he pinpoints why so many marketers fail to get it right. His generous insights will raise the courageous marketer to a new level of skill and, more importantly, results. This book is a dream come true for the marketer who's ready to have an honest, critical look at how they do things and to take concrete steps to refine and improve their marketing abilities. Any smart marketer should read this book—fast.

Gilberto Dalesio,
Chief Commercial Officer, SIFI

Richard Czerniawski is a master marketer who leverages his significant experience and expertise to drive home what not to do and skillfully pinpoints what to do to make your marketing matter more. AVOIDING CRITICAL MARKETING ERRORS is a captivating, thought provoking and insightful guide to marketing effectively in today's changing marketplace. Experienced or not, this book will sharpen your saw and propel your ability to deliver results.

Lisa Tollman,
Executive Director, Amgen

This book is a must-read for those marketers who are truly committed to making a measurable and meaningful impact on their business. The lessons Richard Czerniawski shares from his vast experience spanning industries and geographies are universal, so you'll feel he's talking just to you. More importantly, applying the know-how found within its pages will empower you to drive incremental business growth to demonstrate marketing's and your value to the organization. Read this book to take on a more significant role in marketing your brand!

Nikki Sidi,
Vice President, Global Strategic Marketing, Johnson & Johnson Vision

DEDICATION

To my wife, June, who has stood by me and encouraged me for some 50 years and still counting, despite my preoccupation with all things marketing and serving clients with frequent trips away from home.

To my daughters, Katie, Christina and Melissa, whose lofty opinion of me sets a high standard that is always out of reach but I'm forever climbing to achieve.

To my sons-in-law, Gad, Geoff and Cliff, for loving my daughters and gifting (along with my daughters who did and do the hard part of birthing and rearing) June and me with four precious granddaughters.

For my granddaughters, Eila, Zoe, Luna and Ivy, for delighting all of us in our family and filling me with hope of an even brighter future for this world.

For my parents, Mary and Faustine Czerniawski, and brothers Faustine and Walter and sister Jennifer (and their spouses). We are one family, one love.

ACKNOWLEDGMENTS

*But it is not true that I am self-made. Like everyone, to get to where I am,
I stood on the shoulders of giants. My life was built on a foundation of
parents, coaches, and teachers; of kind souls who lent couches or gym back
rooms where I could sleep; of mentors who shared wisdom and advice; of
idols who motivated me from the pages of magazines
(and, as my life grew, from personal interaction).*
Arnold Schwarzenegger

I love the quote from Mr. Schwarzenegger. Here's a person who is larger than life, beyond the bulging muscles, and not just on-screen in action-packed movies but in his real life. He's lived large in his accomplishments and, I feel certain, in his mistakes. But I think he has it right with what he's said about not being self-made. Despite his dreams, drive and hard work, he refuses to accept the compliment that he is "self-made." Regardless of what you think of Arnold Schwarzenegger, I say, in this case, "Bravo Mr. Schwarzenegger. You have it right."

Usually, acknowledgements are reserved for the back of a book. But, I feel, as Mr. Schwarzenegger does, that I cannot take full credit for what appears on these pages, no matter what credit you may bestow (if any) on me. I might like to, but it would be false. There are really many whom I am compelled to acknowledge who continue to this day to lift me in my career and personal development—far too many to mention. I want to acknowledge some of these wonderful, talented and supportive people before we begin our journey together. Up front is where they belong. Up front is what I want to be with you on this matter and throughout this book.

First, I'd like to acknowledgement my business partner of the last 25 years and counting, Mike Maloney. I hired Mike from my alma mater, Procter &

Gamble (P&G), to work at Coca-Cola USA. This was back in 1980, so we've been colleagues and the best of friends for nearly 40 years. When I started Brand Development Network *International* in 1985, Mike hired me as a consultant. He was my first client. At the time, he was Director of Marketing at Tropicana Foods, Inc. Mike has been an outstanding partner, and Brand Development Network *International* would not have achieved the level and quality of success it has enjoyed without him. Mike has been a stalwart contributor and the yin to my yang in managing projects and clients. Together, we are co-authors of two books: *CREATING BRAND LOYALTY: The Management of Power Positioning and Really Great Advertising*, and *COMPETITIVE POSITIONING: Best Practices for Creating Brand Loyalty*. Additionally, we've shared the work in writing hundreds of articles for our blog, *DISPATCHES: Insights from the Marketing Front*. While I might use the pronoun "I" throughout the book, I really believe much of the learning, concepts and ideas in this book may be attributed to "we!" Thank you, Mike. Here's to many more years working together.

Second, I need to acknowledge the bosses, colleagues and friends from the stellar enterprises I've been fortunate to have served. This includes P&G, where I learned the science of marketing; Johnson & Johnson (J&J), where I learned business management; Richardson-Vicks (acquired by P&G), where I learned the sad tale of politics but, admittedly, had many of the values of P&G related to advertising reinforced there; and Coca-Cola USA, where I learned about the importance of managing alternate constituencies. I didn't fall off a pumpkin truck. I learned much from working within these organizations and the outstanding, disciplined talent within each of them.

I can call to mind the direct and indirect learning from people such as Ed Lotspeich at P&G, whose missives shared proven principles. Mike and I often reflect on and discuss these principles as they are as relevant today as they were then, across business sectors and geographies. Then, there is Jim Burke, the late great chairman at J&J, who was a true marketer and driver of the Johnson & Johnson Credo—a code of conduct for that great company. There is Peter Larson and Bob Townsend, also of J&J. Peter was the single-most talented judge of talent and an impressive team leader. Despite taking the "two-by-four" to me many times, he would work to ensure we were on the same page as it related to objectives and strategies and then let me go about my business to execute against them. He was the one manager who when promoted, grew to fulfill that new level as opposed to manage from the previous one.

I can't forget Bob Townsend. He used to come into my office every morning and let me know that he expected me to do great things on that day. He'd say, "Czerniawski, I don't care what you did for me yesterday. I want to know what you are going to do for me today." Then there is Brian Dyson and Sergio Zyman at Coca-Cola USA. Brian was the ultimate master of strategy. He would invite managers to play devil's advocate to a given strategy (often times his own) and listened to their points-of-view. In fact, he would even play devil's advocate to his own thinking. He helped me understand the big picture and the give-and-take needed to achieve it. Sergio Zyman is a creative genius. He is a reminder that marketing is not just a science, but an art. He brought art to marketing in everything he did. If we can marry art to the science, we can create magic. Henry Burdick, of client companies Pharmavite and Pharmanex, a mega, serial-entrepreneur, unleashed my entrepreneurial spirit and drive to be a co-creator and collaborator with the best minds.

There are many, many others too numerous to mention. I like to think of us all as a link in a chain. My marketing chain consists of all those people I've worked with throughout the years, at all levels, from all disciplines, sectors, categories and countries in which I've been privileged to work. Unfortunately, many are no longer with us in the world of marketing or, for that matter, in this world. (What do you expect? I've been a career marketer for more than 45 years.)

I also pay tribute to those agency team members, who while they might not remember me, I remember them for their keen insights and outstanding talent, such as the late, great Frankie Cadwell and Herm Davis (who hold a special place in my heart), Tony Chevas, Bob Jordan, Ed Wax, Andy Langer, Hank Seiden, Phil Dusenberry and currently Robin Shapiro. Some of these folks are deservedly legends. Little might the marketers and agency people, mentioned and not mentioned, in my chain, know how they've impacted my thinking and career. (I'd like to think it would bring a smile to their faces.)

Third, I acknowledge our outstanding clients. (Most client companies do not want to be acknowledged by name.) While Mike and I have worked with many companies, across numerous sectors, throughout the world, it's the people I've had the privilege to serve at those companies who have contributed in a big way to my continued learning and development. It's truly amazing that while they've hired us to assist in developing and growing their brands and marketers, they've trained us in their businesses. They have enabled me to dig deeper, peeling the proverbial onion, to plumb the depths of the science and art of marketing, and to uncover universal principles, best practices and quality processes. Many are not merely clients, but they have become good friends who continue to share their deep wisdom regarding marketing and life.

Fourth, I'd be amiss not to acknowledge those who have served BDNI over the years. This includes Bill Atchinson (my second client and business partner), Director of Operations Lori Vandervoort (who was really our major domo and made our operations run smoothly, regardless of where in the world we were working), Sherry Greve-Engelman, Dave Roche, Rod McNealy, Brenda Bence and Lisa Rhodes. The latter three were former clients, served as BDNI colleagues, and remain dear friends. Special shout out to Krysten Peppmeier for developing the BDNI website and all digital materials in support of this book. I tip my hat to each and every one of you.

Importantly, I want to acknowledge you, the reader of this book. In no way do I believe you are dumb! Some of your behaviors may not be smart, but you are not dumb. I borrowed this word "dumb" from a quote by Charlie Munger, Warren Buffet's partner, a fount of experience and wisdom. Mr. Munger perceived being dumb as engaging in those things that undermine success. So, doing dumb is making errors that sabotage our ability to make our marketing matter. Also, I use the word "dumb" to be provocative. I do believe that if you put what you learn from this book into practice, and make it your own, you are capable of making your marketing matter more.

Finally, my record, while outstanding, is not perfect. I can step back and acknowledge where I was dumb but learned to do smart from my experiences and from the help of others. And, by the way, I'm still learning and proud to admit it!

PROLOGUE

WHERE/WHY MARKETING DOESN'T MATTER

Once upon a time, there was a land where marketing didn't matter. Oh, managers said it mattered, and they went about their business as if it mattered, but it really didn't matter. What went on in this land where marketing didn't matter?

Successful sales managers were promoted into marketing. Yes, this was their ticket for future promotions in sales and general management. They had to do their tour and get their ticket punched, so they could return to sales, earn a promotion, get a fresh new car, be recognized and, importantly, receive BIG $$$ bonuses.

No, these sales managers did not start at the bottom of marketing to learn the business. Why should they? They had successful sales careers going for them with significant achievements in their field. They were thrown into the kitchen and given the title of "chef" despite the fact that they had not cooked a meal; they had merely served and eaten them. Instead, they were expected to be successful in their new role because they liked to eat and had been doing so since birth. So, they moved into marketing at the product manager level (in this land, they don't appreciate the difference between "brands" and mere "products") or higher. Yes, higher, and they were expected to make a profound impact on the business. The way to make that impact was to support the sales force.

In this land, these new marketers from sales could expect to learn from their bosses. Their bosses were among the anointed. How do we know? Well, they also came from sales and had a couple of years' experience working in the marketing function, so they knew how things worked. Everyone thought so, particularly senior management, who not only supported but promoted this arrangement. What could be so difficult about marketing? Secure KOLs (key opinion leaders), develop consumer advertising, run medical congresses, develop CME (continuing medical education), develop consumer and trade promotions, create viz-aids, gain access or retail distribution—many of the kinds of things they were familiar with from working in sales. And, perhaps, most important, they gave the sales force what they needed. Why on this earth, in this land, would there ever be a need for "professional" or "career" marketers?

According to them, their products were the best, highest quality. Any customer should understand and respect this fact. Yes, products from others were significantly less costly, and more and more customers were buying from these others, but that is because these customers did not know better. They were obviously being fooled by inferior quality. This land knew this to be true. No, not because they had clinically proven, better outcomes or clear customer preferences, but because *they just knew it to be true.* Everyone in this land knew it to be true and made it his mantra: *Our products are the best, highest quality. You should buy them.*

In this land, all customers were treated equally. No, not equally well, but they were treated equally, as in homogeneous. There was no such thing as segments of customers with different needs and values. No, if there was any segmentation, it was, naturally, sales segmentation. You know, segmentation based upon volume. This meant, of course, that there were top deciles and A accounts. Segmentation was established based upon the relationship between the specific customer and salesperson, as in "our daughters play in the same soccer league."

This is the land where marketing doesn't matter. What does matter are sales and finance. Nothing matters more than today's bottom line, and in this land, they will take any path to get there. In fact, they depend upon the sales force to get them there. Operations will do its part. They'll source the cheapest materials and find new ways to slash operating costs. Finance will tumble the numbers and senior managers will cut marketing resources and heads (they call this being "displaced"). Product R&D will concoct the flavor-of-the-month because customers like anything that is "new." It's okay because regardless of what they do, they just know they have the best, highest quality products.

Customers know these products. They know them because they do the same things, and work in the same ways, as all the other products they use in the same category. And, in the hands of an intermediary, such as a craftsperson (e.g., a surgeon), any product differences are washed away. In this land, customer selection has been built upon the relationship with the salesperson. However, this has been changing rapidly. For one, customers are less interested in spending time to meet with sales personnel. They're just too busy, and what the salesperson has to say is just not as important as it once was when everything was so new and real differences existed. For another, the decision makers may not be the end users of the products, and perceiving all of the products to be similar, if not the same, they seek to commoditize the market.

These marketers know what it takes to win, so they say. They will launch their flavor-of-the-month before their competitors. This is their contribution and path to leadership in their categories. In many instances, they'll launch before their infrastructure is in place to even support (and sell) these products. Sure, there will be some snafus along the way, but they "gotta do what they gotta do" to meet Wall Street's demand to feed its insatiable appetite for increasing revenues and driving stock prices higher. This makes alienating the customer, while certainly not preferable, acceptable in this land, particularly since they have the best, highest quality products and feel that, therefore, customers have to return to purchase from them no matter what. "What's good for General Motors is good for the country." What's good for them is good for their customers.

Additionally, deep price discounting, tenders and regulations are growing in significance, casting a pall on everything. Competitors claim "same as the leader but cheaper," making it all about price. Tenders are where different companies bid for the business. It, too, is a price game—one that is believed can be appeased with skillful negotiation or legacy. The only way to win in this land, given this situation, is to cut costs and redouble the sales effort. Therefore, marketing's role is emphasized as supporting the sales force. Who could better handle that role than (former) successful sales personnel? Regulations are a thorn. They interfere with the sales manager's ability to interface with, and win over, customers. Too bad! But what are they going to do? In this land, they are going to focus on this year, this quarter, this month, this week, this day, this hour.

How will marketing assist the sales force? Doing what they've always done. Start with the business objectives of sales, market share and profit that are handed down to them. Next, go directly to the tactics these marketers (or their predecessors) employed in preceding years. How many congresses did they participate in last year? How many promotion periods did they push? Okay, they'll do one more. Don't have the resources? Okay, they'll vow to do what they did last year, only "better" this time around. What exactly does it mean "to do better?" How do they know if they are doing "better?" It doesn't matter. They know they have the best, highest quality products.

In this land, senior management will let marketers know if they are doing their job correctly. How? I'm still trying to figure out this one, and I'm not alone. Forgive me, because I am not from this land. This is a land where there is no market testing of any kind. There is limited or inconsequential marketing research, non-existent or incomplete data on market share and key performance indicators, no adaptive experiments in the marketplace. In this land, all of that is considered to be "non-working" funds. And, non-working funds must be cut to the bone so the organization can achieve its bottom line. ROI (return on investment)? It's irrelevant because there is no way, time, energy, or resources to measure it. Besides in this land, they know their business, and what they've always done is what everyone does, so it has to be correct.

Marketing planning is no more than a launch event with a big party. When the party is over, marketers begin to plan for the next launch and party. If we don't get it right the first time, then it's high time to move on to something else. Marketing plans are business plans. They buoy management with a false sense of confidence that the planned business objectives of sales, market share and profit can be achieved. There is no dialogue regarding behavior objectives and their relationship to business objectives, key marketing objectives, SMART objectives for marketing mix elements and tactics, etc.

In this land, all senior management wants to be told, and can hear, is that you can make the numbers you've been given. How do they know? They just know. It's important for them to know. So, everyone's marketing plan is unique in terms of what elements are addressed and how they are addressed, complete with different formats, nomenclature, etc. If senior management were really involved in understanding and addressing these plans, rather than texting and emailing during marketing planning presentations, they would find them quite bewildering.

Curiously, more than three-quarters of senior managers do not think that marketing impacts sales. They've got that correct because they have done nothing to organize or prepare marketing to have an impact. They would not know how to do it because they do not understand marketing, perceiving its role as sales force support and/or project management. I call this "small 'm' marketing." Unfortunately, it is dumb marketing underscored by costly mistakes of omission and commission.

Yes, they say, "marketing is important." In fact, they initiate marketing training programs under the umbrella of "marketing excellence." They pull together committees of like-minded managers with limited professional marketing experience and give them the title of SMEs (subject matter experts) who undertake a study of needed competencies. They identify scores of competencies that each marketer must achieve and demonstrate. These competencies change more frequently than presidential elections in the US. They are not bound to specific, critically important marketing functions (such as developing high-impact brand messaging and "marketing by 'behavior' objectives" marketing plans) but stand out as isolated competencies, as if one could detach addressing the plate from slugging a baseball for on-base percentage.

There is no distinction in their marketing training given to absorbing information versus developing skills based on proven principles, best practices and quality processes. Moreover, they don't represent "marketing excellence," as they are stretching to achieve marketing "norms." Norms are certainly not representative of excellence. They're average. Also, they are divorced from practice, repetition and reinforcement at the organization level. You see, senior managers do not participate in the training. They cannot institutionalize what they themselves do not know, cannot do and/or don't choose to follow and institutionalize.

While this land clearly exists, it is an illusion. The emperor has no clothes. In this land, marketing does not, and cannot, matter. That's because it has no proven impact, no line of sight to sales.

Certainly, this is an extreme, but no matter where we turn, we observe that marketing is capable of more, much more. We need to get beyond doing dumb, those critical marketing mistakes, to instituting smart marketing practices. We need to get smarter if we are going to best our competition.

How do we do it? This book will show you the difference and how to be smart—or, at least, how to avoid doing dumb!

In this land, management is finally recognizing that in an "age of abundance and sameness" (where we have a plethora of choices but where products and services are basically the same), GAQ reigns and where tenders and promotions dominate the landscape, marketing really needs to matter to make a difference. They are coming to realize what Theodore Levitt taught years ago: everything can be differentiated, even commodities. Smart people like you can make a difference. Your marketing matters if you avoid making critical marketing mistakes and institute smart marketing—proven principles, best practices and quality processes.

THE END (OR IS IT JUST THE BEGINNING?)

If you want to avoid doing dumb marketing and, instead, do smart marketing that has a positive impact in developing and growing healthy brands to create brand loyalty, I invite you to read on. The choice is yours.

TABLE OF CONTENTS

INTRODUCTION

AVOIDING CRITICAL MARKETING ERRORS:
How to Go from Dumb to Smart Marketing

> *We recognized early on that very smart people do very dumb things, and*
> *we wanted to know why and who, so that we could avoid them.*
> **Charlie Munger, investing partner of Warren Buffett**
>
> *We try more to profit from always remembering the*
> *obvious than from grasping the esoteric.*
> *It is remarkable how much long-term advantage people like us have*
> *gotten by trying to be consistently not stupid, instead of*
> *trying to be very intelligent.*
> **Charlie Munger, investing partner of Warren Buffett**
>
> *Marketing is too important to be ignored and/or left to people who*
> *don't know what they are doing.*
> **Richard Czerniawski**

An investment banker was asked why marketing is under-represented on corporate boards. (Only 2 to 3% of board members are former marketers.) His answer was that marketers are "tactical." But there's more to it than failing to be perceived as "strategic." It really has to do with marketers not being accountable for linking their marketing with sales results (and stock performance). Marketing is not providing a clear line of sight in driving sales outcomes. That's not smart. In fact, it's dumb marketing!

There are a number of reasons why marketing is failing to manifest itself. The late Peter Drucker, the father of modern management, proposes it is one of the two most important functions in the organization. He says, "Because the purpose of business is to create a customer, the business enterprise has two, and only two, basic functions: marketing and innovation. Marketing and innovation produce results; all the rest are costs." Hmmm, how curious. Most organizations view marketing as a cost center as opposed to a producer of results.

It appears that marketing has lost its place in the world in "creating customers" AND in "producing results." Our marketing doesn't appear to generate impact, as in generating predictable, incremental sales with highly attractive ROI results. The failure to marry marketing with outcomes is why marketing support budgets are cut deeply and frequently. The ignorance of proven principles and a failure to adopt best practices and quality processes are at the root of the decline of marketing preeminence and relevance. It's poor marketing. Those slip-ups, oversights and lack of predictability of marketing results contribute to retarding versus optimizing brand and corporate performance. To Charlie Munger's and my (and I hope your) way of thinking, that's being and doing "dumb." Let's acknowledge it so we may progress.

AVOIDING CRITICAL MARKETING ERRORS: How to Go from Dumb to Smart Marketing will confront critical marketing errors—those grave blunders, slip-ups and missteps, both of omission and commission, that not only lead to underperformance (versus potential) but threaten brand survival. Importantly, this book addresses what all marketers, at every level, need to do to achieve smart marketing so that it matters where it counts: in the marketplace. I will reveal what comprises and contributes to dumb marketing and provide guidance in the form of an Rx (the healthcare symbol for prescription, although much of this is directional), to show how to avoid and fix marketing mistakes and instead create marketing that lives up to professor Drucker's view of the role of marketing.

The book is divided into three sections. The first section, "Situational Awareness," identifies what is shaping the marketing environment and the leadership role marketing must assume to address it. The second section, "Critical Marketing Errors," tackles 10 critical marketing errors. These are mega-errors that have a profound impact on brand sales and market share performance, such as not having a brand or campaign idea. Each chapter also identifies the myriad of errors that contribute to undermining marketing effectiveness at best, and derailing or rending marketing ineffective at worst, such as an incomplete profile of the target customer. The third section, "Additional Practices for Smart Marketing," will offer suggestions on how to make the pursuit of marketing excellence a practice that can give birth to reality.

Please note, the proven principles, best practices and quality processes shared in this book are universal in nature. Your sector (e.g., pharmaceutical, consumer, medical device, financial, services, etc.), your category, your brand and your geography don't matter. I've attempted to include examples from a myriad of sectors and categories to show what "smart" looks like. Use it as a model for your marketing, but certainly feel free to think for yourself when applying what you learn to your brand and situation. However, and this is a strong *however*, if you are going to choose to ignore or dismiss any of what is offered, make sure you have a sound reason for it and check to make absolutely certain that what you do is truly working for you. When something is working, it generates predictable, incremental outcomes.

My intention is not to offend. It's not in my nature, nor do I take pleasure in doing so. However, I do want to provoke marketers and their organizations to appreciate that there's so much more to learn about doing marketing correctly, so we may utilize it more fully and realize its value. So, consider any of my provocations as serving the same role as the *keisaku*—a flat wooden stick used in Zen meditation. It is used to strike the meditator to reinvigorate and awaken one suffering from fatigue or monkey mind (a mind that is not focused but filled with random thoughts). Just like the keisaku's strike does not, nor is it intended to, hurt, I hope my provocations will awaken you to being and doing more with marketing.

David Packard, of Hewlett-Packard, stated, "Marketing is too important to be left to the marketing people." I'd like to restate his statement: Marketing is too important to be ignored and/or left to people who don't know what they are doing. This book reveals critical marketing mistakes and how to avoid and/or fix them. It also shares how to do your marketing so it will matter more. It is not intended for those marketers who believe they have it all figured out and think there's nothing else to learn or improve upon. Those marketers live in the land of (dis)illusion and, if they are lucky, they will someday mature and wake up to learn that one can always go deeper and do better, no matter how good you are or think you are.

Instead, this book is intended for marketing professionals and organizations who recognize there's ample opportunity for continuous development. In the words of Stephen Covey, they are interested in "sharpening their saw" to create true "marketing excellence" as defined by creating brand loyalty and generating positive, line-of-sight impact on sales in the marketplace from their strategies and initiatives. You have the smarts and resources to do smart, even brilliant, marketing. This book will shine the light in making you aware of what's needed to get there. Now, it's up to you to make it happen.

Richard Czerniawski

SITUATIONAL AWARENESS

According to Wikipedia, situational awareness (SA) is "the perception of environmental elements and events with respect to time or space, the comprehension of their meaning, and the projection of their future status." Furthermore, they state, "Lacking or inadequate situational awareness has been identified as one of the primary factors in accidents attributed to human error."

The purpose of this situational awareness section is to highlight where a product, brand or company stands in the context of its environment: both internal and external. It's about knowing what is going on around your brand and comprehending what it takes to market it successfully. Importantly, it addresses factors that affect state of being, health and competitiveness of your marketing. This situational awareness comprises two rather brief chapters. Together, they address how and why the marketing function and you, the marketer, are losing relevance. My dream is to restore its, and your, proper role in the life of the brand and business enterprise.

- Chapter 1: Why Your Marketing Budget Gets Cut
- Chapter 2: In Defense of (Smart) Marketing

WHY YOUR MARKETING BUDGET GETS CUT

Here's a straightforward and simple question: Does your marketing budget get cut? You may be muttering to yourself, "Are you serious? Of course, it gets cut!" Well, not to make you feel better, but you're not alone. Virtually all our clients, from leading companies throughout the world, experience budget cuts as early as February in the new calendar year (or in the second month of their fiscal year). Often, their budgets are cut multiple times throughout the year. It seems that cutting marketing budgets is a common and somewhat predictable practice of senior managers.

This raises the question: Why does your marketing budget get cut? Why do senior leaders focus so intently on cost-cutting and are quick to shave and slash your budget (repeatedly!)? To answer these questions, it might be a good idea to determine what's more critical to managing the short-term bottom line: growing one dollar (euro, yuan, yen, real, ruble or whatever your currency is) of sales or cutting marketing's budget by the same amount. What do you think?

If you are like the vast majority of marketers, to answer this question, you chose "growth." Sadly, if you did, you chose wrong!

The correct answer is "cutting a dollar of 'marketing' spending." This was brought home to me by Ben Cook, President of Acumen Learning. How can this possibly be so? Let's examine it. We'll start with two columns: "grow" and "cut."

- A dollar of sales has "cost of goods sold" (COGS) associated with it. COGS include materials and manufacturing costs, to name a few. The percentage amount varies by industry and company within a given industry. Average COGS in the US is about 55%, or 55 cents out of every dollar. Therefore, in the "grow" column, we deduct 55 cents. There is no COGS associated with cutting the marketing budget. So, in the grow case, we have 45 cents remaining, but in the cut column, we still have our precious dollar.

- However, there will be additional expenses associated with the sale. After all, there will be sales personnel, sales commissions, distribution costs, marketing-related costs for advertising, promotions, medical congresses and the like. We, therefore, need to consider what is known as sales, general and administration (SG&A) expenses. Again, this percentage of the dollar will vary by industry and company. However, the average is 25 to 30%. We'll deduct 25% or an additional 25 cents in the grow column. So, now the marketer has 20 cents remaining from that initial one dollar of sales.

  Regarding the cutting of marketing's budget, do we have SG&A expenses to contend with? The answer is a most definite YES! We still have the personnel, distribution centers and the like. However, our senior managers achieved their positions by being very savvy businesspeople who know how to manage the bottom line with a life-or-death mentality. To avoid SG&A, they reorganize by cutting (I guess the word is "displacing") all kinds of people in the organization, among other cuts. I'll bet you're quite familiar with reorganizations. It seems they occur every 2 to 3 years or so. Consequently, there are no SG&A expenses, as the company removes them from this line item.

- We should also account for taxes. In the US, the corporate tax rate at this writing is now 21% (down from a whopping 35%). Accordingly, we need to deduct roughly another 4 cents in the grow column, leaving us with 16 cents on the dollar for revenue. By cutting marketing's budget $1.00, we reduce what we keep by 21 cents, leaving us with 79 cents profit after tax. Cutting the marketing budget brings nearly 5 times more to the bottom line than growing sales $1.00. This is why marketing's budget, specifically your budget for building your brand, gets cut.

Here's what it looks like:

	"Grow" Sales	"Cut" Marketing
	$1.00	$1.00
Cost of Goods Sold (55%)	(0.55)	$0.00
Gross Profit	$0.45	$1.00
Sales, General and Admin (25%)	(0.25)	$0.00
Profit before Taxes	$0.20	$1.00
Taxes (21%)	(0.04)	$0.21
Profit after Taxes	$0.16	$0.79

Now you understand why management will ruthlessly cut your marketing budget. It is to preserve profitability and cash when times get tough or when brands aren't performing as expected and demanded.

What does this tell us?

- Unless you can generate nearly $5.00 in growth for every dollar you spend in the example above, it would be better for the CMO (chief marketing officer) to cut spending to achieve the immediate bottom-line profit goals for the company. If the CMO doesn't do it, then the CEO (chief executive officer) will, with or without the urging of the CFO (chief financial officer).
- It is also important to keep in mind that unless we can demonstrate what a dollar of spending will return in incremental sales growth, ROI and profit, then these marketing support funds are vulnerable to budget cutting regardless of whether they are for consumer or retail promotions, advertising, KOL development or medical congresses.
- We need to choose marketing mix elements and launch tactics that not only have a line-of-sight link to sales but will serve to *accelerate* growth rates.

- Also, if we cannot demonstrate any of the things mentioned above, then marketing will be rightly perceived by those senior managers in the organization as a cost, and we marketers will be judged by them as not being smart businesspeople.

Nothing I'm sharing here dismisses the importance of real growth. Pushing the cost-cutting narrative too far could lead to compromising the long-term viability of the brand and organization. It could lead to compromising product quality, market share and, most importantly, the company's brand and reputation. Senior leaders need to recognize the need to strike an essential and delicate balance between driving revenue growth while containing costs, maintaining operating efficiencies and managing the budget.

Tom Peters makes clear the need for growth in his book *The Circle of Innovation: You Can't Shrink Your Way to Greatness.* Growth is essential to the health and survival of the company. When we grow our brands, we generate cash to fund new revenue-producing assets, such as new products. It also fuels the value of the company to stockholders and helps attract favorable financing. The growth of the company will also serve to attract talent. Everyone wants to work with a company or manage a brand that is growing. Life is just sweeter all around, as are the rewards, both financial and psychological, for everyone associated with a growing brand and company.

Instead, I'm establishing the case for you, the marketer, to understand what it takes to make your marketing relevant and to maintain or, better yet, to attract marketing support funding so you may serve your customers better than your competitors. Know what you need to do and prove to senior management that your actions will generate healthy, profitable, predictable incremental sales growth. However, you can't do that if your marketing is dumb.

By the way, this is no different than what senior management has to achieve and demonstrate to stockholders. Dividends are rewards for growth, and stockholders like to receive them. However, if the money to be paid out as dividends could earn for the company and, in turn, for the stockholders more than they could get investing elsewhere, then it would be in the stockholders' best interest, and that of the company, to reinvest the funds in the business (e.g., investing in product development, launch initiatives, hiring of talent, expanding operations, and so forth). It's that simple.

Likewise, if you can demonstrate that spending in support for your brand's strategies and initiatives will generate more profit than cutting the same funding, you will get what you need. Marketers not only compete outside the company, but when it comes to receiving marketing support funds, we compete internally as well. Management will support those businesses with the most promising growth prospects and favorable returns. They will put their money to work funding sectors, brands, initiatives and tactics that will give them the most proven bang for their investment.

If we do not know the sales impact and ROI from our marketing support programs, then we are not managing the business. Instead, the business is leading us! Marketing errors, whether they are errors of omission or commission, undermine the value of our assets, dampen productivity, reduce potential for growth and lead to cuts in resources (marketing budgets). Both errors of omission and commission are indicative of marketing that is not very smart. They erode the relevance of marketing and marketers, limiting our access to resources, both in the immediate and long term, to create brand loyalty.

If we want marketing to matter more, we need to avoid doing "dumb" and embrace doing "smart." We need to do what it takes to deliver line-of-sight sales to our strategies and initiatives. We can't expect to earn our budgets by merely generating a dollar of growth for a dollar of marketing support spending. We need to create a multiplier that will clearly prove we deserve to manage the precious asset that we've been entrusted: our brand. Then, we can take a seat at the boardroom table.

IN DEFENSE OF (SMART) MARKETING

To right the unrightable wrong …
No matter how hopeless, no matter how far …
"The Impossible Dream" (lyrics by Joe Darion)

Our host kicked-off a brand positioning and communications training program we conducted in Europe by having all the participants introduce themselves. In addition to the standard questions such as name, country, title, and brand, she asked each one to share his or her dream. When it came to my turn, I said, "My dream is to dream the impossible dream." Perhaps you are familiar with the song "The Impossible Dream," which comes from the musical *Man of La Mancha* and is based upon the Miguel Cervantes masterpiece *Don Quixote*.

The character Don Quixote is an elderly warrior who, as the expression goes, tilts windmills. He is a knight-errant who goes in search of wrongs with the intention to "right" them. At times, I feel that I'm like Don Quixote, fighting an "unwinnable fight." Along with my business partner, Mike Maloney, I try to assist organizations and their marketers to achieve what they claim to seek, and what we believe is essential: evidence-based "marketing excellence." It is a battle that must be fought on many fronts, among which include the following:

- Management's failure to understand the role marketing can and must play in the organization to create brand loyalty.

- Marketing being run by non-marketers with little training or aptitude for their role, and the misuse of marketing as "service to sales." In the long run, this does a disservice to sales personnel and undermines the ability of the organization to compete effectively in the immediate and long-term.
- Absence of a clear line-of-sight link between marketing strategies and initiatives to sales.
- Lack of institutionalization of sound marketing principles, best practices and quality processes.
- Lack or misuse of marketing research and sound business analysis, failing to create a high-impact, evidence-based organization.

I feel I've lived a dream. I had a wonderful childhood and received a sound education, both formal and informal. I've been a Navy officer and aviator (as well as a "gentleman," according to an act of Congress). I've worked for some of the most admired companies in the world, holding every marketing position from lowly brand assistant to chief marketing officer to general manager. I'm coming on 50 years of marriage with a loving and supportive wife. I have three loving daughters and three fine sons-in-law. I have four precious granddaughters. My business partner and I complement each other, and he's my very dear friend. I have worked with excellent teams over the years that have acted like family, depending upon and supporting each other faithfully and enthusiastically. I've traveled the world and have had scores of friends wherever I've gone. I am a 4th-dan black belt in two martial arts: taekwondo and hapkido. My life has been a dream. What else is there to dream? Win the lottery? That's genuinely improbable, and indeed, it is neither critical nor essential.

There is one dream left; it is what appears to be the impossible dream. In my professional life, my dream is to help restore marketing to its proper role in the corporation and society, and to empower marketers to create new successes that better satisfy customer needs. When I started marketing, which was more than 45 years ago, the company I began my career with, Procter & Gamble, was up there (so I was informed) with the Harvard B-School in producing the most corporate presidents. Moreover, the P&G folks who made it to the top level came out of marketing where they were trained to be *presidents of their brands.*

Today, marketing does not command the respect it did in those early years of my career. In some sectors, marketing is not perceived to be very important, if important at all, other than to provide support to the sales force. As might be expected, this is particularly acute in non-FMCG (fast-moving consumer goods) sectors, such as pharmaceuticals, medical devices and diagnostics, B2B and finance, to name just a few. Nor do marketers run their brands. At best, they own finite projects with little interconnectedness to other disciplines, including their own, in building brands. As a result, marketing is underutilized. It's a vast resource going vastly to waste.

Quite frankly, I'm tired of hearing that marketing isn't capable of building sales and market share. I'm sure you are too. I'm tired of hearing senior managers voice their opinion that they are uncertain of the value that marketing brings to the organization, and question whether they should support marketing at all. On what planet do these managers live? Effective marketing has proven itself in every sector. If marketing is not working, or if it is not working to its potential in your company, then it is not the function of marketing that is at fault; the problem is the way marketing is being done. It is a lack of vision, leadership and/or sound management of those who question the value of marketing that fails the marketing team and their ability to produce results. Quite frankly, it's dumb marketing that's at fault. To live without marketing is to conduct a symphony orchestra without the conductor. It's like driving a car without a driver (or AI software). I'd like to know how these managers who question whether marketing is an essential function in the organization ever got to their level.

The role of marketing is to *create brand loyalty*. "Create" is to bring a customer into existence. "Brand" goes beyond the product to encompass a constellation of values that forge a special relationship and bond with customers. "Loyalty" is about earning the customers' unswerving devotion to the brand. Does this sound unimportant? Is this not essential? It's more important than ever given the dynamic force of markets to commoditize products and categories, coupled with growing price sensitivity in an age characterized by abundance and sameness, particularly when information is so readily available regarding product performance and pricing.

Marketing has never been more essential. And, it's not merely about growing top-line revenues, which is crucial to driving and sustaining business health. It's about serving customers. Many marketers are quite fortunate to be blessed with products that fulfill critically essential physical and emotional needs. The pharmaceutical and medical device and diagnostic sectors are shining examples. While far from perfect, many new products serve to extend life from dreaded diseases and conditions and to improve quality of life. While you may argue the value of select products on the patient and society, one cannot deny that seeking to extend life and its quality is a noble endeavor. This endeavor is becoming more meaningful to me as I advance quite rapidly in age. At Coca-Cola USA, marketing satisfied a need going beyond providing mere refreshment to consumers. It was to put a smile on each of their faces. In this day and age of divisiveness, anxiety, intolerance and rancor, this is a most satisfying goal.

Abandon marketing? Today, it is more important than ever for everyone in the organization to be involved in marketing. When a customer call comes into the company, the person who is handling it is marketing the organization, irrespective of his titular function. Telling the customer the person she needs to speak with is currently at lunch so the customer (yes, the customer!) should call back later subverts the company's ability to forge a relationship built on a positive experience with the potential customer. It will very likely turn off the customer, paving the way for competitors to fill the void.

Marketing is an essential function of everyone in the organization. Having a competent, smart marketing department is *vital to the long-term health of the organization.* However, it's about more than having a marketing function. Marketing needs to drive the organization. It starts with marketers becoming champions of customers and ensuring the organization respects and better serves its customer segment than the competition in everything, *absolutely everything,* it does. It necessitates developing a brand positioning strategy to build brands, not merely sell products, and doing the stewardship to ensure that everyone in the company is undertaking their duties consistent with it. It's about out-thinking the competition today and staying ahead of them into the future. It's about creating relevant and meaningful differentiation to drive customer preference. It's about avoiding critical marketing errors and dumb marketing, and instead doing smart marketing that positively impacts sales growth and delivers a highly favorable ROI.

An argument I hear against marketing from those who do not appreciate its role revolves around their sector or segment. It goes something like this: *Our category is different. It has become increasingly more price-competitive. Governments and purchasers are not distinguishing competitors on the criterion of quality but pricing. Given that we carry premium pricing, competing has become much more difficult, and I don't think marketing can help. We need more sales personnel; we need to rationalize our products; we need a silver bullet.* What we really need is "smart" marketing.

Is it not astounding that these managers did not see or feel price pressures some years ago? Did they think the party of raising pricing to meet sales goals without giving customers anything of added value in return was going to go on forever? Is it not astounding that actions were not taken some time ago to create relevant, meaningful differentiation in their offerings, be it product or brand, physical performance or emotional pay-off? Given that we are at a tipping point in commoditizing many industries and categories, what then do they propose to do? Shore-up the sales force so they can out-muscle the competition in the short-term? What will the smart competitors do? At the very minimum, they will follow quickly with generally accepted quality, claim they perform the same as the leader and drop their prices to squeeze their premium-priced competitors to gain a competitive advantage. So, how will these premium-priced companies, who trade on their reputation, compete with third-world countries who can make and sell products cheaper than the industrialized nations can make them? Oh, it's ugly and only going to get uglier.

Without smart marketing that creates *meaningful* differentiation (as in driving preference despite a price premium), pricing will be driven lower wherever surplus capacity exists, more efficient producers are available, cost of labor and/or materials are cheaper, and the need to curb costs is essential. *It's the way of markets.* Without smart marketing, premium-priced companies will need to reduce or even eliminate their premium pricing to maintain their business. Furthermore, wherever premium pricing exists, there will be ample room for lower-priced competitors to further reduce their pricing, dragging the premium-priced competitors into a downward spiral. *It's the way of markets.* Just look at what is going on in the electronics sector. Products like smartphones, tablets and personal computers (such as the iPhone, iPad and

MacBook Pro) are enhanced while their pricing is coming down. What will happen to the pricing for products whose performance is not improved to deliver added-value and/or lack the appeal of these flashy electronic devices? The answer is evident. They will suffer without smart marketing.

Yet, even within the electronics sector, some brands (such as Apple) will enjoy continued growth despite, and perhaps assisted by, premium pricing. That's a mark of smart marketing.

If senior managers are not taking the lead in avoiding critical marketing errors and ensuring smart marketing in creating brand loyalty and delivering line-of-sight sales growth, then who will undertake this in the organization? Product development? Only if R&D is customer-centric and is a core competency of the organization and has both the focus and the capability to create meaningful differentiation and to marry performance to strategies and initiatives. Sales? Not hardly. They are interested in making the transaction today. Moreover, customer loyalty to a salesperson is not the same as gaining customer loyalty to a brand or its company. We need to go beyond being transactional to being transformational. Manufacturing? They can ensure quality (as in meeting minimum standards) and efficiency, neither of which build brand loyalty. Finance? You don't even want to go there. They will rationalize products and services to bolster margins. They'll also encourage taking price increases without providing a corresponding value to customers, exacerbating premium pricing. Also, they'll inveigh for cutting marketing support funds, especially when there is no proven line-of-sight link to sales (this I support). Whichever way you look at this, it is not a pretty picture.

What would happen if there were no marketing? If we abolished marketing from a given organization, the function would have to take root informally. Most likely, the salesperson would do her marketing. Why? Because marketing is essential in differentiating offerings, influencing customer preference and providing fuel for growing sales. However, the marketing would not be disciplined and strategic but random and spurious. Maybe that's not too far off from what some organizations are currently getting from their marketing department.

Only the marketing function, where utilized appropriately, is in a position to create brand loyalty. I have a problem with senior managers questioning whether marketing is essential to the organization. On the other hand,

I do not have a problem with these senior managers questioning whether they are getting fair value from their marketing department. This question is a real issue—one we can and must address. We need to make marketing accountable for results the same way sales is responsible for achieving targets. We need to establish expectations for marketing, and all efforts should be inspected to ensure these expectations are met. In other words, we must analyze all efforts against concrete goals. I'm referring to practicing evidence-based marketing. If marketing proves ineffective to the organization, it is not that the marketing function is not essential; instead, it is that the marketing in question is not smart. Unfortunately, it's dumb!

We need to undertake this journey to avoid critical marketing errors and to institute smart marketing. As previously mentioned, I'll make clear the critical errors and the individual components leading up to them, and I will shine a light on what we marketers need to do to practice smart marketing in pursuit of authentic marketing excellence. Together, we can win the fight to realize the impossible dream: to fulfill the potential of marketing to be transformational in the organization, for the brand, the market, target customers, and society. Let's avoid doing dumb. Let's do smart marketing to create brand loyalty.

COMMON CRITICAL MARKETING ERRORS: HOW TO AVOID AND FIX THEM

I don't visit mistakes to bewail them.
I revisit them for their learning purposes.
Charlie Munger, Warren Buffet's partner, as told to
Jason Zweig, THE INTELLIGENT INVESTOR, WSJ

Here are the critical errors that reveal "dumb" marketing. These are mega-errors of omission and commission that we must avoid and fix if we are going to do "smart" marketing and make our marketing matter (more). Each comes with a Rx (in the parlance of the pharmaceutical sector, a "prescription") for doing smart marketing.

- Chapter 3: Mis-Positioning Brand Positioning
- Chapter 4: Selling the Product, Not Marketing the Brand Experience
- Chapter 5: Lack of Relevant, Meaningful Differentiation
- Chapter 6: Mis-Targeting Target Customers
- Chapter 7: "Bad" Behaviors
- Chapter 8: Unsights versus Insights
- Chapter 9: Brand Communications That Suck!
- Chapter 10: Overstating Your Capabilities and Underestimating the Competition
- Chapter 11: Lack of Ideas - The Mark of a Dull Brand
- Chapter 12: Eminence-Based versus Evidence-Based Marketing

CHAPTER 3

MIS-POSITIONING "BRAND" POSITIONING

Positioning is the "customer-centric" strategic practice of transforming products, compounds, and services into brands to "create brand loyalty."
Richard Czerniawski

The Most Important "P" in Marketing

Ask anyone who has studied marketing, "What are the four Ps of marketing?" and they'll answer, "Product, price, placement, and promotion." So, where is "positioning?" Unfortunately, it has been relegated as a subset of promotion, yet positioning is the most important "P" in marketing. It addresses the following questions:

- What does our brand stand for; namely, why do we exist? What is our purpose?
- Who's the target customer? (As you'll learn in chapter 6, it's NOT EVERYONE!)
- What's our market (i.e., our source-of-volume; namely, where we will source sales volume)?
- What's our differentiated value-proposition (benefit promise) versus the competition?

- What is our reason-why support that makes the brand's benefit promise credible?
- What is our brand personality, or what we, at BDNI, refer to as brand character?

Positioning is relegated as a subset of promotion. The two creative people who introduced us to this ground-breaking concept, Reis and Trout, were two advertising guys. They conceived "positioning" as what you "message" about your product (as in advertising) to secure a place in customers' minds to win them over to the product. Small-minded marketers continue to treat positioning in this manner. However, we've learned over the years that this notion of brand positioning is so much more than what you communicate in your advertising. *Brand positioning is the "customer-centric" strategic practice of transforming products, compounds, and services into brands to create brand loyalty.* Perhaps, the distinction centers around the word *brand*, which is much more than a product.

As mentioned in the previous chapter, creating brand loyalty is the essence of marketing. Each word is pregnant with meaning, or at least it should be to the smart marketer. I'm repeating it because it is so very important, and repetition is essential to aid learning and, in turn, action.

- *Create* means to bring a customer into existence. This is what Peter Drucker referred to as "the purpose of the enterprise."
- The *brand* is a constellation of shared and fulfilled values that create a special relationship (our bond) with customers based upon their experience with it.
- *Loyalty* refers to commanding unswerving customer attachment and devotion to the brand.

The phrase *creating brand loyalty* captures the essence of what I believe is (and should be) the definition of marketing: *Marketing is the science and art of creating and maintaining customers in a mutually beneficial and compelling relationship.*

Fulfillment of the positioning strategy in the marketplace leads to the establishment of the brand, which then enables us to achieve the aim of marketing: creating and maintaining loyal customers.

There are so many different types of brand positioning strategies. There's competitive positioning, oppositioning, repositioning, and prositioning. These are the most frequent types employed to create and claim a unique and coveted space in the minds, hearts, and souls of target customers and the marketplace.

We define competitive positioning, which serves as the blueprint for the development of the brand, as *to how we want customers to perceive, think and feel about our brand versus the competition.* It serves as the blueprint for the development of the brand. It is not just what we message in our advertising (and not all brands advertise, especially in the traditional way), but it is every choice we make and everything we do to support the development of the brand.

Starbucks was able to establish its positioning to develop a global brand (which has grown to nearly 30,000 locations worldwide, leading all food outlets but Subway and McDonald's) with little to no advertising. They used their choice of retail locations, store layout and décor, menu items, the nomenclature for menu items, roasting style, music selection, coffee cup sleeves, and even stock-ownership for employees, among other actions, to establish their brand. Howard Shultz, the marketect behind Starbucks, firmly believed that it was critically important to treat his employees properly as it would impact how they, in turn, would treat Starbucks' customers. It's about making the positioning strategy real to target customers with all the marketing mix elements available to us in fulfilling the strategy and in driving customer preference.

CRITICAL POSITIONING MISTAKES

I can't overstate the importance of the role of brand positioning and the development of a competitive brand positioning strategy. Unfortunately, there are many mistakes and oversights marketers and their organizations make concerning positioning that thwart the development of a brand and the achievement of its competitive potential. Here are some of the most significant:

1. *No positioning strategy.* Can you believe it? It's true! Many brands lack a positioning strategy. Do you have one? Can you produce it if asked to share it with me? If you can't produce your positioning strategy, then you, like other marketers who don't have one, are merely selling versus marketing your company's offering. Selling is transactional whereas marketing is transformational. Transactions are the outcome of tactics and are episodic. Transformation is built on strategy, and it is enduring. If we are going to gain and maintain customer loyalty, we must get beyond being satisfied with a mere transaction and seek to be transformational with target customers.

   Now the question is, if you don't have a written positioning strategy, does that mean you don't occupy a place in the minds of potential customers? No, you have a positioning. Recall that I defined *competitive positioning* as "how customers perceive, think and feel about our brand." Customers perceive something regarding who you are and what you do. (If they don't think anything of you, then you're in for real trouble. You don't exist in their minds!) However, if you don't have a brand positioning strategy, any positioning that exists in the minds of prospective customers, your "positioning," was not designed by you. Instead, potential customers will conjure your positioning based on a plethora of unrelated tactics, which could result in an impression of schizophrenia. Worse yet, without a written brand positioning strategy—the positioning for your brand, the perception that exists in the marketplace—was most likely established by competitors *oppositioning* your offering. Allowing competitors to position your brand is not being competitive—far from it! It's handing them the keys to your kingdom.

   Moreover, without a written brand positioning strategy statement, you lack a blueprint to guide the development of your brand and to set it apart from the competition. It's akin to building a home without a blueprint. The outcome is not likely to please you. One will not have the specs, a set of expectations, from which to judge every decision and action that affects your brand and its relationship with target customers. Not having a brand positioning strategy is a gross oversight and error of omission, and it's just plain dumb marketing.

2. ***Product versus brand positioning.*** Product positioning is about the product, not the brand. The brand is the more vibrant and more compelling entity given its constellation of values and customer experiences with it. Simply stated, a product positioning promises a product benefit—namely, what the product does. For example, Gatorade restores electrolytes lost from sweating. Eliquis helps prevent strokes from AFib not caused by a heart valve problem (AFib, or, atrial fibrillation, is an irregular heartbeat that can cause poor blood flow and increased risk of strokes and other heart-related complications). Given that each product in the customer's competitive set basically shares the same product benefits—regardless of whether it is a consumer or health care practitioner or B2B purchaser—the resultant product positioning is generic. In other words, it is not competitive in serving to drive differentiation and to inspire preference in this "age of abundance," where we have a plethora of products in each category, and in this "age of sameness," where compounds, products, and services do the same things, work in the same fundamental ways and produce similar, if not the same, outcomes.

At the very least, think beyond the physical product to address the "whole" product, which includes intangibles such as terms, support services, etc. Think about additional benefits that add value to your offering versus your competitors. Consider the customer benefit; namely, what's in it for the customer that will elevate your offering over and above the product benefit. Imagine what your brand, once established, can mean for your target customer that a mere product cannot. For example, the brand Gatorade—not the product but the brand—enables you to perform like an iconic, alpha athlete. With Gatorade, you can perform like Tom Brady. Now that's brand positioning!

3. ***Starting positioning development too late.*** Senior managers share news of potential new pipeline products with the press and Wall Street well before launch and before they unleash marketers to begin positioning development. It's letting the horse out of the proverbial barn. Consider the pharmaceutical sector, where this occurs well before

Phase III clinical trials are completed, or even contemplated, in most companies. What these senior managers report to Wall Street and present at medical congresses seeps into the marketplace. This colors perceptions as to the potential new entry's positioning. Moreover, competitors will pick up on it and begin to opposition your offering.

As an example, my business partner and I worked on brand positioning development with a pharmaceutical client who was about one year away from launch. They were to be the first in a new therapeutic area. Their competitor was approximately one year behind our client. However, senior management had been talking about this new product's positioning in the market well before a brand positioning strategy had been developed. Consequently, the competitor was already *oppositioning* our client's emerging product with prospective target customers, attempting to disparage its efficacy and undermine its viability. The competition was trying to block adoption of our client's product so they could swoop in and take the business when they followed with their product's introduction. Everyone was positioning the much publicized, anticipated offering well before the marketer had his hand in undertaking the most crucial strategic mission facing the launch.

Marketing has to retrospectively develop a brand positioning strategy based upon what product development created and/or clinical studies were designed to show. It becomes a Rube Goldberg approach. If you'll recall, I defined brand positioning as being "customer-centric." It's not about what we can make and then discovering how to sell it; it's about making things that customers need or want. No one in the organization should know and understand customers better than marketers and how to appeal to them. Accordingly, marketing needs to be involved, up front, in uncovering untapped target customer needs and leading product development, including the development of clinical studies, that will support a competitive, meaningfully differentiated positioning strategy—a strategy that will lead to the development of a preferred brand.

4. ***Lacks a BIG brand idea.*** The brand idea is the theme of the positioning strategy. This point is consistent with point #2, developing a brand versus product positioning strategy, yet it's more significant. The brand idea addresses the *purpose* of the brand in a way that is highly emotive to the target customer. It gets to the heart of the WHY of the brand to its reason for existence beyond what is already available in the marketplace. Additionally, the inclusion of a brand idea works not only to ensure our positioning is differentiated but that it is also choiceful, which is evidenced by being single-minded. It's how we serve up our undifferentiated "egg" (another way to say "commodity") in a way that is appealing and inspiring to our target customer.

EGGS-ACTLY BRAND IDEA WORTHY

"The Incredible, Edible Egg"

I love eggs. I have 2 to 3 every morning for breakfast. Given that I adhere to a low-carb diet, eggs are a staple for me. They are incredibly good for you. Each nutritionally dense egg is low in calories yet packs 14 essential nutrients and 6 grams of protein. While it has cholesterol, I'm assured it's the right kind. It's kind of like a multi-vitamin health booster. However, it's real, not ersatz, food.

Nutrition Facts
Per 1 large egg (50 g)

Amount		% Daily Value
Calories 70		
Fat 5 g		8%
Sarturated 1.5 g + Trans 0 g		8%
Cholesterol 190 mg		
Sodium 55 mg		2%
Carbohydrate 0 g		0%
Fibre 0 g		0%
Suger 0 g		
Protein 6 g		

Vitamin A	8%	Vitamin C	0%
Calcium	2%	Iron	4%
Vitamin D	8%	Vitamin E	10%
Riboflavin	15%	Niacin	6%
Vitamin B$_{12}$	30%	Folate	15%

Nutritional Facts about Eggs

Eggs offer the promise of many benefits. There are at least as many benefits from one egg as one might find eggs in a carton. Here are a dozen benefits from consuming eggs:

1. Improves concentration
2. Taste great
3. Aids in weight management
4. Boosts brain development
5. Protects eyesight
6. Provides sustainable energy
7. Contains essential vitamins for better overall health
8. Convenient
9. Affordable
10. Easy and quick to cook
11. Satiating
12. Versatile

This last benefit, versatility, is one that has significant meaning to me, and it should for all marketers. Eggs can be prepared in many different ways, depending on your taste. I, for one, do not like soft-boiled eggs. (They are a bit too slimy.) On the other hand, I love fried eggs—over-easy that is. I'm not a fan of hardboiled eggs. However, I love my wife's deviled eggs. Scrambled eggs are okay, but omelets are better (depending upon the ingredients and the way they are prepared). Same egg, yet different results.

Eggs are not just breakfast food. You can eat them any time of the day, and there's a plethora of recipes for different times of the day and for different occasions. There are egg recipes for appetizers, snacks, brunches, main dishes, holidays and special occasions, among others. Eggs are an essential ingredient in your birthday cake, pasta dish and the salad dressings you love to eat. Eggs are incredible.

Okay, so what does this have to do with marketing? Good question. An egg is an egg is an egg. Or, is it? What about your pharmaceutical compound, medical device, consumer product, financial product or service? It probably is no more different from your competitors' offerings than one egg is from another. However, there are a zillion ways to serve up an egg. Likewise, there are many ways to serve up your offering to deliver relevant, meaningful differentiation versus your competition and to connect with potential target customers. We refer to this way of serving up your egg as the brand idea. It's eggs-actly what you need to make your marketing matter more.

THE BRAND IDEA

The brand idea is a crystallization of the positioning, or theme, for your brand. Take the antiperspirant category, for example. Do you know eggs-actly what the active ingredient is in each of the many brands that line the retail shelves? It's aluminum zirconium octachlorohydrex gly 16% (anhydrous), or some variant of the compound. That's right, each of your antiperspirant brand choices contains the same basic ingredient.

Yet, if you choose AXE, you can become a "chick magnet" (brand idea). If you choose Secret, you are likely to value that it is "strong enough for a man but made for a woman" (brand idea). The very same active ingredient is in both deodorants. but each has a distinctive brand that appeals to different target-customer segments.

Just as the egg may be transformed into many variants, depending upon individual tastes, so may your compound, medical device, product or service. Without a brand idea, your offering is destined to become a commodity. The marketplace will commoditize it and reduce choice to price or availability. The brand idea is eggs-actly what you need to make your offering distinctive and competitive, regardless of your category.

WOLFGANG PUCK KNOWS EGGS-ACTLY THE MARK OF A GREAT CHEF

You probably know Wolfgang Puck from his restaurants and many appearances on the Food Network. He is a celebrated chef and businessman. He created the Wolfgang Puck Companies, which, at one time, encompassed over 20 fine-dining restaurants, top 40 restaurants in the U.S. premium services category, more than 80 Wolfgang Puck Express operations, and kitchen and food merchandise. He has been the official caterer for the Academy Awards Governors' Ball. He's become quite the celebrity. I often stopped for a breakfast of a 4-cheese or vegetarian omelet at the Wolfgang Puck restaurant when it was located in Terminal 3 at O'Hare Airport whenever I had an early morning flight (which was rather frequently).

Wolfgang Puck believes that the real test of a great chef is a simple egg. He judges chefs on their ability to expertly cook an egg. He will request that they make him an omelet, and if the result leaves something to be desired, then they lack the fundamentals to be great chefs. Likewise, if there is no brand idea, your offering will not likely be a great (i.e., leadership) brand. Similarly, if we are unable to work with brand ideas, it is unlikely that we are great marketers.

WHAT COMES FIRST, THE CHICKEN OR THE EGG?

Let's not get into a philosophical debate. Your guess is as good as mine. However, when it comes to developing brand positioning strategy statements, I believe it is best to start with the brand idea. There are many significant advantages to this:

- It enables a big-picture approach to strategy development.
- It helps us get beyond the product (egg) to the brand we can make of it (outcome).
- It is choiceful and encourages the development of a single-minded theme.
- It suggests options, which we can use to dialogue with customers and iterate our way to success.
- It provides a solid anchor for the full brand positioning strategy development (i.e., target customer, competitive framework, core differentiated benefit, the reason-why support, and brand character).
- It is eminently testable.

5. *Converging on the "right answer."* I've observed from my years of practice working with leading companies throughout the world that the right answer is the same for all of them. It's "the first *executional expedient* answer that has *consensus.*" Unfortunately, it is typically not the correct answer when it comes to establishing a successful brand positioning in the marketplace. The first answer usually reflects a product positioning as previously mentioned, which more often than not, does not serve to differentiate your offering. To get to the appropriate competitive brand positioning strategy, the marketer needs to diverge with many potential brand ideas, reflecting differentiated positioning strategies, before converging. The potential differentiated brand ideas may then be used to engage and dialogue with the marketplace (i.e., real prospective target customers) so the marketer may iterate his way to a

brand positioning strategy that will work to create preference. By the way, this is a best practice. It improves your likelihood of success!

6. *Launch versus aspirational positioning.* Positioning needs to go beyond launch to envision the future life stages of the brand. This is particularly important to effectively guide management of the lifecycle of a brand and to realize its full potential. As mentioned previously, the brand positioning strategy is our blueprint for the development of the brand. It guides everything we do (see next point). If we merely position for the launch, which typically stems from using positioning for messaging only, it's like creating a blueprint for the first level of a multi-level home as opposed to the entire house. We need to envision what we can make of the brand and where we can take it over its lifetime. Developing a positioning strategy that encompasses the lifecycle of the brand and its many stages is critical, particularly where we expect to launch product improvements, share compelling findings from new clinical studies, introduce product line extensions, and seek new uses or indications. Regardless, we need to be responsive to changes in the marketplace and to shifts in target customer needs. Once we have created that guiding, brand positioning strategy, we then need to make it happen. On the other hand, our specific communication strategy will guide the development of the launch communications and those of line extensions and new indications.

7. *Advertising versus power positioning.* Positioning in the marketplace takes root from everything we do, not just what we say. When we relegate positioning merely to advertising, we are not leveraging its full potential to create and establish the brand in the minds and hearts of target customers. We, marketers, are not only responsible for creating a positioning strategy but also for using it as our blueprint for transforming the product, compound or service into an enduring, competitive brand. Accordingly, we must take on an additional role: serving as stewards for brand development. The positioning strategy is used to guide and filter everything we consider doing, and do, to ensure that all the choices we make and marketing initiatives we undertake are consistent with

the brand positioning strategy and to bring the brand idea to life. It impacts not just advertising but promotion, clinical studies, product development, and absolutely everything we choose to do.

8. ***Repositioning versus prositioning.*** Repositioning is reactive. Repositioning typically occurs when a brand has been losing market share, category growth has slowed and/or revenues are declining. (It also happens when someone new joins the brand team and wishes to make his mark.) Most often, it is not initiated until many years into the brand's decline. Repositioning is desperate and is manifested by revolution as opposed to evolution. Most repositioning attempts fail because the change is too dramatic, leading to a loss of identity with customers, and/or the brand is too far gone before repositioning is undertaken. Repositioning requires significant investment, and management has little patience with it, nor do they have the propensity to spend behind it. (If you doubt this, go back and reread "Chapter 1: Why Your Marketing Budget Gets Cut.") So, the organization typically gives up on it shortly following its launch, well before it is seeded in the marketplace.

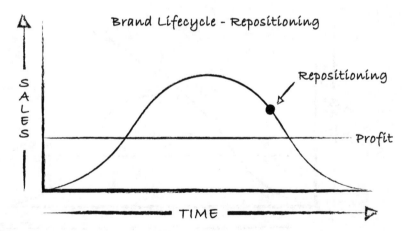

"Prositioning" is responsive. It is also proactive. It is an evolution of the brand's positioning that is triggered by: a slowdown, or anticipation of a slowdown, in the rate of growth; new brand development (e.g., product improvements or new clinical outcomes);

or new developments in the market (such as a shift in customer needs or introduction of new products).

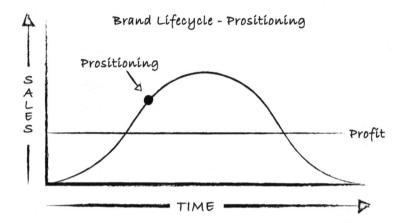

It serves to help move the S-curve (the curve that shows rate of growth over time) up and to the right, increasing sales and extending brand viability.

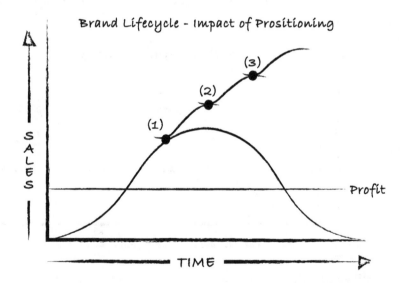

Beware of repositioning. I would only consider repositioning if my brand was bleeding revenues and profit, or if target customers were not aware of what the brand represented in the past and I didn't have more attractive investment options within the organization. A brand such as Old Spice was popular some 50 years or so ago, only to fall into obscurity. (It was my dad's brand, which probably makes it your grandfather's or, perhaps, great-grandfather's brand.) P&G brought it back to new generations of men (perhaps, even you) through repositioning. On the other hand, any attempts to reposition SEARS is likely to meet with failure. They are too far gone. (SEARS should have prositioned back in the early 1970s.)

9. *Extraneous garbage.* The core elements of the positioning strategy are the following:
   - Brand idea
   - Target customer
   - Competitive framework
   - Benefit (product, customer and emotional)
   - Reasons-why (support for the benefit)
   - Brand character

   Anything less is incomplete. Anything more is garbage. It's superfluous and, as such, an energy drain. It dilutes one's focus on what is relevant and meaningful to create a compelling brand positioning strategy. "What about customer insights?" you might ask. Customer insights are undoubtedly critical. However, it is a lead-in to the development of the brand positioning strategy, the start of which is the brand idea. We may also capture and reflect customer insights in the target customer's attitudes about the category and her/his telling behaviors. Additionally, customer insights can assist us in articulating the benefit, consistent with the brand idea.

10. *Poor technical skills.* It is incredible to witness the lack of technical competence among many marketers in professionally addressing the core elements in their development of a brand positioning strategy. For example, they will often do the following:
    - Define the target customer too broadly (like EVERYONE), provide an incomplete target profile, and/or fabricate the target,

which bends reality or leads to a lack of focus on what's needed to drive preference with real people.

- Merely listing the standard of identity or class of product (e.g., statin, energy drink, overnight delivery service, et al.) in the competitive framework, leaving out the "perceptual competitive framework" (how you want to be perceived as different from your standard of identity or category class or products or compounds such as "THE Ultimate Cholesterol Reducer" for Lipitor or "Cholesterol Regulator" for Crestor or "Ultimate Liquid Athletic Equipment" for Gatorade, etc.), which serves to genericize your offering in the minds of target customers by linking it to every other offering in their competitive set and your framework.

- Articulate multiple benefits that obfuscate the brand's meaning.

- Use "fat" words (i.e., words that have many meanings, such as the words "efficacious" and "great tasting") for the benefits.

- Offer generic benefits (i.e., the same that competitors are promising).

- Stuff benefit claims in the reason-why section, which neither supports credibility for the proffered benefit nor promotes single-minded focus.

- Do not use legitimate reasons-why (which are features, attributes, clinical outcomes, ingredients, and design, among others) to add credibility to the benefits.

- Use cost-of-entry reasons-why that do not differentiate the brand but merely reinforce target customers' perceptions that it performs the same as competitors.

- Do not develop extrinsic reasons-why, such as endorsements from recognized authorities, which could serve to meaningfully differentiate your offering.

- String a litany of adjectives for the brand character, which are the same descriptors (or synonyms) used by *everyone*. Whew! And, these are just a few of the technical errors that riddle the vast majority of brand positioning strategy statements.

RX FOR SMART POSITIONING

What might we do to fix these significant positioning mistakes to make our positioning more productive? Here are a few thoughts that address each of the points mentioned above:

1. ***Develop, or pressure-test, your competitive brand positioning strategy.*** If you don't have one, create one! It should be your first order of business, as it is the most important "P" in marketing. Start by pulling together a multi-function (i.e., marketing, R&D, agency, sales, clinical, marketing research, etc.) and broad geographic team that works to support and market your offering. Conduct a workshop and address each of the preceding five core elements, plus the brand idea, that comprise a competitive brand positioning strategy. Stick with the core elements and nothing more. Start with the brand idea, as it represents the WHY of the offering and the big picture, and it will anchor the brand positioning strategy.

   If you do have a positioning strategy, conduct due diligence to pressure-test it for competitiveness (distinction and preference) and identify what you might do to make it more productive. Take notice of how the marketplace and competitors are positioning your brand. Note, too, your competitors' positioning strategies by learning how target customers perceive them. Then, identify ways in which you might position your brand offering, so it is relevant and meaningfully differentiated from your competitors, and identify how you are currently perceived. Note the gaps between where you stand today and where you want to be in the future, then identify what you need to do to fill any gaps.

2. ***Get beyond the product to develop a brand positioning strategy.*** We need to get beyond the physical product we sell and think about the whole product and experiences we intend to deliver. Apple has a genius bar staffed by real people you can deal with face to face; this is outside of MacBook Pro but part of the whole-product offering. Amazon Prime

provides free shipping and, in many cases, will deliver your purchases to you by the next day. It goes beyond tangible merchandise to help differentiate and make your experience a winning one!

3. ***Get to work on positioning development before the horse is out of the barn.*** Senior managers should be taking their cue from marketing when it comes to positioning the asset. If you market pharmaceutical products, begin positioning development before Phase III studies. Ideally, you should be involved in the strategic dialogue dealing with the objectives of your clinical research and how you might use the outcomes it generates. Consider whether you want the clinical study to prove your product merely works or if you wish to demonstrate superiority over the competition. Unless your company is content with its fair share of the market, we should direct outcomes research to ensure it produces meaningful differentiation (even if that's focusing on different needs).

   Ideally, consumer, financial and service companies should develop products from winning positioning concepts to fill gaps in the market and to better satisfy target customer needs rather than relegate marketing to selling what the company makes. Work closely with R&D to address real target customer dissatisfactions and needs. Tide Laundry Detergent, whose sales in North America exceed the next nine laundry detergent brands combined, addresses real target consumer needs through R&D and marketing collaboration, often long before consumers can even express those needs. For example, there's the Tide Wear-Care line extension. It works to keep fabrics from fading and fraying in the wash, so they look newer longer.

4. ***Start with creating a BIG, emotive brand idea.*** The brand idea is the way to serve up your egg, so it does not become a commodity. Dig deep to define the purpose of your intended brand and direct it at target customers who, in the words of executive coach Simon Sinek, "believe what you believe," so it will inspire, compel and drive their preference.

   We, at BDNI, approach brand positioning strategy development by starting with the brand idea. Working with the client, we will develop many different brand ideas for their "egg," regardless of the category. It is not unusual for us to generate more than a dozen potential brand ideas for the same product, compound or service. Certainly, we cannot work on 12 ideas. Instead, the client team selects those few (3 to 5) that its members believe have the best potential for commercial success and are consistent with what they will be able to support in the future. We work with the client team in our Navigator workshop to marshal the collective wisdom of the participants in "intelligent collaboration" to develop brand positioning strategy statements for each of those few. We adapt the positioning strategy statements and brand ideas throughout the workshop. At the conclusion of the workshop, the team selects 1 to 3 brand ideas and strategies it develops that they judge to have the best potential for success with the target customer. These are further adapted and put into marketing research to assist in deciding on the most strategically appropriate brand idea and positioning strategy statement to guide the development of the brand.

5. ***Diverge before converging.*** Seek many potential brand ideas. If you feel you have an appropriate brand idea and positioning strategy early in the development process, put it aside and see what additional strategic options you might generate. Use these in an attempt to best your first solution. This practice will help you overcome group-think. Additionally, it will lead you to peel the onion, enabling you to uncover key issues and to reveal what matters to target customers within the context of their needs and those of the market.

   Contrary to popular belief, your first choice is rarely the best or even correct choice. It is typically substandard or highly flawed. As Ray Dalio states in his book *Principles*, "There is almost always a good path that you just haven't discovered yet, so look for it until you find it rather than settle for the choice that is then apparent to you." Once you have more options, use them to dialogue with prospective target customers and adapt to iterate your way to success.

6. ***Go beyond the launch to capture the full potential for the brand's life.*** Our blueprint should guide the development of the brand over its life,

including product development, clinical studies, and so forth. On the other hand, use the communication strategy to address your launch messaging. The communication strategy might focus on a subset of the target customer identified in your brand positioning strategy. Messaging, too, will address those messages that you can currently support, as you await outcomes from additional clinical studies, product improvements, etc.

7. ***Reflect your positioning strategy in everything you do.*** The brand idea and positioning strategy will guide all choices and marketing initiatives, which in turn, will serve to establish the positioning in the marketplace. We refer to this as power positioning. Power positioning addresses product development, clinical studies, advertising, promotion, continuing medical education, medical congresses, retail promotion— EVERYTHING! The target customer needs to see, hear, and feel the brand positioning strategy. (For more on power positioning, read *CREATING BRAND LOYALTY: The Management of Power Positioning and Really Great Advertising* by Richard Czerniawski and Mike Maloney.)

8. ***Prosition your brand for success.*** Don't rest on your laurels. Satisfaction will open the door for active inertia and complacency to set in. It's the way good companies and brands go bad. Instead, be sensitive to lifecycle management, marketplace dynamics, and competitive developments. Respond to shifting dynamics to keep the brand fresh and relevant. Avoid repositioning, as it requires significant investment, which an impatient management (and virtually all are impatient) will cut if it does not produce immediate results. Instead, prosition the brand to lift and move the S-curve up and to the right to help extend the brand's lifecycle.

9. ***Cut out all non-essential elements from your positioning strategy.*** Do not entertain any elements beyond the brand idea and the five components highlighted in this chapter. Devote your attention to using each essential part to reinforce the brand idea and to drive differentiation. Here's a template (with a rudimentary explanation

of the components) you can use to develop your brand positioning strategy:

BRAND POSITIONING STRATEGY – ESSENTIAL ELEMENTS

ELEMENT	EXPLANATION
Brand Idea	This is the theme of your competitive brand positioning strategy. It's your WHY, your purpose, your reason for the brand's existence. It needs to differentiate your brand versus your competition. It also needs to be aspirational to cover the brand's lifecycle, and emotive to generate target-customer preference.
Target Customer	This addresses those people who believe in your brand idea. See "Chapter 6: Mis-Targeting Target Customers" for an explanation of each element that comprises the target-customer profile. • Demographics • Psychographics • Patient-condition, life stage or usage occasion • Attitudes regarding (treating) condition, life stage or occasion-state • Current usage and dissatisfactions • Telling behaviors • Needs (physical and emotional)
Competitive Framework	• Literal: This is where we source volume. • Perceptual: The perceptual competitive framework (PCF) is a label that captures how we want to be perceived. It's as if our offering were a new segment in the market.
Benefit	• Product: What the product does. • Customer: WIIFM or "What's In It For Me (i.e., the customer). • Emotional: How it makes the target customer feel.

ELEMENT	EXPLANATION
Reasons-Why	• Intrinsic: Evidence such as clinical study outcomes, ingredients, materials, modalities, etc. • Extrinsic: These are outside the product, such as endorsements, survey results, and so forth.
Brand Character	This refers to the personality of the brand. Use an analogy complete with label and explanation. For example, "The Lifeguard: There to watch-over and protect you from harm."

10. ***Develop a technically correct positioning strategy.*** The brand positioning strategy must be technically correct. It is not just about being professional, but it will enable you to more clearly assess whether it is competitive. We, at BDNI, use the 5 Cs to check for technical competency. Here are the 5 Cs:

- **Clear:** We've articulated all elements of the positioning strategy in a way that is incapable of being misunderstood.
- **Complete:** We've addressed all the essential elements. It is also robust.
- **Competitive:** The positioning strategy and its elements are relevant and meaningfully differentiated versus competition for the target customer you've chosen.
- **Cohesive:** All elements are aligned perfectly. For example, the benefits should fulfill the target-customer needs. The benefits must also be consistent with the brand idea. The reasons-why support the benefit. By the way, it's okay to repeat words.
- **Choiceful:** There is one, and only one, theme. In other words, the positioning strategy is single-minded.

If you haven't already done so, read *COMPETITIVE POSITIONING: Best Practices for Creating Brand Loyalty*, a book I co-authored with my business partner, Mike Maloney. It will provide you with in-depth instruction to help you make your positioning development work more productive in creating and marketing brands, not products.

It's only smart to embrace the most important "P" in marketing and to do it right if we are going to fulfill our role as marketers to create brand loyalty.

CHAPTER 4

SELLING THE PRODUCT, NOT MARKETING THE BRAND EXPERIENCE

It's time to get beyond the product you sell and think about the customer experience you deliver.

It's the experience, stupid!
Richard Czerniawski

I define enchantment as the process of delighting people with a product, service, organization or idea.
The outcome of enchantment is voluntary and long-lasting support that is mutually beneficial.
Enchantment **– Guy Kawasaki**

No, I'm certainly not calling you stupid when I declare, "It's the experience, stupid!" You've evidenced that you are not stupid by merely purchasing this book, and more importantly, reading it. Obviously, you are interested in self-development and in your role as a marketer and in enhancing both. I sincerely expect you will take what you learn and apply it to your brand marketing in your way to achieve new levels of success.

Instead, this is drawing, for dramatic effect (which is always essential for high-impact marketing), from the Bill Clinton versus George H. W. Bush 1992 presidential campaign where the economy was the critical and deciding issue in the election. Today, people still confirm the rather obvious learning, "It's the economy, stupid," that helped Bill Clinton clinch the presidency.

However, when it comes to bonding with customers—creating the kind of loyalty where customers go beyond preferring, to insisting, on your brand of product or service or, even, you—it's their experience that is the critical and deciding factor. Far too often, marketers overlook the experience of the customer, stopping most frequently at the point of delivery with the basic product and/or service. To do so is a sure path to short-changing the development of brand loyalty, leaving the product vulnerable to becoming a commodity. We need to get beyond the physical product we sell and think about the experience we want customers to enjoy.

THE WHOLE PRODUCT

I might have titled this chapter, "Selling the Product ..." or, perhaps, "Selling One-Half of the Product..." because that's what many marketers do. They sell the physical product, ignoring the support and services that complete the offering and create the experience. Our product offering needs to be more than the physical product. It needs to create a favorable experience for our target customers. Is there truly a difference between what you offer versus your competitors in the same category or segment?

You all occupy the same space. As stated in the previous chapter "Mis-Positioning 'Brand' Positioning," your products do the same things. They work in the same ways. Despite your protestations, they produce the same results in satisfying basic needs. In other words, they're interchangeable and, therefore, subject to commoditization.

Here is where "whole product" thinking and the creation of target-customer experiences with the brand come in. The physical product is one part of the equation and typically does not offer real differentiation. It's the part that is developed by R&D. It may not be enough to meaningfully differentiate your offering and engender loyalty. The other part of the product offering consists of the intangibles such as the support services you provide. Intangibles include servicing, terms of the sale, and anything and everything beyond the physical product that helps you *meaningfully differentiate* your complete offering from competitors and leads to target-customer preference for your brand. This support, or the added-value services you provide, originate with marketing. In other words, marketing is the R&D for the added-value offerings. It is one of the most compelling drivers of the brand experience, along with the physical product performing up to expectations. It is the part that will help customers bond with your brand, not just with your product. It's the part they will talk about.

When I think of my MacBook Pro*, I can come up with a listing of the many attributes of the physical product. I'm not sure what they all mean, but they provide reassurance that I possess a quality product. On the other hand, it's the services they did not include in the product or box, in which I received my MacBook Pro, that make a real difference for me. It's Apple Care, the Genius Bar and their many varied, hands-on workshops that shape my experience, preference, and evangelism for all things regarding the Apple brand.

TANGIBLES	INTANGIBLES
• 13-inch and 15-inch laptop computers	• Complimentary support
• LED-backlit retina display	• AppleCare protection plan
• Force touch trackpad	• Genius Bar
• High-performance technologies (Intel Dual-Core and quad-core)	• Free workshops
• Turbo Boost	• Free two-day delivery
• Two Thunderbolt 2 ports, two USB 3 ports, and an HDMI port	• Pick up today
• PCIe-based flash storage	• Special financing
• Intel Iris Plus Graphics	• Get help buying
• Meets ENERGY STAR 6.1requirements	• Apple retail stores
• Rated EPEAT Gold	
• FaceTime HD camera	

*These attributes and services are undoubtedly already outdated.

FAILING THE CUSTOMER, FAILING THE BRAND

There are myriad ways marketers fail the customer and the brand. The first way is by selling—not marketing but selling—only the product, or more precisely one-half of the product, as already mentioned. This is a purely transactional relationship, so purchasing becomes the result of habit, or special pricing, versus any real commitment on the part of the marketer or customer. There is nothing of distinction to create a bond between the "brand" offering and the target customer.

Another way that marketers will fail the customer and the brand is through poor execution of the offering. Poor execution typically results in a negative experience that turns off the customer, which can lead to the customer bad-mouthing the offender, thus tarnishing reputations and scaring off potential target customers. Let me provide an example to which many business travelers can relate.

Our story starts on a business trip with a flight from O'Hare to Newark Airport on a leading carrier. Already, the traveler is at a disadvantage having to deal with two of the geographical areas with the heaviest air traffic in the country. The aircraft, originating from Austin, arrived late into Chicago. However, that's par for the course these days. If you check the records for many of these flights, you'll find that on-time delivery is only about 30%. Now, that's not just a problem for specific airlines. It's an embarrassment!

The story doesn't end here. A gate attendant announces that the aircraft has developed a mechanical problem. However, the attendant also announces that he does not have information regarding the specific problem since maintenance has not yet informed him of it. He tells us that "maintenance" will get back to him and he will, in turn, get back to us in "about 15 minutes" (which is never *only* 15 minutes).

Not being able to pry any additional information from the attendant, I make a call to my travel agency. "Back me up on the carrier's next flight to Newark."

"That's a 3 o'clock flight," comes the reply, "but the aircraft is out of service."

Accordingly, my travel agency backs me up with a competitive airline. When you positively need to be there, you do what it takes to get there.

Fifteen minutes stretches into forty. No new information is forthcoming other than my carrier is looking into getting another aircraft. Eventually, and to their credit, they do secure one. So, it is off to Newark. But, as you might guess, with a change in equipment and late departure, the aircraft and its "valued" customers experience further delay. This latest delay is exacerbated by the need to reassign seating, which delays boarding and consequently departure, and by issues with slotting at the destination airport.

Finally, I arrive at Newark. Thank heavens all I had was carry-on luggage. Newark is notoriously slow with baggage handling. It is not uncommon to have to wait an additional 30 to 40-minutes when one arrives at baggage claim.

So now, it's a mad dash to the rental car counter via the tram system at Newark. As I get off the escalator, a tram pulls away from the station. Nothing to be concerned about as the digital billboard flashes an announcement that the next one will arrive in just 3 minutes. I've waited a long time to get to Newark, so an additional 3 minutes is nothing to be concerned about. Unfortunately, several minutes later, the masses that have gathered, of which I am a part, are notified that there is a temporary problem with the tram. Twenty or more minutes later, an attendant calls out that the problem is rather significant, and he doesn't know when the next tram will be available. (At least he didn't promise 15 minutes.) However, he goes on to say that the rental car area is just a short walk, and if we follow him, he will lead us there.

I follow, even though it is not in my nature to do so. The short walk turns out to be about a quarter of a mile. Walking a quarter of a mile is usually no big deal, but I was schlepping luggage across grassy medians and up and down curbs. Did I mention it was raining? Alas, finally, we make it.

By this time (being more than 2 hours late), the rental car company has removed my name from the "Preferred" screen. I have to go to a special counter where the manager says she needs my special identification number. Dummy me, I should carry it, but it's another one of those infrequently used cards that, together with other infrequently used cards, causes my wallet and back pocket to bulge such that an observer might conclude I'm wearing an incontinence diaper. "Try my name," I suggest.

"Sorry, sir, but the system doesn't respond to names. I need your number; otherwise, we will have to enter all your information."

"Well," I say, "here's my confirmation number."

"No, that won't work either."

"Then why don't you just enter the information?" After the manager assesses blame on my innocent travel agency rep, she finally hands me the documents and points me to a space.

Guess what? There's no car in the space. So, I return for another vehicle. After I store my luggage in the trunk of the second car, I take a seat and begin to buckle-up. However, the seat belt harness doesn't work. *Perhaps it's me,* I think. I call over an attendant and ask him to check out the seat belt for me. While I was, at one time, a naval aviator who was confident strapping into military aircraft, it now seems I have my doubts about my ability to lock into the seat belt harness of an automobile.

"It's broken," he confirms. "We'll get you another car," which they do following another trek back to the counter schlepping my luggage.

The brand is more than flying passengers from point A to point B or providing late-model cars. It is more than the product or service you offer. Instead, the brand is the inclusion of services and quality that comprise the totality of the experience, forging a relationship between it and customers. It's the smile and pat on the back from the Walmart greeter who makes you feel welcome; it's Tiffany's blue box and satin ribbon that signals a special gift; it's the ease of access that ensures your prescription will be filled and covered; it's free delivery; it's vendor postage paid returns; it's someone who will carry your luggage back to the counter for you and then escort you to your vehicle. The brand is all of this and more.

Perhaps, you are familiar with the debacle on a major airline carrier that caused headlines in the news a couple of years ago where a passenger on an overbooked flight was dragged, yes, "dragged," off the plane following boarding. This proved to be a negative experience not only for this passenger, who was bloodied and bruised, but for all those passengers aboard the aircraft who witnessed the rather violent and alarming incident, and for those millions of people who viewed it on the news and on YouTube. By the way, the airline compensated the passenger after a lawsuit brought on a settlement for an undisclosed sum. Not only was this financially damaging, but it resulted in tons of negative publicity. Unlike Hollywood, negative publicity is not beneficial in the airline industry. I imagine it is not beneficial to your brand either!

This incident may be attributed to rigid policies and blind obedience, gross errors in judgment and hiring the wrong people who, in this case, apparently, are not customer-centric.

While the incident mentioned above is indefensible, we need to recognize things can and do go wrong on occasion. They always will. However, the marketer's ability to anticipate and handle these exigencies defines, and impacts, the brand's relationship with customers and ultimately how it will be perceived. The late Jim Burke, Chairman of the Johnson & Johnson Company, stood by the company's credo, which put customers first, during the dark days of product tampering with the Tylenol brand, to earn a deep and abiding trust with customers that continued for many years. By the way, the credo was not packed into the Tylenol product. Likewise, Disney knows how to serve patrons in its theme parks who encounter long lines and delays for its more popular events in a way that creates a favorable experience and keeps families coming back for more.

BRAND EXPERIENCES THAT MAKE A DIFFERENCE

Do you need to have a brand-new idea or invent something radically different to create difference?
No, not necessarily. Starbucks didn't invent coffee, and Apple didn't invent the smartphone;
these companies simply created new experiences of them,
which in turn created a whole new set of meanings that we attached to what were once commodities.
Bernadette Jiwa

Some marketers recognize the importance of the brand experience. Here are a few that offer valuable lessons:

American Airlines: When we think about experiences, most of us don't think too fondly of our experiences with the airlines. We have to deal with baggage fees, overcrowded aircraft, lost luggage, delays, cancellations, surly flight attendants, poor (if any) food, overbooking, long security lines, the need to strip down to get through security, limited seating area, limited overhead space for bags—the list goes on. We endure rather than relish the experiences of air travel.

American Airlines provides exceptional services to its elite customers (i.e., those who fly and spend the most) to deliver a more pleasing experience to keep them loyal, beyond the miles they earn towards upgrades and free flights. American ConciergeKey is an "invitation only" program to their most elite flyers. It offers a plethora of airport and airline services to make the air travel experience special. Its many services include the following:

- Dedicated check-in kiosks. In Chicago and Los Angeles Airport, this is Flagship Check-In. It is a private area where you are greeted and escorted to (and even through) security, leap-frogging TSA-approved fliers.
- Escort onto the plane before anyone else boards so you can get your bag into the overhead compartment before it becomes full.
- Free upgrades to the next class of service when flying domestically. While this service is available to other frequent fliers, the ConciergeKey members go to the top of the list.
- 4 VIP upgrades wherever American Airlines flies. So, you might use a VIP upgrade from business to first-class on a flight to Asia.
- Complimentary drinks and snacks (even if you are traveling in coach).
- A dedicated telephone number to call for assistance.
- Free membership to the American Airlines Lounge.
- No baggage fees for up to three bags.
- Welcomed at the jetway and escorted through customs and into baggage claim.

Imagine landing at London Heathrow en route to St. Petersburg, Russia, and being met on the jetway and personally escorted (i.e., driven by an airline's car) to the appropriate terminal for the flight to St. Petersburg. No rushing through the terminal. No busses. No waiting. Nothing but concierge service.

Alternatively, imagine checking in at Los Angeles Airport, separate and far from the maddening crowd. There, you are greeted by someone in a top hat, escorted via private elevator to security and whisked through security, ahead of those who have TSA clearance.

That's American ConciergeKey. That's a remarkable experience. By the way, United Airlines has a similar program called United Global Services.

One final note, American Airlines staffs its program with their best agents who are pre-disposed by personality to be eager and are trained to assist you in having a favorable experience.

American Express Platinum: American Express customers are not cardholders but "members." In addition to meeting financial criteria, you pay a fee to become a member. There is American Express Black, Green, Gold, and Platinum, each with different financial criteria and fees. The fee to be a member of the American Express Platinum Card, of which I'm one, doesn't come cheap. It is $550 per annum. If you think about these credit cards, they are identical in their physical makeup, except for their color. Generally, they are the same size, made of the same material and work in the same way. What makes the American Express Platinum Card warrant $550? It's the privileges and experiences it affords.

Some of the services one receives with being an American Express Platinum Card member include the following:

- One year of Amazon Prime membership valued at $119 (discussed below).
- No foreign transaction fees.
- 24/7 service.
- Membership Rewards Program where you get points for spending that you can use for air travel and hotel stays without blackouts or travel restrictions.
- Airport Club Access and Priority Pass Select, providing access to over 600 domestic and international lounges where you may chill out, get work done, have a meal, etc., before boarding your flight.
- International Airline Program that enables you to enjoy savings on a companion ticket when you purchase business or first-class travel for yourself.

- $200 airline fee credit annually for incidental fees charged by the airlines. It can be used for baggage and flight change fees, etc. By the way, some of these services do not amplify an experience but alleviate or forestall what might otherwise be a poor or irritating experience.
- $100 credit towards the Global Entry program that provides for "expedited clearance" through customs when entering the U.S. (This is a rebate of the $100 application fee.)
- Fine Hotels & Resorts Program that includes availability-based room upgrades, early check-in, and guaranteed 4:00 pm check-out, complimentary breakfast, and credits for expenses like meals, beverages, spa treatments, etc. Booking through American Express will also get the card member the best room rate.
- Purchase protection up to 90 days after the date of purchase if your merchandise is lost, stolen or damaged, throughout the world!
- Platinum Card Concierge (there's that word again, "concierge") staff serves as a personal resource to provide advice on selecting the right gift, picking a restaurant (which comes in very handy when you are in a new city), etc.
- Entertainment Access provides exclusive access to ticket presales for concerts, sporting events, and card member-only events.

American Express Platinum offers so many additional services. These added services are not so much about making your card usage experience a favorable one. Instead, it is about providing meaningful "life experiences."

Amazon Prime: Amazon.com is a godsend for avid readers. They have scores of titles from which to choose. Based upon your purchasing history, they even recommend books. You can also take recommendations from Amazon readers. The books are delivered to your doorstep or immediately to your e-reader.

Amazon Prime* is a fee-based service from Amazon that currently costs $119 per year. What might you get from it?

- Free two-day shipping. My wife has an Amazon Prime account. She does much of her holiday shopping (and shopping throughout the year) through Amazon with her Amazon Prime account. It saves her time and money. Importantly, it helps her complete her shopping early and get our gifts out to family and friends well before the holidays. This two-day shipping is not just for books; it is for all the merchandise Amazon offers. I think the only thing that can beat this for speed and instant gratification is downloading e-books (for books) and drone delivery (when it becomes available) of merchandise. In many cases, you can get "next day" and even "same day" free delivery on orders of $35 or more. Incredible!

- Prime Now provides two-hour delivery of qualifying items, such as groceries. Need it in an hour? You can get that too for $7.99 extra.
- They offer unlimited "instant" streaming of 41,000 movies and TV episodes. "Instant" provides immediate gratification. The wide selection of titles pretty much ensures that what you want to view will be there.
- Borrow one book for free each month from more than 350,000 Kindle titles. You not only save money but a trip to the library.
- Now that Amazon owns Whole Foods, you can get receive a 10% discount on purchases there.

*Prices and services may have changed at the time of your reading.

One of my friends needed a wheelchair for a family member during a vacation. At the vacation locale, wheelchair rental was going to cost $250 for the week. As a member of Amazon Prime, he bought a wheelchair from Amazon for $150 and had it shipped to the vacation site. He received it in two days, exactly when he needed it.

Amazon Prime is about the ease of the shopping experience, a virtually unlimited selection and near instant gratification with its delivery of your order. It is an online or digital business that attempts to make the delivery process more gratifying in many ways.

Apple: Okay, Apple is not without its flaws. It doesn't always play nice with non-Apple products. When new software is launched, it sometimes requires patches (but then that's the case with virtually all software providers). BUT

Apple has focused on the user experience with its products. For one, Apple optimizes all its products for performance. Keynote works superbly with your Mac. iTunes works better on a Mac than with a PC. Neither is compromised for your Mac to make it work for a PC. (That's one of the many ways in which it doesn't always play nice with others.) Additionally, Apple hardware products work seamlessly with each other. My Mac connects to my iPad, and iPhone, and Apple TV. Even if a competitor were to develop better technology, it would take a lot more to move me from Apple given its ecosystem of interconnected products and devices that serves to deliver a *seamless user experience.*

Additionally, Apple provides terrific support for its products. The Genius Bar provides you with real people, who speak your language and with whom you can deal with face to face, versus over the telephone with someone thousands of miles away, to help solve any technical problems you may experience with one of their devices. Then there's Apple's workshops that offer valuable instruction on using and gaining the full benefits from each of their many products. The workshops provide instruction on creating a video using iMovie or a podcast using Garageband, or on making the most of your photo experiences. These are additional services that ease migration to Apple and make the experience more rewarding. They are available at all Apple retail stores where the staff are not only knowledgeable about Apple products, but they are huge fans. They share the passion of Apple users for Apple products.

Coca-Cola: The world's most popular soft drink focuses on the user experience. Enjoying Coca-Cola is more than a taste sensory experience. When I was a young marketer at Coca-Cola, some 35 years ago, I honestly felt my mission was to put smiles on consumers' faces with Coca-Cola. The brand is all about creating a joyful experience, as celebrated in key advertising campaigns like "Things go better with Coke," to "Coke adds life," and "Open happiness." However, Coke is about more than slogans. The "Hug Me" talking vending machines implored passersby to stop and hug them. Then there's the Coca-Cola Freestyle Fountain vending machine. Rather than 6 to 8 beverage choices, the Coca-Cola Freestyle has an easy-to-use screen that dispenses more than 100 individual flavor combinations, some of which aren't available anywhere else. It must be a positive experience; otherwise, how would one explain the increase in traffic and sales at the restaurant locations that carry it?

Coca-Cola distribution has enhanced life, moving from "around the corner from everywhere" to "arms reach from anywhere." It is "the pause that refreshes," going beyond liquid refreshment to bodily and mental refreshment.

One of the novel developments to attempt to create a positive user experience in Asia is the Coca-Cola Sharing Can. The can is made of two half-size cans that you can detach for sharing. As they say in their advertising, "Half the size. Twice the happiness."

USAA (United Services Automobile Association): USAA reports they have a 98% retention rate and nearly all their members plan to stick with USAA for life. That's impressive. It's not mere habit or inertia that drives these members. It's outstanding service and the immense satisfaction and trust derived from it. I ought to know. I've been a USAA member since 1969 (that's 50 years and counting!).

USAA provides insurance for military, former military, and their family members. Cost of its insurance is competitive (and, in actuality, is likely to save you money) with service that is exceptional and the peace of mind that you are protected. According to Forrester's, the US Customer Experience (CX) Index, which measures a brand's CX experience and its influence on loyalty, USAA is in a category of elite brands, which generates "an average of 22 emotionally positive experiences for each negative experience."

When you call USAA, you are greeted by a knowledgeable agent who treats you with the utmost respect. You're not just a number but a member of their military family. They welcome me when I call with the title "Commander," which delights me to no end. (I completed my US Naval service with the rank of lieutenant commander.) There's no quibbling with claims, and they handle all claims most expeditiously. If you have USAA, you can be assured they have your back! I not only have USAA for my two autos, but also for my home and household items, health supplemental, business, and life insurance. I even have a USAA credit card and savings account.

The Steve Foley Cadillac Experience: We lease a Cadillac from Steve Foley Cadillac dealership in Northbrook, Illinois, and have been for more than 30 years. My wife recently brought our car in for servicing. She came home and *raved* about the service she received. "Raved" is typically not a word one uses when describing experiences. Customers rarely talk about the experience, unless it is negative. Moreover, there usually isn't much positive to say about the physical product, unless it is a novelty or a lemon. As per physical products, we purchase and use them more out of habit. We use them without any real emotional connection. They work, so what's there to talk about?

I interviewed Cathy Foley, Marketing Director of Steve Foley Cadillac, to learn more about their attitudes and practices about making a meaningful difference in creating a winning experience. Here's the interview:

- *What does "experience" mean to you?*
  CF: We want to treat our customers the way we want to be treated. This needs to extend through every touchpoint in the customer's journey. (It's practicing the Golden Rule.) These touchpoints include phone contacts, the moment the customer walks through the door of the showroom, porter service (which includes moving and cleaning cars, etc.), the business office experience of financing and insurance, maintenance, the cashier, the after-sales experience, etc. We want to over-deliver every step of the way.

- *How did you come to identify with the need to move beyond product to "experience?" What inspired you?*
  CF: This is fundamentally a Cadillac-originated program. There was a need for something more to effectively compete with other luxury brands. It started in 2012 and was labeled "Defining Moments." It was inspired by the hospitality industry, most notably Ritz Carlton. They're about treating people in an extraordinary way. (Ritz Carlton employees resonate to their mantra "We are ladies and gentlemen serving ladies and gentlemen.") Today, it has been rebranded as "Cadillac Moments."

- *Who's responsible for this?*

  CF: The key managers responsible for implementing the Cadillac Moments strategy are the general manager, the new car sales manager, the service director, and me. However, *every* employee is responsible for making this happen.

- *Who do you view as the competition? Who are you trying to differentiate against?*

  CF: Luxury brands outside of Cadillac, such as Lexus, BMW, Mercedes, etc. Domestically, Lincoln seems to be doing very well currently and represents another luxury competitor. And, then for us, there are the other Cadillac dealerships. We have so many dealerships within Chicagoland that offer the same product. We want to stand out to attract new business.

- *What is the Steve Foley difference?*

  CF: It starts with our customer- and service-focused people. We have low employee turnover. We provide them with training. Each of them has been with us for many years, so customer focus and service focus are ingrained in our culture. Also, we treat our employees with respect. You can't have respect for customers without having employees who are treated with respect.

  Additionally, we have a dedicated product specialist (VIP of Customer Relations) with 30 years of experience, in the service aisle. Many of the dealerships do not have anyone in this role. Our specialist demonstrates to customers how to utilize the features of our loaner cars. It makes the technology accessible. His goal is to provide a positive experience to cultivate relationships. This helps us to sell customers who purchased elsewhere but service with us. It gets maintenance customers to switch to Steve Foley Cadillac for purchasing. We are grateful for our customers' business, and we thank them frequently. We can't thank them enough times.

- *What are your goals?*

  CF: Well, we want to do whatever it takes to earn and retain business for life.

- *How do you measure success?*
  CF: Cadillac provides measurements and rewards. There's a CSI (customer service index) to measure customer satisfaction. Our dealership is in the top 90-percentile. We also have more than 70% retention. We are among the top in the nation.

- *Is this a fad or a permanent shift in the culture of the organization?*
  CF: This is about continuous improvement. Like Six Sigma, we define our objectives, analyze our processes and practices, measure results and adopt controls to make improvements.

RX FOR CREATING A WINNING BRAND EXPERIENCE

So, what does it take to create a winning brand experience and to forge a loyal bond with customers? Here are some thoughts for your consideration and action:

1. ***Segment your customer base.*** Our brands cannot be all things to all people, nor can they afford to do so. We not only need to segment the market, but we should also consider segmenting our customers. American Airlines with its ConciergeKey services for their most elite fliers, and American Express with their Platinum Card offering premium services for their wealthier, higher spending members, are both involved in segmenting their customer base. So is USAA with their servicing of current and former members of the U.S. military and their families. They are providing special treatment to those whom they consider being among their best or most profitable or, perhaps, most influential customers. These represent the customers who mean the most to their franchise. I'd wager that despite the higher cost of serving these customers, they are amongst their most profitable.

2. ***Get in touch with the customer experience.*** Experience the experience. Put yourself in the shoes of your customers. Call the toll-free number or visit the website provided for getting additional information. Purchase

the product to live and feel the experience. Experience what it is like at every touchpoint from pre- to post-sales. What does it feel like to be on the receiving end? Is there an experience? What can you learn that will lead to strengthening the brand and its bond with customers?

However, don't stop at experiencing your brand. Experience your competitors' brands. How do they compare? What can you learn from your competitors to improve upon the experience your brand delivers?

Benchmark brands that deliver a world-class experience in other categories. A Qantas Airlines agent shared with me that her airline holds Ritz Carlton as its model for customer service. So did Steve Foley Cadillac. The Ritz Carlton vision, "We are ladies and gentlemen serving ladies and gentlemen," has been adopted to service customers. It's in the DNA of its employees. In practice, Qantas agents are treated to the Ritz Carlton experience so they can appreciate the experience they are targeting for their customers. Learn what you are capable of achieving and be inspired to achieve it.

3. *Create added-value services to develop a whole product offering that is differentiated from competition and preferred by customers.* Airlines, electronic devices, credit cards, online retailers, insurance companies, auto dealerships, and even soft drinks are pretty much commodities. I'd wager so is your product. There is not much difference in one product offering versus another in the same category. Oh yes, there may be some minor differences in features, but remember, they all do the same sort of things and work in the same basic ways. Services and special terms, on the other hand, add to the physical product to create a whole-product offering that delivers a user experience. Services are non-material elements such as terms, training, etc. Mac is more than a physical computer. It includes its Genius Bar support, workshops, Apple Care and even its retail outlets, among other services. When one purchases a Mac, one receives much more than a personal computer. Mac is a whole-product offering that serves to create a favorable experience. ConciergeKey is not part of the aircraft, the physical entity, that American Airlines uses to whisk its customers

from one point to another. There is nothing physically material about its services, but it has a material impact on the experience its elite customers enjoy. R&D provides us with the tangible elements of the product. However, we marketers are the ones who develop the services to create a whole product that drives differentiation and preference through a rewarding experience.

4. *Create a customer-focused culture within your organization.* Serve the customer well, and brand loyalty is more likely to follow. But, you can't just dictate special handling for customers. If it's not part of the culture, you've got to create it. It starts with hiring people with the right attitude. They're not there for a paycheck or to be served, but instead, they are there to serve others. They have empathy with customers and choose to treat them as they would like to be treated. This extends to how you treat everyone in the company. It won't play out well with customers if employees are not treated with respect. Airline management and labor tend to be antagonistic and often lock horns. Is it any surprise then that management skimps with customers or "labor" engages in disruptive strikes that hold passengers hostage?

USAA views its members as part of a family. Those of us who have served in the military share the perspective that, because of our service, we are part of a proud, devoted and loyal family. USAA is an extension of it. They promise to "stand by you during every stage of your life," and they live up to that promise in deed, not merely in word. One out of every four USAA employees are veterans or military spouses.

Do not forget that we are all in a battle to win customers for life. Customers are not, nor should they ever be viewed as, an inconvenience. Nor should we attempt to bend customers, through manipulation or inconveniences, to satisfy operational needs and practices of the company. Instead, it is the company and its people that need to bend its operations and practices to meet the needs of its customers. This is being there for the customer when and how she needs.

5. *Make your values your code of conduct, and reject anything and everything that is not consistent with these values.* Marketing is not about using "smoke

and mirrors" to make a transaction. Instead, it is about operating with integrity to create an enduring, transformative relationship. Values are foundational to a relationship. If you have a set of values within your organization, live up to them to create lasting relationships rather than a series of transactions. The late, great James "Jim" Burke, former Chairman of Johnson & Johnson, worked with his senior executives throughout the world to rewrite and recommit them, and all employees, to the company's credo. He stated that if managers were not going to honor the credo, then it was hypocrisy to keep it. He said something along the lines of, "If we are not going to be governed by it, we should tear it off the damn wall." Never compromise on values to satisfy strategy or chase a transaction.

6. *Solve people's problems. Don't be wed to dogma.* Customer service is an extension of marketing. If they don't report to marketing, perhaps they should! When we don't deal with customers as human beings but as things to be manipulated, we create problems for them and for our organizations. We destroy trust. Those in customer service need to be able to resolve customer problems or to connect the aggrieved customer with someone who has the authority to resolve the issue to the customer's satisfaction. Believe it or not, satisfactorily addressing a customer's issue (particularly one we have caused) can serve to revitalize the bond and relationship with that customer, as we've witnessed with the Coca-Cola Company following its reintroduction of Classic Coke and Johnson & Johnson with its recall and relaunch of the Tylenol brand following tampering back in 1982. This takes "true" versus "blind" obedience to the principle of being customer-centric. Do what it takes to create a *transformational* relationship.

7. *Consider "exclusivity" to engage and reward customer performance.* There is inherent value in "exclusivity" (as in exclusive membership), especially when tied to performance. The fact that the experience isn't for everyone and requires performance makes selection and membership all the more valuable to the customer. It conveys a level of status and prestige and affords the customer bragging rights. In the

2009 movie *Up in the Air,* George Clooney plays an executive who has amassed more than *ten million miles* with American Airlines. He uses his ConciergeKey card to seal his seduction of a fellow frequent-flier woman traveler he meets at the hotel bar (that's Hollywood for you!). She is in awe of his status and the miles it has taken to achieve it. As per the American Express Platinum Card, it seems to elicit more attention and better service from merchants. They perceive the cardholder to be particularly valuable regarding his ability and willingness to make (many) purchases of premium brands. However, it is important to be transparent about the requirements. If not, you could turn off those target customers who "don't make the (perceived arbitrary) grade."

8. ***Create value-added pay for play.*** Many of these experiences cost the brands that are offering them. The services that contribute to winning experiences don't necessarily come cheap. So, some brands require payment, which makes membership "self-selective." Actually, this can be an excellent practice. It is sort of like separating the wheat from the chaff as it relates to the quality of customers and the ability to attract and service them. It also means there must be a favorable perceived value to these services and resultant experiences. The American Express Platinum Card is $550 per annum. No, that's not cheap! However, when you tally the benefits and services, it seems to be well worth its cost and premium versus the Green and Gold Cards offered by the same issuer. Amazon Prime costs $119 per year. Why pay $119 per year when Amazon is free? Once again, the services and experiences derived from this membership are perceived to more than offset the costs of participation for these customers.

9. ***Attract, retain and encourage usage.*** Many marketers focus on attracting new users, but they neglect retention. Can anyone here say "J.C. Penney?" The goal of creating brand loyalty demands that we retain customers. If we don't, we lose their loyalty! It also encourages the frequency of use or, as characterized in some categories, increased utilization. The Coca-Cola Freestyle Fountain vending machine dispenses more than 100 individual flavors, some of which aren't available anywhere else,

to enable consumers to create their own unique beverage experience that's a refreshing change of pace. It helps keep consumers thirsting for more and coming back to satisfy that thirst.

The Apple ecosystem of interconnected products and devices delivers a seamless user experience that serves to encourage the purchase of other Apple product offerings. It helps immunize their customers from migrating to newer technologies offered by competitors. Their Genius Bar staffed by real people speaking your language, whom you can deal with face-to-face versus over the telephone with someone thousands of miles away, to help you resolve any technical issues you are experiencing, is quite comforting and rewarding. So, even if there is a glitch with the product, the very opportunity to speak and work with someone helps make what may have been a negative experience a positive one.

USAA treats its members like family, and it is available to support you throughout your lifetime. Likewise, Steve Foley Cadillac dealership provides exceptional service to retain customers, recognizing they can get the same product from other Cadillac dealerships in the Chicagoland area.

10. ***Thank your customers in deeds, not just in words.*** Words are cheap! Demonstrate through deeds that you appreciate their business and relationship. This certainly includes saying thank you, but it also includes *doing* something that is unexpected, like gifting your customers. It's not a bribe! (We don't nor should anyone do business that way regardless of cultural norms. It is not an ethical norm!) It's merely civility. It could be a VIP upgrade on American Airlines flight or a coupon handed to you as you enter the airline's lounge for a complimentary beverage at the bar. It may be the presence of snacks and refreshments in your hotel room when you arrive, with a note of appreciation for staying at the hotel (using your American Express Platinum Card). It could be something as simple as a representative looking you in the eye and saying, "Thank you for your business. We appreciate it." All these ways of giving thanks help create favorable experiences that serve to engender loyalty.

11. *Fess-up and correct mistakes.* On a recent flight from Newark to Chicago, the flight was two hours late on an already long day. It was a great relief when the plane finally departed. Weather delays happen. However, what doesn't always happen, thank goodness, are mechanical problems and more specifically engine problems that are discovered mid-flight, which is what transpired. Consequently, the aircraft diverted to Cleveland. The passengers were boarded on another plane and flown to Chicago in the wee hours of the morning. The day had started at 4:45 am and ended at 3:00 am the following morning.

American Airlines promptly sent out a letter (not an email) apologizing for the aircraft problem and for the inconvenience it had caused. However, they went one step further. They credited my account with an additional 20,000 air miles (not that I need them). Did this correct potential engine malfunction problems? No, but one would believe, given how infrequently flights need to be diverted due to engine problems, that they are continuously working on it. However, they apologized and, unprompted, attempted to offer some token of restitution. None of us are immune to making mistakes or causing inconveniences. The key is to fess up and then do something about it. (By the way, it would have been a big mistake, not merely an inconvenience, to continue to fly to Chicago with an engine problem, jeopardizing the safety of all those souls on board.)

Then there was the Tylenol crisis of 1982. Several people died in the Chicago area from ingesting tampered Extra-Strength Tylenol cyanide-laced capsules. The late Jim Burke, one of my heroes, decided to pull some 31 million bottles of Tylenol from retailers' shelves and offered free replacement product. Within a couple of months, Tylenol relaunched with tamper-proof packaging supported with an extensive advertising campaign. The company spent more than $100 million for the recall and relaunch of the brand. These courageous actions on the part of Mr. Burke and the company fueled consumer confidence in the brand and company.

A "classic" mistake was the introduction of New Coke. Don Keough, who was president of the Coca-Cola Company at the time, fessed up, apologized and gave consumers what they wanted: "Classic" Coke. A festering wound with consumers was closed and healed. All was forgiven (even with the press). If you make a mistake but fess up and treat customers right, it could serve to strengthen the brand as customers will give you the benefit of the doubt and forgive you for it. (Just don't keep repeating the same mistakes! Customers will tolerate only so much.)

12. ***Brighten your customers' lives.*** Whoa, this is a bit much. How are we going to do that? Well, Coca-Cola finds ways to delight its customers, not only with its refreshing beverage but also in its marketing activities. The talking vending machine, the Freestyle Fountain vending machine, the Coca-Cola sharing can in Asia, and fun promotions are examples of the many ways the brand attempts to create and spread happiness. Coca-Cola sponsors festive sporting events such as the Summer Olympics, the World Cup, local professional teams and even local high school sports, to our enjoyment! Coca-Cola is present where people go to experience happiness, and it contributes to their delight. Even Coca-Cola advertising serves to brighten the spirits of consumers. Just thinking about any one of the Coca-Cola Polar Bear commercials elicits a smile from me. It doesn't matter your age; Coca-Cola is at work to help brighten your day with its quintessential beverage and marketing-related activities.

13. ***Avoid doing what you ought not to do.*** There's a quote about golf that goes something like this: "Golf has too much walking to be a good game, and just enough game to spoil a good walk." The worse the game, then undoubtedly, the more the walk is spoiled. Marketers need to beware of things we do to ruin the game or the walk. These are negative actions that diminish the brand experience and, therefore, we should avoid them at all costs, such as:
    * Bombarding customers with messaging
    * Haunting customers with mobile messaging
    * Falsely posing as friends

- Promising the improbable or unachievable (such as "get your life back")
- Making false or misleading claims
- Overcomplicating things for customers (e.g., packaging, promotions, etc.)
- Talking down to customers
- Serving your organization at the expense of your customers
- Using call-in centers that take customers through several automated commands before connecting with a human being
- Passing off a customer call from one rep to another requiring the customer to retell his issue
- Not solving the customer's problem or inadequately addressing the issue
- Wasting the customer's time by having them talk with a representative from the company who is not authorized to solve the customer's problem but merely repeat false apologies
- Suggesting that, perhaps, the customer did not use the product appropriately (when it doesn't work correctly or malfunctions)
- Over-engineering the product
- Insulting and infuriating the customer by suggesting that she doesn't know how to use the product correctly
- Designing the product so it takes an engineer to assemble or use it
- Attempting to trade-up a customer from a disappointing purchase to another item, as opposed to correcting the problem
- Not honoring terms
- Delaying service
- Not providing suitable quality control to ensure product integrity
- Not apologizing for mistakes
- Staffing with poorly trained or incompetent service personnel
- Not having product in stock
- Understaffing (which results in problems for the customer, such as long lines or wait periods to deal with an issue)
- Not refunding returns
- Issuing store credits versus refunds for returned merchandise

- Deep discounting product after a customer purchases it, for which she will not be entitled to a refund or return
- Selling shoddy or inferior products
- Slapping the customer with enormous penalties for changing an airline reservation

Those adverse actions mentioned above can transform an even relatively mindless experience into one that customers will remember, most unfavorably!

14. ***Treat the customer as if she is always right.*** We're all familiar with the maxim "the customer is always right." However, you may argue that this is not always true. But, really, who are we to argue one way or the other? It is a slogan that was coined to encourage workers to be attentive to customer satisfaction. Our goal should not be to make a transaction, particularly at the risk of damaging a relationship, but to create brand loyalty. We have a vested interest in customer satisfaction. If we don't treat the customer with the utmost respect, truly listen to and hear their issues and look for ways to satisfy the customer, we are certainly going to dampen her experience and risk losing her. By the way, it is so much costlier to win a new customer than to keep one who is already on board with your brand. Regardless of whether you hold it to be entirely accurate, it's a critical maxim to heed if you are going to retain customers and win converts.

This is not to suggest, by the way, that all the brands talked about in this chapter are perfect. They're not! One is liable to have a poor experience with any one of these somewhere along the line. However, they are clearly thinking "whole-product customer experience" and attempting to make it a positive one to build a relationship as opposed to tally up a mere transaction. They are exhibiting a desire to better serve their customers than competition, going well beyond their physical product offering.

HOW NOT TO TREAT (LOYAL) CUSTOMERS
A customer is more than just a number on a balance sheet.

A LOYAL CUSTOMER DONE WRONG

I anxiously awaited news from American Airlines, like a kid awaiting the arrival of Santa Claus, that my ConciergeKey membership had been renewed. ConciergeKey is an American Airlines loyalty rewards program offering special added-value services to what it refers to as its "elite" customers (i.e., those who fly and spend the most). The program is designed to deliver a more pleasing experience to reward and maintain customer loyalty. It consists of a plethora of highly relevant and meaningful airport and airline services such as:

- A dedicated check-in area at airports (e.g., busy airports like Chicago and Los Angeles) where members are greeted and escorted to (and even through) security, leapfrogging TSA approved fliers.
- Being escorted onto the aircraft before boarding anyone else so you can get your bag into the overhead (by the way, no baggage fees) before it is filled.
- Free membership and use of the Flagship Lounge.
- Receiving priority for upgrades.
- Being met at the jetway upon arrival from international flights and escorted through customs and into baggage claim.

Given these wonderful services (there are even more special services than those listed), you can certainly understand why I was excited about receiving confirmation that American Airlines had renewed my membership.

There was no reason to expect that it would not. During the year, I had flown 157,999 EQM (elite qualifying miles) and had EQD (elite qualifying dollar) purchases of $36,055. This is significantly more than the requirements for receiving Executive Platinum status, which is on the next lower rung of the ladder. Executive Platinum status requires 100,000 EQM and $12,000 in EQD purchases. I blew through those numbers and figured I was guaranteed to have my ConciergeKey membership renewed. However, much to my disappointment, it did not come to pass.

GOB-SMACKED!

On 11 January of the new year, I received an email from the President of the AAdvantage Loyalty Program informing me that my travel "wasn't quite enough." What!?! To put it mildly, I was gob-smacked. This was extremely disappointing and disturbing news as I credit the service with helping extend the longevity of my career slogging around the world to service our clients. I've been part of the American Advantage loyalty program since 1985 and an annual ConciergeKey member since its inception (or close to it). I've flown more than 7 million miles with American Airlines and its partners, which is equivalent to flying around the earth more than 300 times. As a result of many years of frequent, extended travels, I know the American Airlines personnel working at O'Hare better than I know my neighbors (and even some of my family members). And, now I'd been dropped! I felt desperate. What to do?

THE CUSTOMER SPEAKS (BEGS)

I took to "pleading" for reinstatement of my ConciergeKey membership. I started with calling ConciergeKey, as members have a special line. But, alas, no one there could help me. They not only didn't know who received membership, but they had no inkling regarding criteria for selection. (I guess I was a member of a secret society.) So, I took the next step and emailed my petition, only to have it summarily rejected once, then twice. I suspect these rejections were "form emails" since they did not address the details of what I had written. Instead, they stated that they needed to limit the number of invitations "to ensure adequate resources are available for the services offered." Finally, I wrote a letter to the President of the AAdvantage Loyalty Program, and I also emailed her. I felt that, surely, she could empathize with my case and would be a final benevolent authority on a very loyal customer's petition. You don't get to be president of a customer loyalty program without caring genuinely for your customers and how to treat them. Or, do you?

In my email to the president, I cited my long history with American Airlines. I also informed her that my stats don't even tell the whole story, as I fly my family (three daughters, their husbands and our four granddaughters) to and from family functions (of which there were four during the previous year) via American Airlines and its partners, all at my expense. I felt certain I'd get the benefit of the doubt, especially since they informed me that my travel "wasn't quite enough." I figured "quite" meant slightly off and shouldn't be a deal-breaker. Also, I had booked all my flights through ConciergeKey services, and no one informed me at any time during the year that I was (slightly?) behind in either EQM or EQD, or both. If they had, I might have taken a holiday with my wife to a distant and exotic locale to snag the additional miles needed.

I received a response within a few days, not from the President of the AAdvantage Loyalty Program, but from an executive liaison, who was asked to correspond on behalf of the president, saying, "Thank you for your many years of business and loyalty." While at the least, I expected the president to have someone write for her signature (as opposed to the liaison's signature), I did nonetheless find the response was more thoughtful than previous emails in that it directly addressed points for consideration contained in my plea.

RESPONSES TO THE SITUATION

When I informed colleagues, friends, and family of my predicament, they responded thusly:

- "Wow! Is that what they did?!"

- "I can't believe it. American Airlines dropped you."
- "It's like a slap in the face."
- "You've been kicked to the curb."

Well, perhaps the responses I received were a little over the top. After all, I did receive Executive Platinum status, and it has significant perks recognizing frequent customers. (In fact, at this writing, I learned that American Airlines upgraded me on my flight to Newark on Monday. However, they are nothing compared to ConciergeKey.) I'd be less than truthful if I said that I did not feel let down, abandoned, and stung in my heart. Am I overreacting? How might you feel if this happened to you?

You might think I'm acting like an elitist, but those who know me know that I am far from being one. Alternatively, you might think I'm spoiled. My wife and daughters might agree with this last assessment. I admit to having been spoiled by ConciergeKey's special services, which reduced the burden of my frequent travel. Taking it away for not flying *quite enough* during the year, when I blew through the numbers for the next lower status, seems severe.

What is the impact of my being rejected for ConciergeKey membership on American Airlines and OneWorld? It undoubtedly will not have a significant impact on them. I'm only one of many travelers. But, consider this: we recently conducted work in Zurich, Switzerland. My choices were to fly American Airlines to Heathrow and their partner, British Airways, to Zurich (two legs each way) or to take Swiss Air direct to Zurich (one leg each way). The costs being the same, I chose to fly Swiss Air to make the travel easier on me. Had I remained a ConciergeKey member, I undoubtedly would have taken the American Airlines OneWorld option. As such, OneWorld lost around $9,200 in revenue. Also, in November, I made an around-the-world trip to Osaka then on to Barcelona and, finally, to Zurich before heading back to Chicago. I flew several legs to travel within the OneWorld network. Had I known that I would not have my ConciergeKey membership renewed, I would have taken an alternate itinerary with fewer legs, as I had already achieved the QEM and QED levels for Executive Platinum status. I'll most certainly not do that again.

A MODEL WAY TO TREAT LOYAL CUSTOMERS

My last business trip of that year was in December on an American Airlines co-share with Cathay Pacific to Phuket. An ad for a bank played on the inflight entertainment. It showed a college-educated son working with and advising his father on the family greengrocer business (which likely paid to put the son through college). He makes sure his father gets a cash register versus dealing from a money box. The son also takes exception to a customer whom, after she pays for her produce, picks up another item with an acknowledgement that she will pay for this last selection next time. When the customer leaves, the son expresses his exasperation that his father is letting the customer get away with something that is detrimental to the profitability of the business. The father listens patiently.

The customer returns to the store on another occasion. She pays for her produce and this time she makes a point of acknowledging payment for the item for which she had previously not made payment. The father points this out to the son and counsels him that he should trust (and empathize) with customers. The commercial closes with the father opening the cash register. However, there is no cash in the register, only lollipops that he distributes to the children of his customers, and he offers one to his son.

Ah, empathy with (loyal) customers.

CHANGING THE STORY, CHANGING THE RESULTS

Marketing is the science and art of winning and maintaining (loyal) customers. Here are some of the things American Airlines could have done that would have kept me a highly vocal "champion" of their services:

1. Informed me during the year that I needed to do more (and what specifically I needed to do) to maintain ConciergeKey membership.
2. Entered into a direct dialogue with me, not send me a form email with the company line of needing to limit the number of invitations "to ensure adequate resources are available for the

services offered," nor delegating the task of responding to my petition to someone lower on the ladder.

3. Provided me with the benefit of the doubt by extending membership for the first half of the new year with specific EQM and EQD goals that I would need to achieve for maintaining it throughout the year.

HOW TO TREAT LOYAL CUSTOMERS

Here are a few simple suggestions for your consideration in winning and maintaining customers:

- **Treat customers special, so they don't feel like they are only a number on a balance sheet**. This means to get a feel for the whole cloth not just one measure of it. I'm worth so much more than what I spent on my travel to include my family's (three daughters and sons-in-law and four granddaughters) extensive (and expensive!) travel. I have a history going back to 1985 with American Airlines. I'm more than a one-year pony.
- **Be empathetic**. Follow the Golden Rule. Treat them the way you would want others to treat you. Remember, customers are made of flesh and blood and have feelings that affect their loyalty. Companies, while having identities, don't always act humanly. Larger companies tend to be somewhat inhuman. Smaller companies generally serve more empathetically. American Airlines behaved like a behemoth company (which they undoubtedly are). If we follow the Golden Rule, we are going to be more human regardless of the size of the enterprise.
- **Adopt "true" obedience to policies regarding customers**. Don't be rigid but adapt to ensure you are doing your utmost to find a solution that will satisfy your customers.
- **Get beyond the product you sell and think about the customer experience you deliver**. Make every customer interaction a winning experience for them and it will be one for you.

- **Adopt the following policy:**

It's time to get beyond selling the product, or one-half of the product, to marketing a brand experience one can only realize through the development of "whole product" thinking and action that is inspired by empathy for, and devotion to serving, the customer.

CHAPTER 5

LACK OF RELEVANT, MEANINGFUL DIFFERENTIATION

Differentiate or die.
Jack Trout

Differentiate to thrive.
Richard Czerniawski

Our goal is to win astutely selected target customers to our offering. Have you considered how you might win the battle for the customer in this age of abundance and sameness where generally acceptable quality reigns? Well, there are four fundamental ways:

1. Having a lower price than competitors.
2. Exerting more muscle than the competition.
3. Creating relevant and meaningful differentiation versus the competition.
4. Superior execution.

NEED FOR DIFFERENTIATION

For our clients (large multi-national corporations), pricing is never, ever lower than their competitors. It's just the opposite. They are engaged in premium pricing. Moreover, our clients do not flex more muscle than their competitors. More muscle equates to putting more feet on the street, outspending competitors in key areas such as advertising, launching more marketing initiatives, providing more marketing funding that exceeds their share of the market, etc. Where there is the inclination or promise of using more muscle, it is frequently sabotaged by budget cuts and reorganizations.

Additionally, outmuscling the competition is no guarantee of success and is generally inefficient, particularly where evidence is not provided to support line-of-sight impact on sales. While superior execution has been frequently declared in corporate corridors over the years as the principal weapon to winning, it is a real crapshoot. It seems that achieving the most basic execution is a challenge for nearly every marketer and organization. The only fertile area remaining that we may use to win in the marketplace is differentiation. However, differentiation is the exception versus the norm.

Stating the obvious, "differentiation makes a difference." Differentiation sets your rather generic product offering apart from all the others and counters the "way of the marketplace," which is to commoditize your, and all other, offerings in the same category of products. It's the nature of the marketplace to commoditize the plethora of products available in this age of abundance and sameness where GAQ reigns.

There are so very many offerings in virtually all categories. As mentioned repeatedly, these product offerings do the same things, work in the same general ways and get the same basic results. They are, in reality, somewhat generic. So, to make choosing from among the plethora of offerings available easier, prospective customers classify them as being interchangeable, exerting downward pressure on pricing. In this case, Mr. Trout's proclamation, "Differentiate or die," is prophetic.

Even if your product enjoys an advantage in pricing, or muscle (execution), or any combination, or all the aforementioned, it is still wise to differentiate. Differentiation serves to help your offering stand apart and out from the herd. It defies commoditization because, well, it is different! It enables you to opposition your competitors as being part of the "rat pack," those substandard offerings whose performance is not worthy of your target customers.

Moreover, differentiation applied properly bolsters the growth acceleration rate of your offering and the ROI for your marketing initiatives.

Additionally, differentiation immunizes your offering from competitive inroads. It may even provide a basis for premium pricing. In this case, I proclaim, "Differentiate to thrive."

But, it's not about differentiation for differentiation's sake. Instead, it needs to be relevant and meaningfully differentiated. Differentiation needs to be relevant, not to the marketer but to the target customer segment. Being relevant means it is both pertinent and important to them, such as representing a compelling, unfulfilled conscious or subliminal need. "Meaningfully differentiated" means the target customer segment can perceive and unequivocally appreciate either the kind or degree of differentiation or both.

Importantly, we need to filter down from point of differentiation to POP (point of preference). POP is the objective. It's a compelling notion, as it makes clear to all that the POD (point of differentiation) must not just be different but relevant and meaningful to target customers. There are those COE (cost of entry) needs that are already being fulfilled by category competitors. Then there are those POD needs that we might fulfill. However, beyond that are POP needs that we can satisfy that will stimulate the target customer behavior changes we need to generate incremental line-of-sight sales. Keep in mind, target customer needs and benefits are two sides of the same coin. A POP need requires a POP benefit. Stated another way, a POP benefit must fulfill a POP need.

CRITICAL MARKETING MISTAKES WITH DIFFERENTIATION

Mistakes concerning differentiation include errors of omission and commission. With omission, differentiation isn't there, which is all too common. In commission, there are a few missteps that obfuscate, dilute or thwart differentiation. Here are some noteworthy mistakes:

1. *Following the herd.* This is about doing the same things in the same way as competitors. Category practices serve (consciously or unconsciously) as the default standard operating practices for nearly all competitors. Marketers accept this as the way of life and the way to success. It's jumping off an undeniable cliff into obscurity. As an example, competitors make the same promise to prospective target customers

and execute them in the same way because it is the accepted belief that this is required to be successful in their category. With everyone in the category doing the same, it is no small wonder that prospective customers perceive them as being the same. It becomes so easy for target customers, therefore, to commoditize them.

2. ***Trying to be all things to all people.*** There's no doubt that many of the marketing mis-steps I'm sharing with you are interrelated. We'll address this error and many of its consequences in the next chapter, "Mis-Targeting Target Customers." When we attempt to go too broadly with our target customers, or try to be all things to them, we dilute any differentiation that our brand offering might possess. All too often, we hear pharmaceutical marketers promise efficacy, safety, and tolerability so as not to miss anyone or anything. Marketers are not making choices with whom they want to establish a relationship and what they stand for, thereby, losing any distinction and advantage they may have in any one of the areas mentioned above with a specific target customer segment.

3. ***Success.*** Sometimes, past success(es) can be a problem. In a 1999 *Harvard Business Review* article, "Why Good Companies Go Bad," which could easily be titled, "Why Good Brands Go Bad," Donald N. Sull writes, "Success breeds active inertia, and active inertia breeds failure." This is as true, perhaps, even more so, as when it was written 20 years ago. Virtually every marketer can point to a company, brand and, even, an industry that was once perceived as impregnable but now lies buried, felled by competitor innovation (many times coming from outside the category).

   Success can lead to hubris, a false sense of security and complacency, all of which undermine those successful ones' willingness to adapt and build upon any advantage they might hold. Also, a contented marketer is an easy mark for a determined, aggressive competitor to topple (see point 6). The determined competitor will neutralize the differentiation and may go on to win on price or some other factor (perhaps, using intangibles, such as terms of purchase or free delivery).

4. ***Participate versus compete in the marketplace.*** Most marketers would claim they are competing in the market with their offerings. After all, they face "competition." That's what they do. However, to compete, one must put the brand into a position to outperform. A new entry in the marketplace is not competing if it doesn't differentiate or attempt to differentiate in either the product offering or the marketing of it. In reality, these entries are merely participating in the market to get a piece of the action, and despite proclamations to the contrary, that's all they intend to do. This is evident by launching a new product that is not differentiated from existing products or brands. Differentiation is not in the eyes of the organization; it is the eyes of the target customer. It's the target customer who is the final judge of whether you have differentiation, and whether it is relevant and meaningful to her. And, importantly, whether it leads to preference.

5. ***Cutting investment needed to create and maintain differentiation.*** Many organizations have narrowed their time horizon to quarterly to satisfy Wall Street's expectations and demands. Some organizations we know have contracted their time horizon even further to monthly (with significant scrutiny of weekly and even daily sales results). To meet profit expectations, deep and frequent cuts are made throughout the organization (e.g., R&D, manufacturing, marketing, quality control, etc.). As a result of cutting investment, meaningful differentiation and the ability to differentiate erodes. Cuts in investment also allow shrewd competitors, who pursue a strategy of being "fast followers," to match or even leapfrog your offering. At minimum, they will erase any differentiation between them and your brand, obliterating former advantages you may have held. These aggressive competitors may up the ante by offering discount pricing, thereby contributing to intensifying the nature of the market to commoditize and then capitalize on it to capture market share. They will claim they are the same as the leading brand but cost less. Worse, they will establish

relevant and meaningful differentiation for their offerings. While the focus may be quarterly, the consequences of cutting investment are significant and prolonged, putting the future in danger and doubt.

6. ***Rationalizing the product.*** This is related to the previous point. In this case, an ongoing string of reductions is conducted on the product offering (e.g., formulation, packaging, terms, etc.) over some time (usually years). Something is removed or diminished (sometimes, multiple things). The apparent reason for rationalizing is to cut costs. It is characterized by a series of minute changes that evidence no statistical difference versus the previous rendition. However, when viewed in the aggregate, these reductions represent a significant compromise in product quality and/or the customer experience from the original offering. This is what's referred to as *creeping decrementalism*—a term coined by Leo Kiely, former President of Coors Brewing Company. At the very least, it narrows "meaningful differentiation." At its worst, it eradicates it.

7. *Misuse of marketing research.* I genuinely believe in the value of marketing research. I wouldn't want to leave home without it. However, it is often misused in ways that contribute to driving sameness and undermining differentiation. To illustrate, when a needs analysis is conducted, the needs are prioritized in order of importance to the customer. The most important needs typically become generic needs, as virtually all competitors are compelled to work to exploit them. As such, they tend to be needs that are already being satisfied.

Often, it is a need further down the listing of perceived importance that will make a difference just because it is, well, different. As an example, relief from a debilitating condition is more important than the convenience of dosing. However, if customers perceive all competitors as equally satisfying the need for relief, then convenience could prove to be a relevant and meaningful differentiator. Yet it may go unexplored or untapped because it is not one of the key needs (which have become generic) and so, it's erroneously overlooked or ignored, particularly when viewed absent of specific target-customer segmentation to which it could prove important.

Also, marketing research is a snapshot in time. It's a picture of the marketplace at the time the snapshot is taken. Every competitor with the same type of research study has the same snapshot and, therefore, sees the market in the same, identical way. As a result, everyone is directed to pursue and promote the same things (and in the same ways).

8. *A culture of consensus.* Unfortunately, originality (a requirement for differentiation) is not always appreciated in many corporations, particularly those large ones and those cruising on past successes. It tends to scare managers, as they fear to make a mistake that might cost them their jobs. Accordingly, responsibility and accountability are dispersed via consensus. Consensus is about gaining approval to something. It is not the same, nor as valuable, as collaboration.

    Collaboration recognizes that everyone has a piece of the puzzle. People contribute their diverse experiences, knowledge, perspectives, and insights to create a mosaic, with one person holding the responsibility and accountability for the decision and results. With consensus, it's a group decision and outcome resulting from the members' desire and willingness to compromise in reaching an agreement, going along to get along with the herd. There is scant exploration into what could be. It is more about what will please senior management, what will keep us out of trouble, what will help us get along, and what will be approved. The outcome of consensus, and resulting compromise, far too often contributes to a lack of differentiation.

9. *Focus on the physical product.* As noted in the last chapter, the physical product is only one part of the whole product. It represents the material aspects that comprise the physical product, such as features. The other part of the product lies outside both the literal and figurative box, compound or device. It consists of elements, such as services and terms, and the way you go about doing business. As you'll

recall, physical products competing in the same category are often undifferentiated, thereby predictably resulting in the same generic benefit promise around what the products do. In other words, no differentiation!

10. *Using "fat" words.* Fat words are imprecise. They open the door to many interpretations. As such, they lack focus and distinction. They lack the power to induce behavior. Take the word *efficacy* which is frequently used as a benefit promise by pharmaceutical and OTC brands. What does it mean? Is the marketer referring to the speed of action? Duration of action? Quality of action? Some combination of these? Something entirely different? Or take the word *healthy*. What does it mean? Absence of negative ingredients? Low in fat? Loaded with essential vitamins and minerals? Fat words obfuscate the meaning and any distinctions in the offering.

Moreover, when competitors employ the same fat words, the collective messaging is like wallpaper. It blends into the background and target customers can't distinguish one product from another. It doesn't move them to act other than, once again, to commoditize the category and your offering.

RX FOR CREATING RELEVANT, MEANINGFUL DIFFERENTIATION

1. *Audit your offering for relevant, meaningful differentiation.* Marketers and their organizations miss the big picture as it relates to whether they have differentiation, and whether it is relevant and meaningful to their target customer segment. To avoid this, check your offering versus the competition for product performance. Get beyond features to include the value proposition and customer perceptions. Then, map the category based upon performance "P" and differentiation "D." So-called better performance is often considered puffery and

is inconsequential, as customers cannot perceive a real advantage. "Differentiation" trumps "better," as long as it is relevant and meaningful. The place to occupy is the top right corner. The top left and bottom right corners are nearly a wash. Some target customers who purchase out of habit may believe (or rationalize) "better" whereas some target customers may choose that which is merely different just because it is not the same, or merely to be contrarian, or to declare themselves as different.

DIFFERENTIATION MAP

"P"		
BETTER but Not Meaningfully Different and/or Relevant	RELEVANT, MEANINGFUL DIFFERENTIATION
SAME or Less	DIFFERENTIATED but Not Meaningful or Relevant

"D"

2. *Avoid doing what all other competitors are doing.* Resist the lemming-like urge to follow others over the proverbial cliff. In the words of brothers Chip and Dan Heath, co-authors of *Made to Stick,* "Resist the usual." Question standard category operating practices to determine if they will make a difference in your brand's health and performance. If the practices are not essential, find a different way. Take a different path. Challenge all assumptions. The goal is not just to look different but to be different in a way that the target customer perceives to be relevant and meaningfully differentiated over the alternative offerings. Importantly, it needs to be a point of preference. In other words, it has to work in achieving specific purchasing behavior objectives. Warby-Parker, Amazon, and Starbucks represent companies who departed from conventional wisdom and took a different path concerning their business model—one their target customers prefer. And, they've succeeded. (However, they need to continue to evolve if they are to remain relevant, different and preferred!) Do you have the courage to

do the same? The change need not be radical, but it must demonstrate a favorable impact on target customer perceptions and experiences.

3. ***Choose to be and not to be.*** This is taken from the next chapter, "Mis-Targeting Target Customers," as we cannot divorce the target from differentiation. It is essential for us to make choices regarding whom we will target AND whom we will not target. Keep in mind that we are targeting those potential customers for whom our brand will have strong appeal (i.e., those who "believe what we believe"), with the anticipated impact of a faster growth acceleration rate (i.e., the speed of growth at which we achieve target financial goals) and more favorable ROI.

   Also, this means making choices regarding the reason for our brand's existence (the brand idea and brand positioning strategy) and what we will and will not stand for, what product developments we will and will not pursue, what we will message and what we will not, and what marketing activities we will undertake and what we will not do. When we don't make clear choices, we undermine marketing effectiveness.

   Also, we'll find that in identifying and making choices, our research is likely to give us a different view of the marketplace, revealing distinct differences from segment to segment in target customer attitudes, behaviors, value systems, needs, etc., that we may focus against and capitalize upon to drive differentiation.

4. ***"Stay thirsty, my friends."*** I recently delivered a keynote presentation to a large, multi-national pharmaceutical company on the subject of marketing excellence. Before preparing this talk, I was told that a segment of the target audience already felt that they had achieved, and were currently engaged in, marketing excellence. Okay, wonderful. Curiously, in researching the company, I learned their average cost for bringing a new drug to market was the highest in the pharmaceutical sector, nearly four times higher than the most efficient pharmaceutical company. Therefore, I warned that these marketers could not afford to be self-satisfied. I counseled them that their marketing should

probably be at least four times more productive than their competitors' marketing if they hoped to either compete effectively or to optimize the value of their very precious assets.

Any competitor who is self-satisfied is one who is vulnerable to failure. This is where "active inertia" sets in and the quest for additional ways to differentiate begins to falter. If you want to be a winner, then you ought to take to heart the words of the most interesting man in the world, the former Dos Equis spokesman, who in the brand's advertising advised, "Stay thirsty, my friends. Stay thirsty." Don't allow yourself to become complacent. Participate in war-gaming to identify ways in which competitors may best your offering and marketing. Then, find ways to immunize your brand from the most significant and likely of these potential initiatives. Be relentless in your search for ways to differentiate and forestall more thirsty competitors. Importantly, act to increase your bond with your target customers and (leadership) position in the marketplace.

5. ***Compete to win target customers***. What the marketplace doesn't need is another entry that doesn't have anything new and different to offer. If you are going to enter, compete! Give target customers something new that they perceive has value. Build differentiation into your offering. Differentiation can be built into the product offering, the business model, your strategies, the choices you make, even the execution. There are so many places to seek and create differentiation. In our communications to target customers, we can differentiate in each part of the communication strategy: the target customer we choose, the communication behavior objective we seek, the legitimate and productive customer insight we discover, the key thought we promise (i.e., the point-of-difference benefit that creates preference), and the reason-to-believe we provide to add credibility to the POD, or better stated, "POP" (point of preference) benefit promise. We can also differentiate in how we deliver the communications, which includes the development and choice of a campaign idea, and where and when we communicate our message. Vie for target customer preference in each and everything you do

6. ***Invest in the future of the brand.*** We understand that if quarterly expectations are not met, there will be no future for the brand or for your employment within your current organization. However, indiscriminate cutting will hurt the brand's ability to compete in the future. It will enable those hungry, aggressive competitors to narrow or close any gaps, technological or otherwise, eradicating advantages in differentiation you may have possessed, leading to commoditizing (undermining the value of) your offering with target customers. Indiscriminate cutting also opens the door for competitors to leapfrog you. The choice is clear: invest now or pay for it later. Regardless, the marketer and his organization will pay for it one way or the other! If the marketing support funds can be directed at providing or enhancing preferential differentiation, and growing incremental sales, then it is important to invest.

However, before investing, as marketers, we must know the behaviors we seek and whether the proposed activities will achieve those behaviors to generate incremental sales and a favorable ROI. The only way we can determine this is to inspect what we expect: we must conduct marketing research and measure everything we do for productivity. Anything less will result in a cost at best or a gamble at worst. Either way, it is not an investment and deserves to be cut. (More on this subject in a later chapter.)

7. ***Avoid creeping decrementalism.*** Certainly, it is important to cut unnecessary costs, both in the product and its delivery. However, when it comes to rationalizing the product, it is a good idea to follow the carpenter's maxim: "Measure twice. Cut once." Specifically, check out the change from the most recent proposed rationalized offering with target customers before launching it. But, don't stop there! Check out the proposed change versus the original product to ensure it has not drifted south (i.e., resulted in a decline in preference with target customers) from the original offering. Also, ask, "What added-value will this bring to our target customer?" If the answer is nothing, think twice.

8. ***Think like a marketect.*** I coined the term *marketect* by combining the words *marketer* and *architect* since the marketer is the architect of the brand. She is responsible for developing the blueprint for the brand (the brand positioning strategy) as well as for providing the stewardship to ensure it is built to specifications. However, there is a quality that one needs to demonstrate to be crowned with the title of marketect. A marketect is well aware of the marketing research and how the market landscape appears to prospective target customers. However, the marketect recognizes the need, and acts, to change how target customers perceive the marketplace to drive and win preference with her brand.

The marketect doesn't see herself as a slave to what is current, but instead, as one who can shape the future. The marketect of our generation is the late Steve Jobs. He ushered in the personal computer industry, which has revolutionized how we work and what we (can) do. He changed the mobile phone industry and video animation. Steve Jobs also commercialized computer tablets and set in motion the multi-billion-dollar app industry. He wasn't content with, nor was he daunted by, what was; he looked to what *could* be.

Use marketing research wisely to inform rather than to decide, to inspire rather than to restrict. Get beyond the numbers and look into the souls of real people, those in your target customer segment. Read between the lines to discover legitimate and productive customer insights. Use marketing research to explore concepts for product improvements, new products, marketing campaigns, etc. Go beyond learning the "what" to learning the "why" so you may develop new hypotheses and adapt, and in doing so, iterate your way to success.

Again, make sure your marketing research is directed at addressing your target customer segment. Use it to better serve your target customer versus your competitors. Do not concern yourself, nor allow yourself to be pulled off track, with less favorable responses from those people who are not in your target customer segment.

9. ***Welcome and explore diverse perspectives.*** Don't seek consensus. Consensus is about compromising to gain agreement. This process

promotes convergence as opposed to divergence. It's about quickly settling on an idea and getting everyone comfortable and satisfied with it. Yet achieving success in creating differentiation is a creative endeavor. If we are to improve the likelihood of success, it requires that we attempt many shots from many different angles. Inviting the team members from diverse functional areas (i.e., disciplines such as finance, access, product development, sales, etc.), who together represent a broad range of experiences, unique insights, and invaluable perspectives, will result in more ideas and more diversity of ideas. In other words, there will be many more shots from many more angles. Additionally, this approach will enable you to resist premature judgments based on the diversity of the participating managers and their unique perspectives.

As Theodore Levitt, former professor of business administration at the Harvard Business School and author of *The Marketing Imagination,* states, "Nothing drives progress like the imagination. The idea precedes the deed." Try to be "the only one who ..." Use your imagination. Focus the resources of the team not on gaining consensus but on creating many different ideas to achieve differentiation that will positively impact target customer perceptions and behaviors towards your offering. How many ideas? Think BIG. If Navy Seals believe you are capable of 20-times more than you think, we need to apply some multiple to the number of intended ideas. At a minimum, whatever you believe, triple it! You can and should do so much more than you currently think.

10. ***Get beyond the physical product you sell.*** The physical product we sell is rather generic. It might have different features and attributes, but when it comes down to it, our physical products do the same basic things, and they work in the same fundamental (or accepted) ways to generate the same general results. Ho hum! Consider both the whole product and the customer experience. The whole product includes things outside the purchased physical product that comprises our entire offering to potential customers. This would include training our customers on ways to maximize the use or performance of our offering.

It could include warranties regarding reliability and outcomes, special financing arrangements and even servicing. These should be created to help differentiate the whole offering versus competition in either kind or degree.

However, as legendary pitchman Ron Popeil would say, "Wait, there's more!" Think of creating differentiation from the perspective of the experience you deliver. Pose and address the following questions:

- What is the experience of customers with my product and competitive products?
- What experience would be truly meaningful to them?
- What might I do to deliver that experience?

The internet enables consumers to shop without leaving home. Membership to Amazon Prime provides next-day delivery service (and, in some instances, even same-day delivery) on orders. They have been experimenting with drones to offer delivery service within a few hours. Experiencing instant gratification takes on a whole (product) new meaning.

11. ***Opposition the competition.*** This is commonly conducted by politicians. It is also attributed as a primary cause for failure by nearly every marketer whose offering is losing to competition. "The competition is making false claims to target customers about us." In brief, it is the practice of positioning a competitor in an unfavorable light to establish your brand's positioning, difference or superiority in the marketplace. Now I'm not suggesting you openly trash the competition. In many parts of the world and categories, it is illegal to engage in comparative communications. Instead, I am proposing you use this as a creative exercise to uncover where your brand has meaningful differentiation by identifying the weaknesses of your competition. Simply answer the following:

- Competitor "A" will or does not ... (negative or incomplete performance).
- This is true because ... (support for oppositioning claim).

For example, "Competitor A will damage fabrics and wear out your clothes. This is true because it contains abrasives, not fabric softeners." This would then lead to our differentiation: "We keep your clothes looking new, wash after wash. This is because our products contain fabric softeners and no abrasives."

12. ***Fast-forward to create the future.*** We need to be able to see where the future is headed and capitalize on it. Identify those emerging forces that signal a "sea change." In other words, these trends represent a significant and lasting impact on the marketplace, everything from business models (how the business operates), to product offerings, to customer wants versus needs. This may be fueled by new technologies, social changes, regulations, changing demographics, etc. Then, make it your business to create the future by aggressively participating in and racing to be the first to get there. Ask yourself:
    - What (societal, technological, etc.) trends are impacting our category?
    - Where will the market be in 5 to 10 years?
    - What are the core differences from today?
    - What must I do to drive and capitalize on achieving those differences?

13. ***Be precise in expressing differentiation in word and deed.*** State clearly and unambiguously what you promise your target customer. Take a stand. Do not use fat words. Check whether you are expressing differentiation by asking target customers these questions:
    - What is the promise?
    - Is this important to you?
    - Is it meaningfully differentiated versus competitive?
    - What is your likelihood of purchasing, prescribing, and using the offering?

Importantly, fulfill your promise to them through your actions. One way of doing this is to examine beliefs and practices. Identify the belief (as it relates to differentiation) and state the current practice.

BELIEFS VERSUS PRACTICES

Beliefs	Practices
•	•
•	•

If belief and practice are not aligned, then it is important to change one or the other. We must back up our promises with our actions.

14. ***Implement kaizen.*** Kaizen is the Japanese practice of continuous, incremental improvements. It's the absolute opposite of rationalization. It is about finding ways to add value to your offering or to the way the organization does things that will have a positive impact on target customer preference. It's also the corporate manifestation of the maxim "a journey of a thousand miles begins with a small step." The sheer scope of the journey to where we need to reach to deliver meaningful differentiation could appear overwhelming if we attempt to do it all in one fell swoop. Instead, identify where you want to take differentiation, and then map out the series of steps it will take to get there. Start at the beginning with the first step then build upon it. Make it a continuous process, each year building in a higher degree of differentiation. When you begin closing in on your destination, establish a new one.

15. ***Seek preferentiation.*** Here's a new word and term for you: *preferentiation.* What does it mean? Well, this chapter has been about seeking relevant, meaningful differentiation. Remember, our brand's differentiation should lead to preference among our chosen target customer segment. Cutting to the chase, we should seek among our points of differentiation the one that leads to preference, our POP (point of preferentiation).

The choice is yours. Differentiate or die. Alternatively, differentiate to thrive. Regardless, seek to create relevant, meaningful differentiation that leads target customers to prefer your brand, your POP, which creates brand loyalty. That's smart marketing.

CHAPTER 6

MIS-TARGETING TARGET CUSTOMERS

Target: goal, somebody aimed at
Customer: supporter and benefactor

THE TARGET CUSTOMER

The target customer refers to whom we intend our brand to appeal. It represents those people with whom we want to establish an ongoing, mutually beneficial relationship, not just of a transactional nature but a transformational one. These are the people we want to win over to our franchise. These are the very people whom we intend to serve better than our competition so that we might earn their financial support in the form of purchasing, usage, and lasting devotion. It's a mutually beneficial and enduring relationship. They receive a relevant, meaningful and perceived unique benefit from the brand experience in the form of physical and/or emotional pay-off and we reap the financial reward and the expectation that they will return over and again to repay us with their business.

It's rather simple when you think about it. It's the people with whom we will form a connection and, better yet, a tribe or community. It's all about mutual attraction and beneficial relationship. While the brand is undoubtedly a significantly important asset, we should not take lightly the importance of the customer. Without the customer, there is no brand. Dismiss, ignore or mistreat customers, and the health of the brand will deteriorate, brand loyalty will erode, and sales will shrink. It's critically important that we get this right.

CRITICAL MISTAKES IN TARGETING TARGET CUSTOMERS

There are many mistakes and oversights marketers and their organizations make concerning targeting target customers. Here are two of the most significant:

1. ***Trying to be all things to all people.*** As Northwestern Marketing Professor Philip Kotler, whose textbooks you probably studied in college, says, "If you're not thinking segments, you're not thinking marketing." It's so very true. I say, that while there is no one way to success, one sure way to failure is to try to be all things to all people. We must segment and segment strategically.

   The fact of the matter is that people aren't all the same. We don't share the same values, have the same needs or respond in the same way to a given brand or message. The online insurance company Essurance ran a clever campaign that communicated significant differences among people who share the same basic demographics. One of their television spots shows a parental couple meeting with a "Mr. Craig," their child's elementary school teacher. However, they're greeted by someone who looks like someone who recently escaped from a federal penitentiary, where he was locked-up for committing a violent crime. Upon seeing him, they declare, "You're not Mr. Craig." He replies, "I'm sorta Mr. Craig. We're both between 25 and 35 years old. We both like to save money on car insurance, and we're both really good at teaching people a lesson," as he crushes a pencil, terrifying the parents. The announcer voiceover states, "*Sorta you* isn't *you.*" We need to be more explicit regarding who our target customer is, and for that matter, who it is not. This will require that we use additional measures beyond the broad demographics cited above.

   Neither Toyota nor Nissan could make a significant dent in the U.S. truck market. They failed to get beyond the broad demographics and consider "telling behaviors," like where truck owners shop and what they do. Telling behaviors represent a finer cut of the population, leading to better targeting of those consumers who are more likely to purchase a truck versus a car or an SUV. As a result, the Big Three, who go beyond demographics to focus on the important "telling behaviors," have been able to maintain more than a 90% market share of this lucrative market.

THE FOLLY OF TARGETING EVERYONE

TRYING TO WIN EVERYONE IS COUNTER-PRODUCTIVE

If you think about it, you'll realize we don't need everyone in the known universe to create a brand or to win. For example, I hold two potential brand ideas, "N" and "P." These ideas could be for any product, service, compound, device, etc. It doesn't matter. I test them with 1,000 potential target customers. These could be consumers, health care practitioners, surgeons, whatever. Again, it doesn't matter for purposes of this example.

The study employs a 5-point scale for purchase/use/prescribing (Rx) intent. The specific type of intent is dependent upon your sector or category.

- "5" signifies the respondent "definitely will" purchase/use/prescribe
- "4" signifies the respondent "probably will" purchase/use/prescribe
- "3" is "maybe/maybe not" purchase/use/prescribe
- "2" signifies "probably not" purchase/use/prescribe
- "1" is "definitely not" purchase/use/prescribe

As shown in the table below, both brand ideas elicit the same mean rating for purchase/use/prescribe, 3.0. Curiously, all 1,000 potential target customers rate brand idea "N" a "3" for maybe/maybe not purchase/use/prescribe. Whereas for brand idea "P," 500 target customers claim they "definitely will" purchase/use/prescribe, and 500 rated it a "1," meaning they would "definitely not." Are these brand ideas, with the same mean rating for purchase/use/prescribe intent, the same? If not, which one would you choose?

Intent – Purchase/Use/Rx	"N"	"P"
Mean Rating	3.0	3.0
5 – Definitely Will		500
4 – Probably Will		
3 – Maybe/Maybe Not	1,000	
2 – Probably Not		
1 – Definitely Not		500

No, they are not the same. And, yes you would (or should) choose brand idea "P" because you have 500 potential target customers who claim they definitely will purchase/use/prescribe that brand. If you look to black box marketing research testing, which correlates intent to purchase/use/prescribe to volume (based upon analysis of linking intent with marketplace results), they attribute something like 96% of the weight to the top box (i.e., "definitely will") plus ½ of the second box ("probably will"). The action is in the top box ("5") and half of the second box ("4").

Now, here's what happens: senior management concurs with the selection of brand idea "P." However, they ask, "What might we do to move some of those who claim 1—definitely not—up on the purchase intent scale? After all, we have a rather significant sales forecast that we need to achieve (like who doesn't?)."

There's only one thing you can do, and that's change brand idea P. However, when you change it, some of those claiming "definitely will," will drop on the rating scale, and some of those claiming "definitely not" will rise. Keep in mind that those who rise to "probably not" or "maybe/maybe not" will have virtually no impact on sales. Whereas, if just one respondent moves down on the scale for claimed intent of "definitely will" or "probably will," this will negatively impact volume.

In the 2016 Republican Primaries for President, Donald Trump had around 35% in the top two boxes. He probably had the remaining 65% or so at the very bottom. Yet, he was able to beat out 16 qualified candidates to secure his nomination for the presidency. You don't have to win everyone! If you try, you will lose and, in President Trump's words, lose BIG.

SEGMENTATION

Therefore, we must carefully segment our market. In order to be successful, we must segment to identify those prospects with which we have the best chance of establishing a mutually productive and beneficial relationship. It's both a matter of appeal and economics. When we don't segment but try to appeal to everyone, we dilute our positioning strategy, messaging and many marketing activities. Instead of spurring the passion of target customers, we elicit a feeling of apathy, making them indifferent to our brand, which retards the growth acceleration rate and causes them to be susceptible to the lure of competitive messaging and activities.

By the way, this applies to identifying and choosing from among many potential segments. First, there's the choice of a constituency. Are we going after purchasers, users, influencers, health care practitioners, payors, and non-clinical targets such as hospital administrators, patients, consumers? Then, within a given constituency, which segment?

Segmentation is a creative exercise. I joke with my business partner, Mike Maloney, that in the next lifetime, we should come back to market and sell segmentation studies. They all produce very similar segments. In the health care area, there are the evidence-based, pragmatists, the traditionalists, the patient-centric practitioners, etc. So, all we'd need to do is one segmentation study, and we'd have it to sell to the world over and over again with each new client. While this is an obvious exaggeration, there is a disturbing element of truth to it. Wouldn't you agree?

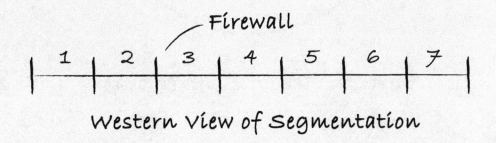

Western View of Segmentation

Once a segmentation exists, one must choose a specific segment to target. Now, you might have more than one segment to address, but please, no more than two. At one time, a client company had two overlapping psychographic segments it was targeting for its pharmaceutical brand. How was this possible? I like to think of segmentation as a circle. It's more like my favorite food, pizza, with slices containing overlapping toppings. For example, when my wife and I order a pizza, we'll make it one-half pepperoni and the other anchovies. My wife likes pepperoni. I don't. I go for the anchovies. She doesn't. When we bite into a slice of our selection, my wife might say that my anchovies are on her slice of pizza, to which I reply that her pepperoni is on mine. They overlap.

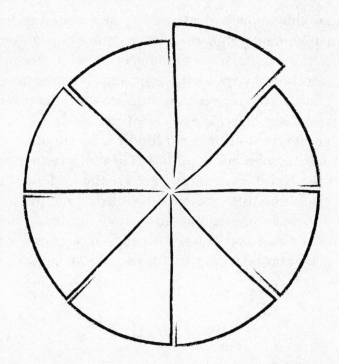

Eastern View of Segmentation

MORE LIKE A PIZZA

Now back to the pharmaceutical brand with the two overlapping segments. One was "stoic soldiers," namely those who sought relief so they could fulfill promises made to others. The other was "successful boundary setters," who needed relief to pursue things they wanted to do. One of the commercials in their campaign featured a grandfather who found the relief he needed to fulfill his mission to "purchase a big-boy bed" for his grandson. Think about it: he was the stoic soldier delivering on his promise to his grandson. He was also the successful boundary-setter in doing something that would delight every grandfather. As a grandfather myself, I understand and empathize with the grandfather in this commercial. By the way, this segmentation study was quite meaningful as it accurately revealed psychographic segments that connected the condition and product performance with the customer's needs.

I remember an assignment I recently led in Europe. It was for a pharmaceutical brand in a therapeutic area that health care practitioners did not treat until the patient suffered consequences (the result of not treating a progressive condition). The team had conducted a segmentation study, and the same several segments turned up that you'll find in most segmentation studies conducted for pharmaceutical companies. Not only was the segmentation rather meaningless, but out of the seven segments, they were choosing to go after all but two. I repeatedly advised them against it and supported my conclusion. While they intellectually understood what I was advocating, they could not bring themselves to limit their choice to no more than two segments. Finally, I raised an important question. I asked, "Might we label those HCPs who treat prophylactically (i.e., before an event so their patients might avoid it) 'difference makers'?" They replied, "Certainly." In that way, we got it down to one segment—a very meaningful and potentially large segment. Importantly, it would help establish a community that HCPs would want to earn membership.

ECONOMICS OF SEGMENTATION

As per the economic reasons for segmenting, we need to address the growth acceleration rate. This refers to the speed of growth. A slower growth rate means it takes us longer to realize the sales and market share potential for the brand. This slower growth rate translates to opportunity losses of sales and profit that could have been used to fund additional marketing initiatives and organization developments. Moreover, when the brand's appeal is diluted, particularly when it lacks perceived differentiation, we are forced to provide discount pricing or exert more muscle in terms of higher levels of sales and marketing support, which reduce margins and profitability.

There's also a drag on efficiency. For example, when I inquire of pharmaceutical or medical device sales personnel about the "mean" number of calls they need to make on the target customer before they effect a change in customer behavior, they typically respond "8 to 11." The accuracy of the actual average number isn't the point (e.g., 8, 9, 10 or 11) as it is a starting point for this example. (Certainly, if you average 11 calls when your competitor takes only 8 calls on average to make a sale, then they are 27.7% more efficient, and you are 37.5% less effective!)

What is essential for marketers to understand is that there will be a wide range within whatever the average is for your brand depending on the specific target customer. For illustration, let's say the number varies from 1 to 20 calls for a given customer to achieve a mean of "8" for a group of customers. Some customers will change behavior on the first call whereas it may take 20 sales calls for other customers before a behavior change occurs, if ever. The exact number of sales calls required is dependent upon the appeal of our brand to them, which differs by customer segment, and even customer to customer within a given segment. It's both irresponsible and foolhardy if we cannot identify and do not first approach the low-hanging fruit since the brand's growth acceleration rate and ROI (from our sales calls, messaging, marketing activities) will be significantly impacted by our ability to match our brand with the most appropriate customers.

When we fail, by targeting too broadly, the growth acceleration rate becomes a growth deceleration rate. The upstart is not just a reduction in profit but leads to cutting budgets that support growth. This, in turn, leads to a vicious cycle that can plunge the brand into decline or, worse yet, a death spiral.

2. *A superficial understanding of the customer.* This is the second crucial mistake in targeting customers. Data regarding the target customer is helpful. However, it is not enough. It mostly deals with broad demographics, which can be very misleading, as made clear by the Essurance example of Mr. Craig, shared earlier in this chapter. For instance, if we were to talk about men 25 to 49 years of age earning $40-$50,000, we could be speaking of a schoolteacher, a truck driver, a technician, a Hell's Angel, etc. They all have very different lifestyles, values, beliefs, behaviors, needs, and so forth. The same goes for thinking about HCPs' practices (e.g., oncologists versus internists). We need to get below the surface of the skin (i.e., go beyond the broad, superficial numbers) to understand the following:
   - The full dimensions (or specs) of our target, such as telling behaviors (where they shop, what they purchase, and what activities they pursue).
   - What our target customer thinks and feels.
   - Her journey.
   - Choices available to her.
   - Dissatisfactions we might exploit and needs we might capitalize upon.
   - How she perceives the world in which we compete.

So many target-customer profiles are vague or too broad and do little to help us understand who it is, at heart, that we intend to serve and win.

RX FOR SMART TARGETING TARGET CUSTOMERS

Here are a few suggested actions regarding what we should do to avoid or fix these significant blunders to make our target customer selection and profile more productive:

1. ***Get to work on target-customer segmentation.*** What we are looking for are those potential customers who, in the words of executive coach Simon Sinek, "believe what we believe." In other words, we are looking for those segments of the target market population who find our brand idea, our "why," compelling. Certainly, we can try to get at this via marketing research. Keep in mind that, as previously stated, this is a creative exercise. What I mean is, two people addressing market segmentation may segment, and label the segments, differently. When I looked at the pharmaceutical client in Europe and suggested "difference makers," I was addressing segmentation differently. I like doing "differently." It is what marketects do (or at least should do).

    By the way, in those sectors and categories, where the sales force calls on the target customer, you may use your sales personnel to identify segments in their market based upon the differing values (psychographic profiles) of those whom they call upon. You'll be able to construct a map of the segments. What you can't do is get at the precise size of each of the segments. For that, you'll need marketing research. We can perform this same exercise with consumers.

    Please don't identify the segment as "early adopters." This is something they teach in business schools, but it's pure poppycock! Think about it: you don't need to find early adopters. They'll find you. As a result, they don't require much marketing. Also, since they are early adopters, then guess what? They're early exiters! They'll quit your brand as soon as the next new thing comes along.

2. ***Choose to be, and choose not to be.*** It is essential for us to make choices regarding whom we will target AND whom we will not target. Keep in mind that we are targeting those potential customers for whom our

brand will have strong appeal, with the anticipated impact of a faster growth acceleration rate and more favorable ROI. This means making choices regarding the reason for our brand's existence (the brand idea and the brand positioning strategy) and what we will not stand for, what we will message and what we will not, and what marketing activities we will undertake and what we will not. Failure to make clear choices will undermine marketing effectiveness.

3. ***Identifying the bull's-eye target customer of one.*** Addressing the target-customer profile can be rather abstract, particularly if one is merely addressing data. So, we approach this by answering the following question: "Whom do we know, a real-life flesh and blood human being, who finds our brand idea or messaging to be so highly compelling that it will trigger achievement of the brand's behavior objective (e.g., switching, adoption, etc.)?" Name that person. This target customer will undoubtedly be at the heart of your segment. She will be your bull's-eye target customer. However, as previously noted, what it can't tell you is how large that segment will be. That's a job for your marketing intelligence personnel.

A TARGET-CUSTOMER OF ONE

Everyone who has taken Marketing 101 was taught "you can't be all things to all people." It appears that nearly everyone in the world of commerce, even if they didn't take a marketing course in their life, knows this. However, do they truly understand it? Follow it? The fact of the matter is, marketers and their organizations repeatedly attempt to broaden their target-customer base such that, more often than not, they are violating this proven, basic principle. Even if these marketers aren't going after "everyone," their target segment is too broadly, or poorly, defined. Either of these results in the absence of a meaningfully differentiated positioning strategy and/or messaging to drive brand preference and loyalty. In other words, the brand idea (and brand positioning strategy) and the single-minded selling proposition become diluted in trying to satisfy a too broad or a too-vague target market to the point of losing its effectiveness in influencing behavior and in creating brand loyalty.

So, what can we do? We need to segment the market. This is another one of those principles introduced in Marketing 101. We need to market to a specific grouping or classification of people. (Marketing research can help us identify potential segmentation models for our category.) Typically, marketers define clusters of potential customers based on shared demographics, socio-economic levels, medical conditions, and generic category needs, among others. But this way of segmenting may not be meaningful or it may lack the level of specificity needed to enable us to understand and appreciate the customer.

As marketers, we need to understand our target customer so well that we can accurately predict how the target will react to a specific piece of stimulus. Package design, a promotional event, public relations, reporting of clinical study outcomes, and other marketing initiatives are all pieces of stimuli. *Therefore, we should only feed our target stimuli that will get her to behave in a predetermined manner that benefits our brand (i.e., achieves a customer behavior objective).*

The segment, when approached from the top down with broad labels, becomes another abstraction that is only slightly more meaningful than pursuing everyone in developing the single-minded proposition or any of the brand's marketing initiatives.

So, what should we do? Let's build our target segment from the bottom up by identifying the bull's-eye target customer of one. We take a single customer and through a process of re-orchestration, we create a mosaic that is our segment. Who is the bull's-eye target customer of one" for your brand and what it represents? It's she who believes what you believe. Find that one person.

Once you can see her clearly in your mind, you define her using the seven essential components we, at BDNI, teach in our Power Positioning and High-Impact Brand Messaging workshops. These are: demographics; psychographics; condition or life stage or target occasion, depending upon the category or your unique situation; attitudes about the subject;

current brand/product usage and dissatisfactions; other relevant behaviors; and, finally, needs—both rational and emotional—the brand can use to win the customer. In this way, you identify and profile the bull's-eye target customer of one. This should result in a more relevant and actionable target segment comprised of matching psychographic profiles, a like mind regarding attitudes about the category and/or specific situation, and dissatisfactions with competitors and, therefore, unfilled needs your brand can remedy.

We need to fix this relevant target clearly in our mind. Many a legendary copywriter set a photo of a potential bull's-eye customer on her desk and wrote copy to that specific individual. It helped her relate to an individual, not an abstraction. The resultant message made for a productive stimulus in winning customers and in growing healthy brands. We can achieve a similar end by developing a bull's-eye target customer of one to establish a relevant, actionable segment.

4. *Define the target customer clearly and completely.* This is about displaying and communicating our target customer in such a way that everyone on the brand team understands her. Remember, we should know and understand our target customer so well that we can predict how she will respond to the stimulus we develop, and all our marketing activities are stimuli, to achieve our stated behavior objective (e.g., switching).

   In defining the bull's-eye target customer of one, we need to identify and address the following:
   - **Demographics:** This is purely the data, such as the type of practice and practice size, where practice for HCPs among other data points, and socio-economics, gender, age, and so forth, for consumers. Use of demographic criteria is pretty much a first cut at segmentation.
   - **Psychographics:** This gets at the values and beliefs of the target customer. Psychographics identify and label those who believe

what we believe (our brand idea). It is the one area that is typically most important in selecting your target customer.

- **Patient-Condition or Life Stage or Usage Occasion:** This element addresses for what, and how (and in pharmaceuticals, for whom), the brand will be used. It's a segment within a segment. If we are addressing a patient, it could very well include demographics, psychographics, and attitudes about the condition. As per consumers, their life stage or usage occasion should be the key consideration.

- **Attitudes Regarding (Treating) Condition or Life Stage or Occasion-State:** This element deals with how the target customer perceives the situation. For example, if we were talking about high LDL cholesterol for high-risk cardiovascular (CV) patients (those who have significant co-morbidities, family history of CV disease or who may personally have CV disease), the treating HCP may feel it is absolutely imperative to get these patients' LDL-Cs to safe levels in order to avoid a catastrophic CV event. If we are addressing mothers preparing meals for young children 4 to 9 years of age, they may feel that while it is imperative to ensure their children get proper nutrition, the food must taste good or their children won't eat it.

- **Current Usage and Dissatisfactions:** Here's where we name names. We identify what the target customer is currently using and their dissatisfactions with these other products that our brand can (better) satisfy. Please note that if marketing research does not reveal any customer dissatisfactions, it is our job to find the difference our brand can make, whether it be functional or emotional, that will uncover and create dissatisfaction with the target customer regarding what they are currently using. If you were to ask me years ago if I used a Sony Walkman (a device from the past) and if I had any dissatisfactions with usage, I would have answered yes to the first and no to the second. Along comes Steve Jobs with the iPod, and lo' and behold, I became dissatisfied with my Walkman! Now with the iPhone, I don't even use an iPod. You don't either!

- **Telling Behaviors:** These are things the target customer does, related to our category, that lead to discovering legitimate and productive customer insights. For example, the HCP treating the high-risk CV patient with high LDL-C may provide a dietitian to counsel the patient on food choices and menu planning. The potential truck buyer may be more likely to own a rifle and hunt than travel via airline.

- **Needs (Both Physical and Emotional):** This is the converse of the dissatisfactions. If the dissatisfaction is that current treatment with statins does not lower the LDL-C to healthy levels, then the need is to lower LDL-C to healthy levels. We need to ensure alignment and that new, conflicting ideas are not creeping into our work. In the example of mothers preparing meals for young children, we need to provide these mothers with the nutrition they seek for their children with meals the kids will consume.

5. *Create a tribe.* What I'm talking about here is a community that target customers identify with and want to join. This practice is about pulling together people who believe what you believe and who want others to know it, too. In the example of "difference makers," if you ask an HCP if she is a difference maker in helping heal or remedy patients' maladies, what would you expect she would answer? "Yes, of course!" This psychographic label should link back to the brand idea. At the same time, it should be so appealing as to invite target customers to identify with and join your tribe.

6. *Be faithful to your target customer.* Ultimately, we need to serve our target customer better than the competition. It is essential that we work to win target customers over to our brands each and every day. Be very mindful that it is more costly to win a new customer than to keep one. So, keep the target customer at the forefront of all your thinking and actions. Whenever you are about to decide on strategies or initiatives of any kind (e.g., change of packaging or a marketing campaign), ask, "What would Sue (our target customer identified and profiled in our bull's-eye target customer of one) think and do as a result of

our proposed action?" She is the only one to be concerned about. It's a good idea to "buy insurance," as one of my former managers at Johnson & Johnson, Peter Larson, used to advise me. Namely, check out the answer using marketing research.

7. *Measure everything against your target customer.* The target customer's needs, concerns, and satisfaction must be our primary concern. Remember without a cadre of loyal customers, there cannot be a brand. Measure all actions and intended actions against your chosen target customer. Do not be concerned with those people outside your target as they represent an energy drain and a potential distraction that could knock you off your single-minded pursuit of those you've chosen to serve.

A client clearly identified the brand's bull's-eye target customer of one in his creative brief and undertook creative development against that target with his advertising agency. He tested the proposed creative and shared the results with me. The results evidenced that the agency had developed compelling messaging against the intended target customer. However, the messaging did not fare well against the larger population purchasing the category. He asked me, "What audience should I use to assess the effectiveness of creative work?"

The answer is simple: For whom did you create the messaging? It was developed for his bull's-eye target customer of one. Therefore, that's the audience response he needs to assess the effectiveness of his messaging. That's it and nothing more!

Choose your target customer through thoughtful segmentation. Go below the surface of the skin to really know and appreciate her so well that you can predict how she will respond to the stimuli you provide. Define her to everyone so there is a complete understanding of whom the brand is targeting and who they are not. This will lead to developing compelling marketing. It's important to choose wisely if we are going to create brand loyalty. Peter Drucker also said, "The aim of marketing is to know the customer so well, the product or service fits him and sells itself."

CHAPTER 7

"BAD" BEHAVIORS

Behavior objectives are the "keystone" habit to building high-impact, performance-driven cultures, and brands.
Richard Czerniawski

keystone (noun) *key-stone:* central stone in an arch

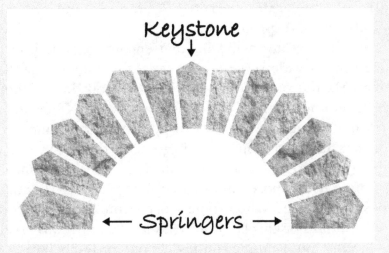

According to Wikipedia: "The term is used figuratively
to refer to a central element
of a larger structure (such as a theory or an organization)
that locks the other elements in place and allows the
whole to be self-supporting."

Charles Duhigg, author of *The Power of Habit: Why We Do What We Do in Life and Business*, introduces the concept of "keystone" habits. Keystone habits are bedrock habits that cause other habits to arise and flourish. According to Mr. Duhigg, "Cultures grow out of the keystone habits in every organization, whether leaders are aware of them or not." Marketing can capitalize on this idea of keystone habits to develop a high-impact, performance-driven culture.

THE POWER OF KEYSTONE HABITS

Keystone habits have the power to trigger change. Exercise is an example of a keystone habit. When people begin to exercise and achieve results, whether it is a loss of weight, increase in energy, or a feeling of achievement, it triggers other healthful habits. Exercising spills over into making conscious choices about nutrition, getting sufficient rest to aid recovery and even taking more care in our hygiene and appearance.

Keystone habits create small wins that encourage widespread changes. These small wins provide rewards that serve to promote change in other related areas. Having your running clothes laid out in the morning and putting them on when you get out of bed, regardless of how tired you may feel, is a small win that serves to help inspire you to continue out the door. Telling yourself that today you are only going to do a slow mile keeps you from getting back into bed, and once your jog begins, that small win helps propel you on to doing more mileage than intended. These small wins lead to other positive changes. When you get back from a jog, it encourages you to pass on the donuts or bagels and instead have a nutritious breakfast. One small win—having your running clothes laid out for you before awakening—cascades into another beneficial action, and then another, etc.

THE KEYSTONE HABIT: BEHAVIOR OBJECTIVES

To ring the cash register (i.e., make a sale), we first have to trigger customer behavior. We refer to these behaviors as "marketing objectives," or its derivatives at the marketing mix and initiatives level (e.g., communication behavior objective for messaging). Stimulating customer behaviors drives performance in the marketplace. Yet, few organizations and marketers think about or make choices regarding the customer behaviors they need to drive incremental sales, achieve their business objectives, generate a positive return on investment to leverage resources and measure performance against a SMART expectation (i.e., specific, measurable, attainable, relevant, and timebound). As a result of not focusing on behavior objectives, these organizations and their brands wallow in ignorance, squandering precious resources, mounting opportunity losses and eroding organization and brand health.

"BAD" BEHAVIORS

Everything we do in marketing should be to stimulate, or contribute to, the achievement of a target customer behavior. In this manner, we can engineer the growth of our brands, and hopefully, grow them faster and increase profits more than the market and individual competitors. Unfortunately, many marketers are engaged in "bad" behaviors.

1. *For one, they pursue activities without making a rational connection to generating specific, essential behaviors for growth.* They're blindly doing things for the sake of doing things since that's what has been done in the past and is expected of them now. If they're involved in the use of social media, retail promotions, medical education or medical congresses, then they continue to pursue these inherited activities, never questioning whether they are leading to essential behaviors. Perhaps then, these marketers do not fully appreciate the relationship between target customer behaviors and sales. Specifically, we all need to understand an activity must trigger an action, which is a specific behavior, to make a sale. It's that simple, but it's not necessarily easy to do.

2. *For another, they misstate or misidentify behaviors.* For example, they might use the term *trade-up* or *upgrade* to identify the behavior they seek from moving a user of a competitive product to their product. The thinking is that the customer is moving from an inferior to a superior performing product, hence their use of this term *upgrade.*

However, this is not an upgrade. This move from a competitive product (regardless of whether you believe it is inferior) to yours is a *switch*. A true upgrade is an internal switch from one of the organization's brands to another of its brands (that is typically premium-priced, offers higher margins, affords more extended patent protection, creates new market segments, etc.). Going from a competitive product (no matter the perception of lesser utility or value) to your brand is a switch, plain and simple. It is not an upgrade.

3. *Third, they confuse subordinate objectives with superordinate behaviors.* For example, they may state "trial" as a behavior. However, "trial" is not a superordinate behavior. Instead, it is subordinate to achieving behaviors of adoption and switching. We seek trial as an objective to generate one of the previously mentioned superordinate behaviors. Trial is typically an objective of promotion. *Awareness* and *access* (or distribution) are also often confused as behaviors. Again, these are subordinate objectives. Awareness is a media, call-frequency or promotion-schedule objective. Both access and distribution are worthy subordinate objectives, for without them, the results from any attempts we make on generating behaviors will be retarded.

   Penetration is a strange one that straddles misstatement and confuses subordinate objectives with superordinate behaviors. Like trial, we need to think about what we are doing. Does penetration pertain to household penetration or to HCP penetration of our brand? Might consumers or HCPs already be using a competitive option? If the consumer or HCP is not using options to our offering, then it is *adoption*. If they are using a competitive option, then what is referred to as penetration of households or pharmacies or HCPs of our brand is, in fact, a switch. Both adoption and switching will lead to penetration. So, penetration is a result, just as sales is a result, of achieving specific behaviors.

4. *Fourth, they will ask their marketing initiatives to do more than they are capable of; namely, achieve more than one behavior.* For example, they may demand that advertising achieve both adoption and switching

112

behaviors. However, the messaging needed for each is very different. If the desired target customer behavior is adoption, then the messaging should be about the benefit of using or prescribing (namely, taking up) the product. If it is switching, then messaging must be about the advantage of using your brand versus already established competition. We need to make choices. If we don't, it is highly unlikely we will achieve either since we will not have the proper focus or proposition to target customers.

Unfortunately, this focus on one behavior objective is essential for senior managers to recognize because in many cases where marketing managers make a choice, their senior managers will push them into doing more than the initiative can handle.

5. *Foisting needed behaviors in developed countries on undeveloped nations.* This is typical bad behavior of global marketers. Specifically, global marketers will establish switching as the critical behavior since it is usually the way to incremental growth in developed countries, where they are headquartered. However, adoption is often the essential behavior to growth in undeveloped nations. A message created to stimulate switching will likely not work in an undeveloped country where adoption is the needed behavior.

6. *Finally, there are no goals established for essential behavior objectives.* Therefore, there is no attempt to measure the impact of marketing activities on their ability to generate the achievement of the behavior objectives. So, neither the marketers nor their organizations know if anything is working, no less the level of productivity of their efforts. More will be forthcoming on this subject in "Chapter 12: Eminence-Based versus Evidence-Based Marketing."

AUTHENTIC BEHAVIORS

Every marketer should learn and employ authentic, or "good," behaviors. Here is a listing of authentic behaviors and their meaning:

- **Adoption:** This is about getting customers to begin using a product or service from a new category or class. It's all about taking up something that they hadn't been doing or using before. For example, it could be getting consumers in China, who previously never used dental floss or mouthwash, to begin using these products. It could also be getting healthcare practitioners who treat ADHD in children to begin treating and prescribing medication for adults with ADHD. Alternatively, it could be getting surgeons to start body sculpting for their bariatric patients whose significant weight loss has resulted in layers of sagging skin.

- **Switch/Convert:** Virtually every marketer, particularly those in developed countries where market growth is slowing, flat or declining, is familiar with switching behavior. This behavior is about getting consumers and surgeons to change their usage from a competitor's product to your brand. As it relates to HCPs, it's all about getting them to switch their prescribing behavior and choose your brand versus other competitive options.

    While switching and conversion are interchangeable, I prefer the term *convert*. It suggests more than an episodic change to one that is more durable and, hopefully, permanent. Furthermore, it suggests an epiphany of sort, as in a spiritual experience, and conjures the notion of creating brand evangelists. Yeah, I like to convert prospects. I love the idea of unleashing evangelists for my brand.

    More worth noting regarding adoption and conversion: A patient who begins treatment for a new condition is adopting it. For example, if you are diagnosed with high levels of unhealthy cholesterol and the HCP prescribes statins, and you comply with the HCP's treatment, then you have adopted it. On the other hand, if the HCP prescribes a treatment for a newly diagnosed patient, it is only adoption for that HCP if he has never treated for that condition. If he has treated for that condition, then it is converting (or switching) from what he would have prescribed to a different drug brand. Again, sticking with this example, if the HCP had been prescribing Lipitor to newly diagnosed hyperlipidemia patients but instead begins prescribing Crestor in its stead to new patients, then he has switched.

So, what about going from one class to another class of products? This is an excellent question to ponder. Let's say you have been using glasses and begin using contact lenses. Is this adoption or switching? For what it's worth, I'd classify it as switching. Wearing glasses represents adoption of a vision correction device. Moving from glasses to contact lens would constitute a switcheroo (or to use the proper term *switch*). While it may not seem like it, this is a big deal. It has all sorts of implications. For example, should messaging be directed against glasses or other contact lens products? Might our messaging be different if we are attempting to stimulate a switch from glasses versus contact lens? Think about it!

- **Trade-Up or Upgrade:** Either term is acceptable. Some prefer the term *upgrade* since it suggests superior performance. Just try to keep it consistent in your organization to avoid confusion. Keep in mind that this is internally focused. It is about getting current customers to move from one of your products to a newer, improved version or product. A trade-up could be moving to a replacement product or to the next generation of products. The new product is usually premium priced, affords higher margins (or, better yet, both!) or replaces products losing patent protection or those going out of production.

  It is far less costly to retain rather than attract new users. Trade-up is a crucial behavior to keep customers from straying. It is particularly a priority with high market share brands whose marketers realize incremental value sales and profit growth from the trade-up. The automotive and medical device industries are prime examples where trade-ups are a priority behavior. In fact, I recently traded up to another Cadillac, our seventh or so in the last 20 years.

  There's also a trade-up to a larger transaction size. It's getting customers to purchase (and consume) more on each occasion. At one time, a 6.5-ounce bottle of Coca-Cola was the standard serving size. Then it went to 12 ounces and on up to 16 ounces. We packaged Coke in larger sizes and drove consumers to them: 1 liter, 2 liters, and 3 liters.

Whereas we used to purchase a 6-pack to take home to the family, today, we are buying a case or two. Our families aren't getting bigger; they are just growing thirstier. Research shows that for many food and beverage categories, the purchasing pattern drives consumption. If you purchase soft drinks weekly, then you will consume what you have purchased for the home between scheduled shopping excursions. If you move from buying a six-pack or two to a case, then consumption will likely increase accordingly.

- **Adjunctive:** This is a behavior favored by healthcare marketers. In its purest terms, it is about getting HCPs to add to their current therapy for a given condition. It's really about making therapy more complete to deliver either better quality of efficacy and/or efficacy for additional symptoms of the patient's condition. As it relates to the former, imagine for a moment a patient suffering from depression. The HCP prescribes anti-depression medication. However, the patient continues to suffer from unresolved depression. In comes Abilify. It's used as an adjunctive therapy to help remedy the patient's unresolved depression.

  However, again, it's important to be clear if this is purely adjunctive or if it is switching. The HCP has additional choices in treating a patient's unresolved depression. She may titrate to the highest tolerated dose of the first line of therapy or switch to another antidepressant. If the HCP's practice was to do either but instead, adds Abilify, then in reality, we have a switch (from what was her standard behavior).

  In providing efficacy for additional symptoms, allergy meds may offer a fruitful example. Let's say the HCP recommends an OTC (over-the-counter) antihistamine for the relief of her patient's seasonal allergy condition. However, the patient continues to suffer from nasal rhinitis. So, the HCP adds an (adjunctive behavior) OTC or Rx nasal-administered remedy. While the patient is feeling significantly better, she continues to complain of itchy, watery eyes. Ah, an opportunity for another adjunct: an ocular allergy med!

Keep in mind that adjunctive therapy complements a treatment. It may not work effectively as a single therapy to provide maximum relief for a given problem or to cover the total spectrum of symptoms or contributing causes to a condition. It's an additional measure to complete therapy. Please don't confuse labeling with behavior. A specific treatment may be approved as adjunctive because it is not sufficiently efficacious as a single agent, or it was clinically tested in a treatment regimen as adjunctive therapy.

- **Increase Utilization:** This is about a broader application and is also highly relevant in healthcare marketing. It's about getting the HCP to treat more patients. Let's assume that for every ten patients a given HCP diagnosis with high cholesterol, he only addresses four with cholesterol-lowering pharmaceutical agents. In this case, the marketer may want to increase utilization by two patients for a total of 6 (in a given period, such as one year). Just by increasing utilization to six patients, the marketer has generated incremental growth of up to 50%.

  Increased utilization can also be an important behavior objective for FMCG (fast-moving consumer goods) brands. It may be manifested by getting consumers to use a given product in more ways than originally intended. Consider Arm & Hammer Baking Soda. The marketers encourage us to use it to satisfy a broad spectrum of needs from neutralizing unwanted food odors in our refrigerator to whitening our teeth.

  Alternatively, it could be about getting consumers to use a product for different occasions or day parts. An example of this is McDonald's taking Denny's lead to make breakfast available at any time of the day. Another example of daypart usage to increase utilization would be Diet Coke, or for that matter Dr. Pepper, encouraging morning (breakfast) usage.

- **Frequency or Repeat Purchasing Rate:** This is about getting customers to repurchase and increase their rate of purchasing. As an example, let's say consumers replace their toothbrushes every 7.8 months on average. However, wear tests demonstrate that toothbrushes lose their cleaning power after just 3 months of usage. For the remaining 4.8 months of usage, consumers are getting the brushing effectiveness of a wet noodle (okay, a bit of an exaggeration, but you get the point). In this case, the behavior goal is to get consumers to purchase quarterly for the sake of their oral health and for the health of the business.

- **Compliance:** This is about using the product as directed. In the healthcare world, it is dosing as prescribed by the HCP. If the HCP prescribes that the patient take the medicine twice daily, once each with the morning and evening meal for 10 days, then anything that deviates from this is non-compliance. Daily contact lenses should be worn, well, daily. That is, one should not wear a daily contact lens for more than one day. The consumer is not to keep a daily lens he has inserted in the eye over the course of two days. If the marketer builds his growth and sales forecast upon compliance, but consumers use the same lens for 2.5 days on average, then the actual volume will be down some 60% from target.

- **Persistency:** This is about sticking with a therapeutic regimen for a prescribed period, the term of a given condition, or to achieve a particular goal. It's a continuance of medication, and it's vital in health care marketing. A patient prescribed an anti-hypertensive will need to take it for life. In this case, persistency is taking the medication throughout the life of the patient. If the patient misses one day, then they are non-compliant. However, if the patient stops taking the drug after a certain period (be it a month, a year, whatever), then it is a lack of persistency.

SO, WHAT'S THE BIG DEAL ABOUT BEHAVIORS?

Unfortunately, from my experience with client companies, many of which are among the most admired in the world, few marketers (or their agencies) think about or make choices regarding the customer behaviors they need to drive incremental sales, achieve their business objectives, generate a positive return on investment, leverage resources and measure performance. As a result of not focusing on behavior objectives, these organizations and their brands wallow in ignorance, squandering precious resources, mounting opportunity losses and eroding organization and brand health.

If the marketer doesn't focus on target customer behaviors, then he, and the company are not creating a clear line-of-sight to sales. They don't know what they are trying to accomplish with a marketing initiative or how they are going to get there. In the words of the late Yankee, Baseball Hall of Fame, catcher Yogi Berra, "Any road will not get you there!"

The California Dairy Board's 1992 "Got Milk?" campaign is a classic case in point for identifying and addressing the correct behavior. After years of consistent declines in milk consumption, the Got Milk? campaign was able to arrest the decline. This change came about from getting on the right track with an authentic, strategically appropriate behavior objective, which in turn, led to the development of a compelling campaign based upon a legitimate and productive consumer insight.

Interestingly, the behavior the marketers initially sought out was stimulating adoption, specifically to get people to drink milk. If you were to ask me, "Do you drink milk?" my answer would be an unequivocal "NO!" I haven't had a glass of milk since I was a child, and even back then I was resistant, so my parents forced it upon me. I didn't prefer it then nor do I prefer it today.

If you were to ask me, "Do you eat cereal?" the answer would be, "Yes, I do." The follow-up question is, "What do you put on your cereal, Budweiser?" The answer is, "Of course not. I use milk." Aha! The realization was that the needed behavior wasn't to drive adoption of milk since consumers, like me, have already adopted it. We consume it! The correct behavior was to get consumers to consume it more frequently, known as "frequency of usage."

This insight led to the campaign that linked milk consumption to foods we crave, where the addition of milk helps make the eating occasion more enjoyable. So, they married milk to chocolate chip cookies, peanut butter sandwiches, brownies, Frosted Flakes cereal, many of the foods you consume and enjoy with milk. It is the exact opposite approach of the marketers of Oreo Cookies who declared their brand as "milk's favorite cookie." The resultant "Got Milk?" campaign declared milk as the selected food items' favorite beverage. The campaign produced results. Oh, for want of a correct behavior objective and insight (more on insights in the next chapter).

The big deal is that focus on behaviors will also encourage meaningful dialogue and investigation with other functions (such as the sales force) in the organization. It will help us think through what we need to accomplish more thoroughly and clearly, so we may make the correct choice. It's about identifying those authentic behaviors the brand requires to achieve its business goals and to generate favorable productivity from each of its investments on initiatives in the marketplace. It's about creating a blueprint for a line-of-sight accountability—not just for marketing but also for the sales force and support staff.

THE ESSENTIAL QUESTIONS

Let's apply the practice of KISS, an acronym that stands for "Keep it simple, Stupid." The most important question every marketer should ask themselves is this:

What behaviors do we need to generate?

This question addresses why we are proposing or conducting a given marketing strategy or initiative. However, marketers have not been asking themselves this question because their senior managers aren't asking it. What a pity.

Assuming we can answer the question with an authentic behavior, then the logical follow-up question is this:

What behaviors will the proposed marketing initiative generate?

This addresses whether we are using our limited resources appropriately.

If we can get this far, then we've made real progress because it suggests we know what we want to accomplish and we're using it as a filter to assess everything we do for appropriateness and relevancy towards achieving our business objectives.

RX FOR GOOD BEHAVIOR(S)

Let's keep this simple:

1. *Recognize and acknowledge that triggering customer behaviors results in sales.* The connection is indisputable. Don't just acknowledge it in word; acknowledging it in your deeds is where it really counts.

2. *Adopt good behaviors.* Choose authentic behaviors. Appreciate the difference between superordinate behaviors and subordinate objectives, and apply each appropriately. Use the correct nomenclature so the specific behavior is incapable of being misunderstood and will direct problem-solving, opportunity analyses and resultant marketing activities fittingly.

3. *Get smart and make your behavior objectives* **SMART.** This the acronym for specific (e.g., adoption, conversion, etc.), measurable, achievable (as in realistic), relevant (contributes to the achievement of sales, market share and profit goals), and timebound.

4. *Identify and pursue the most meaningful behaviors.* Specifically, we need to identify and prioritize the pursuit of those behaviors that will lead to the most incremental sales. Do the math!

5. *Get in the habit of asking the following essential questions:*

   What behaviors do we need to generate?
   (What we are trying to accomplish?)

   and

   What behaviors will this marketing initiative generate?
   (Is this an appropriate use of our resources?)

Don't proceed without answering both, to your satisfaction.

IMPORTANCE OF USING SMART BEHAVIOR OBJECTIVES

HOW BEHAVIOR OBJECTIVES BUILD A HIGH-IMPACT, PERFORMANCE-DRIVEN MARKETING CULTURE

Once we adopt the habit of demanding behavior objectives, it should cascade into many other critically essential habits. Asking for the SMART behavior objectives will trigger the following questions: **Target Segmentation:** Whose behavior (as in target customer) are we targeting? Remember Phillip Kotler's words, "If you are not thinking segments, you're not thinking marketing."

- **Plan Achievement:** How will this contribute to achieving our business objectives? We can do the math to determine if it is relevant to, and capable of, achieving our business objectives.

- **Productivity:** What is the expected impact on sales and ROI of the initiative? These provide a financial basis for choosing among the marketing mix elements and initiatives at our disposal to ensure sound stewardship in helping optimize resource allocation.

- **Compelling:** Is the intended messaging and/or execution of the initiative capable of achieving the SMART expected behavior objective? This question should lead marketers and the organization to demand and assess whether they have a relevant, differentiated message appropriate for the behavior objective. The ideas for all initiatives should trigger the behavior that helps achieve the goal.

- **Knowledge:** How do we know the initiative worked or will work? A high-impact, performance-driven culture is an evidence- and knowledge-based culture. It only chooses to do those things that will deliver predictable, positive results. There is no knowledge or predictability without measurement. There is just speculation and ignorance.

6. *Demand to know the following, and accept nothing less, for all marketing proposals, plans, and initiatives:*
   - Who is the target customer?
   - What is the SMART behavior objective?
   - How will this contribute to the development of your business objectives?
   - What is the expected line-of-sight sales growth impact and ROI for the proposed initiative?
   - Does the specific strategy, proposed initiatives and their execution serve to differentiate your offering and contain ideas that will compel customers into action and lead to the achievement of the SMART behavior objectives?
   - What evidence do we have of performance against our expectations?

7. *Make behavior objectives a keystone habit for your organization and brand.*

I'll give you time-off for any bad behaviors you exhibited in the past as long as you promise to model good behavior now and into the future.

CHAPTER 8

UNSIGHTS VERSUS INSIGHTS

A customer insight is a deep-seated truth that reveals important customer needs and values that the brand can exploit to gain a competitive advantage.
Richard Czerniawski

It's not an insight unless it leads to a difference that creates impact!
Richard Czerniawski

THE VALUE OF CUSTOMER INSIGHTS

No one disputes the need for customer insights. Everywhere you turn, senior marketing managers are demanding their marketers discover and build their marketing around customer insights to strike a responsive chord with target customers and to gain a competitive advantage in the marketplace. However, it's not a customer insight unless it leads to a difference in the product, brand, positioning, messaging, a marketing initiative or how we execute our marketing to impact sales. Customer insights are difference-makers in helping make our marketing matter more in connecting with our target customer and generating incremental sales. Here are areas of development where we need and use customer insights:

- **Product:** Customer insights are used in product development to develop products that satisfy important, unfulfilled and latent customer needs. Alternatively, we may use them to design clinical trials that demonstrate an advantage or help us uncover a unique space for our compound versus competition.

- **Brand Positioning:** Customer insights may also be employed in positioning development to create compelling brand ideas and highly competitive, enduring brand positioning strategies to transform mere products into brands that create brand loyalty.

- **Messaging:** Customer insights are applied to message development to arrive at a strategically appropriate, single-minded, differentiated message that triggers essential target-customer behaviors needed to achieve the brand's business objectives.

- **Tactics:** Customer insights can lead us to tactics that boost marketing effectiveness to deliver incremental line-of-sight sales and a favorable ROI.

Customer insights are the *sine qua non*, underpinning relevant and meaningful marketing differentiation.

There are two types of customer insights: strategic and execution (i.e., the "what" and the "how," respectively). I will deal with strategic insights as it is the marketer's responsibility and points to ways we can win in the marketplace. These focus on each of the areas mentioned above. Executional insights are the province of our creative resource teams, and they address how to present specific initiatives to execute our strategies successfully. While it is essential for marketers to recognize and appreciate them, let's leave the discovery of execution insights to those responsible for delivering the execution.

UNSIGHTS

In order to tap into the value of customer insights to drive customer preference and behaviors, we need to *dig deep* to discover an insight. Unfortunately, what many marketers pass off as insights are really "unsights." Unsights are neither legitimate nor productive—two components that comprise an effective insight. Also, it is not effective unless it leads to impact, connecting with the customer and achieving desired results in the form of generating favorable attitudes and, importantly, triggering predetermined behaviors that generate incremental sales.

There are *three classes of unsights:* **accepted customer beliefs**, **facts** and **generic needs**. One of the most frequent unsights is what is known as an **ACB,** or **accepted customer belief**. These may have been insights at the time they were first discovered and uniquely employed to gain a competitive advantage. But today, they no longer differentiate brands. Examples of ACBs include the following:

- Moms recognize the adverse consequences sugar has on children's health and behavior.
- Early detection of (breast) cancer saves lives.
- Smoking kills.
- Moms don't want to use harsh products on their babies that can irritate their delicate skin.

These ACBs don't lead to differentiation. There's nothing original here. They're ancient history, so we must move on from them. They're "unsights."

Nor is there anything original about **facts**. Marketers misuse facts when they declare them as insights. The facts are available to any and all competitors in your category who undertake the same marketing research (either custom or syndicated).

Facts lack connection to customers; they lack understanding. Facts are about the "what," not the "why" that colors attitudes that drive behaviors. A fact specifies the number of times a smoker attempts to quit before achieving success, if ever. Okay, we appreciate it is difficult to quit smoking. However, the insight lies in why it is so difficult (beyond the addiction to nicotine), leading to a specific action the marketer may take, whether it be product development or behavioral programs to help smokers quit once and for all. In other words, it's not the fact; it's the thinking and attitudes that underlie the fact. If you are calling facts insights, then you are undoubtedly advancing "unsights."

Lastly, **generic needs** are a staple of unsights. They're accessible to everyone. So, everyone uses them. Marketing research contributes to the adoption and advancement of generic needs by doing the same studies in the same ways and reporting the same category needs, which are already being satisfied. Everyone then proceeds to fulfill the top needs that customers identify. However, customers cite what they know, and what they know is what they are getting and doing. So, they're rather generic. Keep in mind, needs and benefits are two sides of the same coin. If you latch onto a generic need, you're saddling your brand with a generic benefit.

WHAT'S A CUSTOMER INSIGHT?

When I ask marketers to define a customer insight, I hear the following responses:

- *"An 'aha!'"*
- *"Stepping into the customer's shoes to identify what truly motivates him."*
- *"Understanding the why behind the what."*

These are among the better responses, but there's more to it. Yes, the marketer may feel an "aha" at the moment of discovery, and the customer may also feel an "aha" when he discovers (or rediscovers) the brand and its promise. Certainly, marketers need to step into the customer's shoes to truly understand what motivates them. We know it's not the "what" but the "why" that gives birth to the insight.

I define a customer insight as *a deep-seated truth that reveals important customer needs and values that the brand can exploit to gain a competitive advantage* and win in the marketplace. It is *target customer centric,* going to the core of the customers' belief system. These beliefs reveal important, previously untapped needs that are buried deep in the subconscious level, and values that the brand, not the product, can capitalize on. As a result, the target customer discovers, or rediscovers, the brand in such a way that it drives preference and triggers the behaviors the marketer needs to achieve the brand's business objectives.

If a customer insight is to be effective, it needs to be legitimate and productive. These two requirements provide a guide for discovering as well as testing for insights. They aid us by directing where to dig for insights and how deeply we must dig. Just as engineers use geological surveys to guide them in where to drill for oil, and just as commercial fisherman use sonar to identify schools of fish before dropping their lines into the deep blue ocean, marketers have valuable indicators that reveal likely places for discovering insights. These indicators point us to legitimate or authentic insights as opposed to unsights.

LEGITIMATE INSIGHTS

There are three areas for us to investigate to discover *legitimate* insights. These are the areas where we should direct our digging:

1. Perceived or real weaknesses of the competition
2. Attitudinal barriers regarding our brand or category
3. Untapped compelling beliefs

If what you believe to be a customer insight does not derive from one of these three areas, then it is unlikely to be an insight. Instead, it is highly likely to be an "unsight." Regardless of what one might call it, it won't create an impact and produce the brand performance results you seek. In the final analysis, it's all about getting results.

Note: I labelled the first one as ***"perceived or real weaknesses of the competition"*** as opposed to "our product's advantages." The reason for this tack is to keep marketers and their organizations from continuing their practice of deluding themselves into believing they have advantages where either none exist or they are not sufficiently meaningful to target customers. In this age of sameness, there is little, if any, difference among products.

For example, when dealing with the same class of drugs, all the compounds produce comparable patient outcomes. Ditto for medical devices and so many other areas. Even if one has clinical evidence that the others do not, HCPs are likely to grant them class effect. In other words, they will credit all compounds within a given class of drug with the same clinical results.

Moreover, in the medical device sector, surgeons believe their skills can negate any differences in product performance to produce the same patient outcomes. Fast-moving consumer goods are no exception. Virtually every brand is making the same claims regardless of category. Nearly all believe they are best for target customers despite a lack of evidence to support their claim.

Rather than fabricating advantages the marketer does not have or may possess to a relatively meaningless degree (as perceived by the target customer), it is more productive for him to address how target customers perceive, or can be made to perceive, competitive performance.

Another point of note is that we include "perceived" weaknesses. Customers perceptions are their reality. For all practical purposes, perceptions and reality are the same. The introduction of the brand Lipitor is a case in point. Lipitor was a mega-blockbuster, achieving something approaching $15 billion in sales before turning generic (i.e., the compound, not the brand). HCPs prescribe statins not merely to lower cholesterol but to help the patient avoid a cardiovascular event. While two existing brands, Pravachol and Zocor, had evidence from clinical studies that they reduced cardiovascular events (that Lipitor did not possess at the time of its launch), these brands were not able to lower cholesterol to healthy levels for as many patients as Lipitor could. Keep in mind that the goal isn't merely to reduce cholesterol but to protect against events that imperil life. Yet, many HCPs perceived these proven brands as less efficacious than Lipitor, intuiting that lowering cholesterol to healthy levels would translate to better protection against cardiovascular events, despite the lack of evidence to support this extrapolation. The rest is history. Lipitor soundly beat both Pravachol and Zocor to become the market share leader.

Often, growth slows or stalls due to an ***attitudinal barrier regarding our brand or the category.*** If we can remove the attitudinal barrier, then the brand has an opportunity for renewed growth. A classic example, which is a torture test of sorts, is Lite Beer from Miller in overcoming a category attitudinal barrier regarding low-calorie beers. Heavy beer drinkers (there's no pun here; I'm referring to high volume consumption, not girth) believed that reducing calories watered down the beer, stripping it of flavor. Miller avoided talking about low calories, and instead, referred to its beer as "less filling." Miller Lite would enable target customers to consume more. This was a meaningful promise to heavy beer drinkers who can easily quaff down a six-pack or two (or three!) at a sitting. Miller was successful where others had failed, by addressing and overcoming an attitudinal barrier.

The final area is ***untapped compelling beliefs.*** These are the obvious beliefs, staring everyone in the face, that marketers have overlooked. The first brand to tap into one of these untapped compelling beliefs gains an advantage. However, to achieve and maintain the advantage, the marketer needs to own what others could also own. The way to do this is to invest, and sustain that investment, behind it. If the marketer does not continue investing, a "fast-follower" competitor could capitalize on what another has surrendered.

An example of an untapped compelling belief is the long-standing reason-why support for the Folger's Coffee claim of being the richest, most flavorful cup of coffee in the world: "Mountain grown." Consumers believe that what's grown in the mountains is closer to the heavens, and therefore, the recipient of abundant sunshine and clean, cold waters—unspoiled by the pollution of civilization. "Mountain grown" makes for a compelling reason-why support for a meaningful benefit whether it is for coffee or bottled water. However, in this case, coffee is grown in the mountains—all coffee! Yet, Folger's Coffee claimed it as their reason-why support, trademarked it (which, by the way, is no longer permitted by current law), and supported it for decades. It is one of the reasons for its incredible success in becoming the number one grocery coffee brand in the U.S.

PRODUCTIVE INSIGHTS

Discovering a legitimate insight is only part, albeit an important part, of the battle in winning with customer insights. Once we have unearthed a legitimate insight, we need to determine if it is *productive*. After all, the discovery of oil doesn't mean the well will be productive, or worth the cost of further drilling and operating. We must determine if the legitimate insights we discover will make a difference to our target customer and to our brand and business. For an insight to be productive, it must meet two conditions:

1. ***The brand can exploit it.*** If the brand cannot exploit it (e.g., the technology is not available, the clinical studies don't bear it out, product

testing doesn't evidence it, customer perceptions or experiences don't favor it, or it is not consistent with the brand positioning strategy, etc.) then it is not productive. Take note that we've specified "brand" not "product." The brand is a constellation of values and perceptions, and it captures customers' experiences with it. For example, Gatorade the brand can deliver more versus other brands in the category due to its strategic sponsorships and endorsements with professional sports, while its formulation is basically the same as its competitors. If what we've found is not productive, then we need to return to our three areas and renew our digging.

2. *It will cause a change in customer behavior.* This, too, is absolutely essential. It fulfills the purpose of the insight. It must lead to stimulating a predetermined, desired behavior objective (e.g., switching or adoption). Moreover, it must achieve a specific level of behavior. In other words, it must meet a numeric hurdle, a marketing metric that ultimately contributes to realizing the brand's business objectives. We refer to this as a SMART behavior objective, which I covered in the preceding chapter. If you've missed this or need more detail, go back to chapter 7 and (re)read it!

We need to discover customer insights that are both legitimate and productive if we are going to make a difference in generating results in the marketplace!

DIGGING FOR CUSTOMER INSIGHTS

There are informal and formal ways of going about digging for insights. Informal ways include the many random times and places we find ourselves struck with an "aha" moment. This might happen in the shower, connecting seemingly unrelated things, connecting the dots to see the big picture, upon awakening with an insight that surfaced from your subconscious mind, or when meditating about or noodling through a problem. The informal ways lack a disciplined approach; therefore, they are unpredictable, mainly since they rely on serendipity for the many who are not accustomed to tapping into and trusting their intuition. In other words, the probability of success is low for the vast majority of marketers.

What we need is a disciplined, quality process to go about digging for insights if we are going to improve our probability of achieving success in unearthing legitimate and productive customer insights. Here's a disciplined, quality process for going about digging for customer insights:

1. ***Pull together a multi-discipline team to collaborate on the discovery of legitimate and productive customer insights.*** This is not merely an individual sport relying on an informal approach to discovering insights. Instead, this is a team sport where everyone has a piece of the puzzle that we want to tap into to create a mosaic that gives us a clear picture of what lies in our target customer's subconscious mind. A disciplined approach involves your team, which would include sales, marketing research, product research and development, and agency personnel among others whose experiences and judgment you value.

2. ***Identify the target customer.*** This starts with thoughtful segmentation and the choiceful selection of a customer segment. Then, we need to seek to genuinely know and understand the customer: his attitudes and deep motivations. To accomplish this, we must put together a clear and complete profile of the target customer. If you'll recall from "Chapter 6: Mis-Targeting Target Customers," this would include:
   - Demographics
   - Psychographics
   - Patient-condition, targeted-occasion need states or whatever is appropriate for your sector and category
   - Target-customer attitudes about the category, condition, patients, practices, etc.
   - Current usage and dissatisfactions
   - Telling behaviors of the target customer
   - Untapped needs, both rational and emotional, that our "brand" can better satisfy than those competitors identified in current usage and dissatisfactions

For more on identifying and defining your target customer, go back and reread chapter 6.

3. ***Determine the behavior objective you seek for the target customer.*** Remember an insight is not productive unless it can be exploited to achieve a specific, predetermined behavior objective that will contribute to achieving your brand's business objectives. These include adoption, switching, increased utilization or frequency of purchasing, increased transaction size, trade-up, compliance, persistency, etc. Make the behavior objective SMART (specific, measurable, achievable, relevant and timebound).

4. ***Scour available sources for a better understanding of the target customer.*** This includes but goes beyond marketing research. On the subject of marketing research, qualitative is significantly more likely to provide a better understanding of the "why" behind the "what" of customer behavior than quantitative research. When using quantitative marketing research, it is important to read between the lines and repeatedly question "why," to develop working hypotheses. Capitalize on your experiences, observations and intuition. Try to make leaps from what you have learned in other categories about customer behaviors and insights to your category and brand. Check out what you discover with quantitative research to confirm and quantify the opportunity.

5. ***Use a variety of tools, approaches, and exercises to develop a plethora of potential customer insights.*** Don't' settle for one. Explore many hypotheses to improve the likelihood of discovering a legitimate and productive customer insight. The process of checking out potential customer insights will provide valuable feedback that will lead to a better understanding of the target customer. This may help you discover an insight that will generate preference for your brand and drive incremental sales growth.

6. *Employ the customer insights litmus test.* I've developed the litmus test tool to help you determine if what you've dug up is a potentially legitimate and productive customer insight. (More on it later in this chapter.)

7. *Assess it in the marketplace.* It's about generating line-of-sight sales growth in the market. Everything is hypothetical until proven. So, test it to demonstrate it has an incremental impact in the marketplace before applying it on a broadscale basis.

CAPTURING THE CUSTOMER INSIGHT

Once we have unearthed what we believe might be a potential customer insight, it is essential that we capture and display it in a manner that we can: a) see what we think; b) share it with others to encourage an exchange of ideas; and c) inspect it for being legitimate and productive. The following BDNI tool will help you determine if you are achieving the aforementioned. The first two rows (dark gray) address whether we have a legitimate customer insight. The bottom two rows (light gray) address whether the insight has the potential to be productive." An explanation for each appears in the tool.

BDNI CUSTOMER INSIGHT TOOL

Class of Insight	Identify and explain the class of insight. • Perceived or real weaknesses of the competition • Attitudinal barriers to overcome • Untapped compelling beliefs
Customer Insight	State the insight in the customer's language. • Put it in quotes • Use italics Get into, and share, the mind of the customer. This represents the voice of the customer.

POD (Key-Thought – Benefits/Action)	The POD is the payoff for the insight. The insight is only productive if we can capitalize on it and the resultant action creates the needed sales impact in the marketplace. This includes: • Either a key thought or benefit promise in messaging and brand positioning • A specific action or initiative (e.g., product development, promotion, clinical study, etc.)
Reality (Reasons-Why/Details)	The reasons-why provide evidence that we can pay off the insight. The insight needs to lead to an incremental sales impact and if we lack proof we are probably rationalizing and talking to ourselves. • Reason-why for the key thought or benefit promise • In the case of a marketing initiative, this identifies the details

EXAMPLES

Seeing examples helps provide a model to emulate. Here are two examples. One is for a pharmaceutical brand, Cialis; the other is for a consumer brand, MasterCard. Both brands have experienced significant marketplace success grounded in legitimate and productive customer insights. A brief explanation for each precedes the example.

Cialis has a nine-fold advantage in terms of duration of efficacy, with 36 hours versus 4 hours for Viagra. However, what does that really mean? After all, most sex doesn't last very long. It would seem on the surface that 4 hours is more than enough to consummate the act. However, planned sex doesn't always go as planned. Also, planned sex does not have the same emotional value as spontaneous lovemaking. So, rather than comparing duration, Cialis found an insight that led to the brand's positioning and subsequent messaging: *men can share and respond to intimacy when the moment strikes*. The

Cialis brand positioning is about sharing intimacy in the moment rather than having sex.

"INFERRED" CUSTOMER INSIGHT EXAMPLE

Class of Insight	Perceived or real weakness to exploit of competitive products lasting only about 4 hours. Therefore, you have to plan and make the decision to have sex rather than let the moment lead to sharing and responding to intimacy.
Customer Insight	*"Don't get me wrong, I think these erectile dysfunction relief products are very beneficial. However, the problem is you have to plan for the occasion. Life makes planning a bit difficult. My partner and I may not be on at the same time, and it just doesn't allow for spontaneity in sharing or responding to intimacy."*
POD (Key Thought – Benefits/Action)	Now you don't need to "plan" for your intimate moments; you can be ready when the moment strikes.
Reality (Reasons-Why/Details)	• Clinical studies – Lasts for 36-hours • Indication/labeling

MasterCard is a parity product. Its card has the same dimensions as its competitors (Visa and AMEX); it is made from the same materials and works in the same ways. In fact, prior to the launch of its "Priceless" campaign, which resulted from a legitimate customer insight, consumers perceived MasterCard as purely utilitarian. They afforded no special value to it other than as a backup when they maxed out of their other credit cards. But, the tides (and times) they were a-changin'. Many consumers faced overwhelming debt in purchasing things they did not need, or that were well beyond their means, in trying to keep up with the Joneses.

On the other hand, there was a growing segment of consumers who perceived themselves as "credit-card pragmatists." (If you're taking note, this is a psychographic segment.) They felt that they, unlike their conspicuous spending neighbors, were fiscally responsible. They demonstrated their responsibility by using their credit cards for those things that truly mattered in life. This was a place that neither Visa nor AMEX could own, since they both occupied prestige positioning in the marketplace. The impact came via the Priceless campaign, which capitalized on the target customer selection and corresponding insight to fuel significant MasterCard brand growth for more than 15 years.

"INFERRED" CUSTOMER INSIGHT EXAMPLE

Class of Insight	<u>Untapped compelling belief</u> into consumers' desire to de-emphasize materialism and get back to what truly matters in their lives.
Customer Insight	*"There are many more important things in life than one's material goods and keeping up with the Joneses. I feel life is more about sharing precious moments with family and friends than accumulating material possessions."*
POD (Key Thought – Benefits/Action)	MasterCard. It's there when you need it for purchases big and small, and to get cash *for those moments that truly matter in life.*
Reality (Reasons-Why/Details)	• Available for use just about everywhere • The marriage of utility with values

Okay, so now you know what makes for a legitimate and productive customer insight and how to avoid unsights. You also know where and how to go about digging for legitimate insights. Additionally, you have a tool and model for capturing potential target-customer insights. Where do we go from here?

HOW TO DEVELOP 1001 CUSTOMER INSIGHTS

The typical approach in digging for customer insights is to go in search of *a* significant insight with emphasis on the "a," as in "one." Marketing research models would have marketing managers pouring over and sifting through the same data that is held by competitors in the hope of finding a rare nugget of gold. Frequently, this leads to marketers being dazzled by fool's gold—some meaningless fact. Others hope an insight will miraculously appear, but as we know, chance favors the prepared, and hope is rarely a reliable strategy. A blockbuster insight is as unlikely to fall out of the sky as a rock is to drop out of a cloud.

The way to go about discovering customer insights is to go in search of a plethora of possible legitimate and productive insights. We need to diverge well before we converge on that consensus-driven, so-called BIG insight, which typically turns out to be nothing more than a rationalization for what we think we know. The name of the game in many sports is "shots on goal." The more shots we take, the more opportunity we have to score. It is no different with the discovery of customer insights. We need to develop 1001 potential customer insights if we are to discover gold—a *legitimately* BIG insight that will have a *dramatically* BIG impact on delivering significant incremental results, regardless of whether it is for a new product, positioning, campaign development or marketing initiative. Here's how we can go about developing roughly 1001 potential customer insights for our brands to improve the likelihood that we will discover gold:

1. **The Basis for Insight:** Start by exploring each of the three sources for legitimate customer insights:
   - Perceived or real weaknesses of competitors
   - Attitudinal barriers to overcome regarding your brand or the category

- Untapped compelling beliefs

Dig deep into your target customer's subconscious mind to unearth a potential insight. Don't settle for digging in just one source area. Explore each one, thoroughly. Dig for as many possible insights *as your mind can imagine*. Discovering customer insights is a creative pursuit. Use your imagination to conjure hypotheses. Try to set a minimum of five potential insights for each source area.

2. **Strategic Elements:** Forget focusing on "how" we do something. That's the role of your support team members, such as advertising agency creative personnel, promotion development specialists or product development managers. This isn't to say that executional insights aren't important. They're critically important, but they are not what we marketers typically do. They fall outside our area of expertise and specialty.

Moreover, executional insights are nothing without an appropriate strategic insight. It's the marketer's job to discover the strategic insight. As per executional insights, it is the marketer's job to recognize their potential value when creative personnel share them with us and, if appropriate, add value to their development to fully capitalize on the potential of the insight and, subsequently, it's impact on brand growth.

Each element of the brand positioning strategy provides an opportunity for strategic insight discovery and for gaining an advantage versus competition in motivating customer preference and in driving incremental growth. Our search needs to include but *go beyond the benefit* element. The insight discovery search should cover target segment identification and selection, target-customer needs, competitive framework (particularly perceptual competitive framework), benefit (of course), reason-why support to believe the benefit, and brand character. There are six elements in all. We should set a goal of identifying "X" (such as 5) potential insights for each element of the brand positioning.

3. **Approach to Insights:** This is about our way of gaining access to insights within each of the sources for legitimate customer insights and strategic elements of positioning discussed in points #1 and #2. It's about our entry into their discovery. We must undoubtedly approach insights from the perspective of the customer, whether it be the consumer, health care professional, patient, payor or retailer, gatekeeper, caregiver, or whoever is deemed essential to our task of gaining insights that will lead to creating brand loyalty. But, there are other approaches to discovering customer insights. Here are some, but by all means, this is not all of the most fruitful:

   - *Product/Brand Investigation:* One approach we should not ignore is our product and what it can deliver. Another is the brand itself, which gives us even more than the product to work with (since it represents tangible and intangible attributes: the whole product, target customer experiences, and a bundle of values in our search for insights). The key is to relate the product and brand back to our chosen target customer in the absolute and relative to competition.

   - *Competitive Analysis:* We must consider our competitors, current and future. Identify where they play, where they don't and where they might play. How might you market against your brand if you were in the role of a competitor?

   - *Company Capabilities:* How about exploring for insights within the context of our company's capabilities? What do we, as a company, do well? What competencies can we capitalize upon to tap into customer needs and or values that have been either overlooked or are better than the competition?

   - *Intuition/Experiences:* We should not ignore our intuition and experiences. Get crazy. Dare to hypothesize. A tree model tool is particularly useful to doodle and use for generating and capturing hypotheses.

4. **Playing the Angles:** While approaches get at entry points, *playing the angles* refers to different positions, or ways, of looking at a given point. For example, in a case study product we worked with in conducting

two *Discovering* customer insight programs in Singapore, one of the core product differences participants identified was that a new non-opioid prescription pain relief product triggered the release of the body's natural endorphins. The perceived benefit of this was that it helped to "overcome depression," something chronic pain sufferers, who are unable to get the relief they seek, often experience. Playing the angles, here are some alternatives we were able to generate:

- Boosts mood
- Gives the patient hope
- Helps the body heal from the pain
- Enables total pain management – physical and emotional
- Enables a better quality of life
- Encourages better patient compliance
- Restores a feeling of normalcy
- Enables the physician to maintain treatment control (as opposed to the treating physician needing to refer the patient to another specialty for treatment of pain-related depression)
- Avoid the use of, and dependency on, opioids

Including the first angle, to overcome depression, there are a total of 10 responses or nuggets from which to extract insights. Let's be clear: not all of these will be supportable or effective. That's not the point! The point is to use your imagination and to go beyond the first expected answer (which is obvious and therefore common) to take more shots on goal in preparing or setting up oneself to discover a truly meaningful customer insight for the selected target-customer segment.

5. **Brainstorm for Insights**: Again, the goal is to take many shots on goal (i.e., identify as many potential customer insights as possible). Thus, at BDNI, we encourage each member of the team to refrain from judging until judgment time becomes appropriate. And, it is not appropriate to judge while participants are attempting to ideate. Nothing will cause the creative pump to seize faster than premature judgment. There will be time for winnowing down the potential

insights using the Customer Insight Litmus Tool (see below) and any other criteria you deem relevant. The few that you select can be captured and assessed with customers through marketing research. Finally, you might want to conduct an *adaptive experiment* in the market to confirm, reaffirm and adapt to optimize the productivity of the strategic insight and the resultant action, and its execution. But first things first: develop 1001 customer insights.

If we have done the minimum, here's what we will generate in terms of potential customer insights:

Strategic Brainstorming

Basis for Insight	Strategic Element	Approach	Angle
1. Perceived or Real Weaknesses of the Competition 2. Attitudinal Barriers to Overcome Regarding the Brand 3. Untapped Compelling Beliefs	• Target Segment • Target Telling-Behaviors • Target Needs & Dissatisfactions • Competitive Framework • Benefit • Reason-Why • Brand Character	• Customer • Product/Brand Investigation • Competitive Analysis • Company Capabilities • Intuition/Experience	• 10 (Taken from Point 5)

Assuming we can "do" for each of the "basis for insight" areas, we would have 3 x 5 (basis for insights), + 3 x 7 (strategic elements) x 5 (approaches) x 10 (angles) for a total of 1065 potential customer insights (over the minimum 1001!). As stated previously, not every one of these is going to be the key to success, but each represents another shot at scoring big with customer insights.

LITMUS TEST

The time has come to winnow down the potential customer insights to determine if we're dealing with gold. Here's the BDNI Litmus Test tool, consisting of a series of questions, each of which must be answered in the affirmative, to determine if we have a legitimate AND productive insight:

BDNI CUSTOMER INSIGHT LITMUS TEST

Legitimate

1. Some form of market research suggests it (i.e., quantitative, qualitative or in-market activity):   YES   NO

2. It fits into one of the following classifications: YES   NO
   - *Perceived or real weakness* to be exploited of a competitive product
   - *Attitudinal barrier to overcome* in the minds of customers regarding your brand
   - *Untapped compelling belief or practice* about the condition, category and/or behaviors, which, if tapped, would lead customers to choose your brand

---

Productive

1. a) Can be paid-off by a strategic element of the brand YES   NO
   b) The above can be done in a meaningful way
      (i.e., category or competitive?)   YES   NO

2. Effects a change in customer attitudes, behavior and/or relationship with the brand, in such a way that leads to the achievement of the marketing behavior objective   YES   NO

If you can answer YES to each of the questions in the BDNI Litmus Test tool, then it is more likely that you have a legitimate and productive insight rather than an unsight.

GUT CHECK

The gut check is another way to check for insights. The reality of the situation is that marketers are good rationalizers. We will find ways to rationalize what we have identified and feel to be an insight. Unfortunately, this is aided and abetted by the conventional wisdom of the organization and/or category. By the way, if it is part of the conventional wisdom, in all likelihood, it's not an insight! Furthermore, it is exacerbated by *consensus*, which is another word for "groupthink." This next methodology to pressure test for an insight relies on honestly connecting with your gut. Yes, your gut can be a good indicator of whether you've struck gold, providing you are truly attuned to your feelings. Here are some questions you should ask of yourself (and, for that matter, others on your team):

1. ***Have you been gob-smacked?*** To be gob-smacked is to be figuratively "hit in the mouth." In other words, you are astonished and awed by what you have discovered. Not merely pleasantly surprised, but knocked off your feet: *Where did this come from?* If you haven't been gob-smacked, it means that you not only don't have a great discovery, but it is probably not an insight at all.

2. ***Do you need to champion it?*** Must you push it up a hill? Do you initially feel organization resistance? This is yet another way to say many or most managers in the organization just don't get it. In fact, it might actually scare them because it flies in the face of conventional wisdom regarding how we do things or what we know. Also, it requires by its very nature that we take a different tack from the way we, and our competitors, have always done things. Now that's really scary. Don't be turned off if you have to champion it. View it as a positive indication that you have something of potential value.

3. *Are there a few astute and savvy managers who recognize its beauty?* There is something aesthetically pleasing about an elegant solution or idea. If you and a precious few others—whose judgment, instinct and experiences you respect—see beauty in the insight, then it is a potential sign that you may be on to something profound.

4. *Do you feel a sense of pride in your discovery?* C'mon now, if you don't feel a sense of pride in a job well done, then you're either dead or in the wrong field. Perhaps, you should consider getting into another field. Imagine what you'd feel if you won an award for "Marketer of the Year" or jumped up two pay grades. You'd be ecstatic, bursting with pride. There has to be a sense of pride in your discovery. Otherwise, keep digging.

5. *Can you envision it leading to, and making a big, difference for the brand?* Something worth discovering must have value. It's treasure. The payout is substantial. The discovery of an insight must lead to and make a big difference in target-customer preference for your brand and in generating incremental sales. It has to make a significant impact to the competitiveness and business-building of the brand. If the insight leads you to where you have already been, or to where you were already going, or to where everyone else is, then you probably don't have a legitimate and productive insight.

REALITY

The aforementioned litmus test and gut check are ways to pressure-test potential insights. However, the real test lies in conducting marketing research of the insight (e.g., messaging, etc.), followed by in-market testing, to determine if it positively impacts target-customer behaviors. Your marketing research team members can assist you in validating your discoveries where it counts, with the resultant solution.

RX FOR DISCOVERING LEGITIMATE AND PRODUCTIVE INSIGHTS

Here are some things to consider in your search to discover, capture and validate legitimate and productive customer insights that will lead to initiatives that have an impact on generating incremental sales in the marketplace:

1. *Undertake a disciplined, quality process for discovering customer insights.* This is not to negate an individual, informal approach to digging for insights. However, I'm encouraging you to go one step further and make it a team sport to improve the likelihood of discovering legitimate and productive customer insights. It will serve to make it a priority, focusing everyone on the importance of customer insights. Additionally, it will capitalize on the unique perspectives and experiences of team members. Adopt the quality process I've shared with you, but feel free to adapt it to better meet your needs.

2. *Avoid unsights.* Do not accept ACBs, facts or generic needs as insights. These are unsights! Don't allow them to lull you into complacency. They will not be productive.

3. *Dig (or drill) where you are likely to find legitimate insights.* Remember, there are three areas in which to dig for legitimate insights:
    *   Perceived or real weaknesses of the competition
    *   Attitudinal barriers regarding our brand or category
    *   Untapped compelling beliefs

    If what you've discovered doesn't fall into one of these classifications, then it is highly unlikely to be an insight. You're probably dealing with an unsight. So, keep digging.

4. *Make sure you can make something out of it.* In other words, make sure it is going to be productive. This means that you can capitalize on it with your brand, claims, reasons-to-believe, brand positioning strategy, etc. You have to be able to pay off the insight if it is to be productive.

5. *If it isn't productive, go back to digging.* Remember, don't just dig anywhere; dig where you're likely to find legitimate insights. Repeat as needed!

6. ***Capture and display your customer insight using the BDNI Customer Insight Tool.*** This will enable you and others to see if it is legitimate and has the potential for being productive. It will also keep the focus on the customer.

7. ***Go in search of 1001 customer insights.*** "One" is not the luckiest number. Discovering one legitimate and productive customer insight takes a lot of hard work. The harder you're willing to work and the more areas you pursue, the more likely you are to discover gold – an insight that leads to creating a positive impact in the market for your brand.

8. ***Wo/man-up.*** Use the checklist to help you winnow down from 1001 potential customer insights to the handful or more that are genuinely legitimate and productive. Many marketers shun using checklists because it is additional work, or they think they already know it, or it calls their professionalism into question, or whatever! As a former military pilot, I am quite familiar and comfortable with using checklists. It helps cut down on making mistakes, ensuring right action and achieving predictable, successful outcomes. Use the litmus test tool and gut check.

9. ***Get real.*** The insight must lead to an action that will positively impact your brand's growth and development in the marketplace. The only way to confirm this is to test the resultant product of the insight in the marketplace. Identify your expectations and inspect for what you expect.

Legitimate and productive insights are within reach. All it takes is knowing where to dig, knowing how to dig, taking multiple shots on goal from all angles, displaying your discovery, checking for productivity and testing for impact. You can do it. Persevere, smartly!

CHAPTER 9

BRAND COMMUNICATIONS THAT SUCK

Suck (suk) verb: to be very bad

High-impact communications stimulate the achievement
of "stretch" business objectives.
Richard Czerniawski

During one of our High-Impact Communications workshops, a participant shared that his team tested their communications and found that it did poorly in convincing target customers to act. As a result, he erroneously concluded that since his brand communications did not work to increase sales, then marketing communications (as in advertising) do not work. There is ample evidence to suggest that, regardless of the category, effective communications can drive target customer behaviors leading to an increase in sales and working wonders in building brand equity.

This participant jutted his chin and threw out a challenge, which he disguised in the form of this question, *"Can you tell me why my communications don't work?"* I responded, *"Yes, of course. Your marketing communications suck!"* His communications were terrible. However, this is not an indictment against this marketer or his communications. Neither he nor his marketing communications are outliers. Instead, it's the norm. Doubt me? Spend an evening watching television (for the commercials), leafing through magazines or journals (for the ads), clicking on banner ads, visiting websites, spending time on a brand page in Facebook, opening an email solicitation, or reviewing any communications developed by marketers directed at target customers. There is a vast wasteland out there, regardless of the medium, filled with marketing communications that suck big time.

Why do the communications suck? This chapter is not about communication vehicles (as in media selection). Instead, this is about a poor process or lack of process. This is about inappropriate and misguided strategic content. It is about execution that fails the strategy, fails to engage the target customer or lacks a campaign idea. (It should also be about being able to assess communications and provide sound direction that adds to the productivity of the messaging. However, I will save this for another time and place.) It is about marketers knowing how communications work and knowing what they are doing. It's all rather simple, but it's not easy.

I could write a book about this subject. Perhaps, I will at another time. But this is too important a subject to wait to do so. If we fail to communicate appropriately and meaningfully, we will not connect our brand with potential target customers. It's absolutely amazing to me that so many marketing training programs at leading companies do not require all their marketers to undertake training in brand communications. If we are unable to communicate or message effectively about our brand, then at worse, it is going to fail, or at best, it won't realize its potential.

Brand communications are vital to connecting with your target customer. It's about sharing your story and telling it in such a way as to resonate with target customers, so they see your brand in a favorable light and act on it. When done well, your communications (your messaging!) will drive incremental line-of-sight sales and build brand equity.

How Communications Work

It's not creative unless it sells.
Bill Bernbach (Doyle Dane Bernbach)

Let's start with how communications don't work. Marketers, agency creative directors, and sales personnel can't develop messaging to grow sales 10% or increase market share by 1.5 points. It just doesn't work that way because there is no clear strategic focus, as in winning the minds and the hearts of target customers to change their behaviors.

Then, how do brands communications work to enhance sales? Marketing communications are about stimulating a specific behavior (the "communication behavior objective") for a strategically selected target customer. To stimulate a behavior, the communication must first instill a belief (which I will refer to as the "key thought"). The agency, creative resource team or sales rep develops the execution (the campaign idea), which is the stimulus needed to instill the key thought in a way that connects on an emotional level with the target customer. The emotional connection triggers the behavior, contributing to the achievement of the communication behavior objective, which drives sales and market share growth.

HOW MARKETING COMMUNICATIONS WORK – Causal Relationship

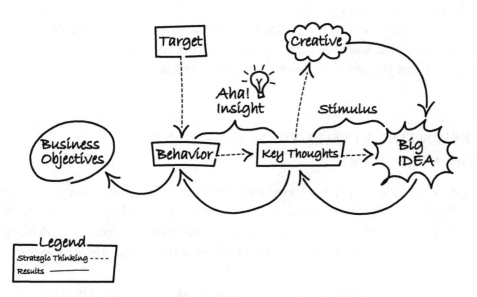

HIGH-IMPACT COMMUNICATIONS

Our goal is not merely to avoid brand communications that suck or just to develop brand communications that are effective. Instead, our goal is, and should be, to develop high-impact brand communications. High-impact communications does the following:

- Goes beyond educating or informing to *achieving stretch business objectives*. By "stretch" I mean exceeding our expectations in driving incremental line-of-sight sales that can be traced to the communications. For example, if the market is growing by 3% and our brand by 5%, our brand communications drive 10% growth.
- *Builds brand equity* by reflecting our "competitive" brand idea and positioning strategy in the messaging so it takes root in the minds, hearts and souls of target customers.
- *Capitalizes on an important customer insight* to offer a relevant, meaningfully differentiated point-of-difference that leads to *preference* for our brand and triggers achievement of the communication behavior objective.
- Incorporates a unique, ownable, provocative, memorable *brand campaign idea* that lasts a long time, across multiple customer touch points and *gets the target customer to take action.*

THE ESSENTIAL ELEMENTS OF EFFECTIVE COMMUNICATIONS

Now that you understand how communications work and what it means to have "high-impact" communications, it's time to tackle how to make it happen. Let's start with the essential elements, identify the critical marketing errors, go beyond how to avoid them and address them smartly. These are:

- The essential creative brief to provide the strategic direction for messaging
- The campaign idea to dramatize the strategic messaging in compelling customer language

- Execution to cut through the clutter to be noticed, to showcase the campaign idea and to establish positive brand linkage.

THE ESSENTIAL CREATIVE BRIEF

The creative brief is the most important piece of paper at the agency.
Andy Langer, Worldwide Creative Director,
Roberts-Langer Advertising

We start at the beginning with the essential creative brief (ECB). The ECB provides the direction for the messaging the creative resource team will use to develop the campaign idea needed to stimulate the behaviors of the target customer that will contribute to the achievement of the business objectives (which are and always will be sales, market share, and profit). It must contain all the essential information and nothing more. It demonstrates a well-chosen target customer, clear intent regarding the behavior that is needed, a legitimate and productive customer insight that leads to a relevant and meaningfully differentiated key thought (which some would say is the benefit, promise or belief), and credibility in the form of convincing reason-to-believe support.

The ECB is the first step. It lays out the assignment. It is a step that requires marketers and their creative resource partners to approach collaboratively to dialogue and thoughtfully address strategic issues. It's about determining the appropriate strategic message (again, the key thought) for a select segment of target customers, based upon a legitimate and productive customer insight to stimulate the achievement of a pre-determined behavior.

Andy Langer, Worldwide Creative Director for Roberts-Langer Advertising, says, "The creative brief is the most important piece of paper at the agency." Yet, many creative briefs are not worth the paper upon which they are written. This conclusion is not merely my opinion. It is a common complaint among senior marketers and agency personnel. Creative briefs suck for any of the following reasons:

- There is no "one" standard creative brief. Just about every brand within a company has a different brief, which makes it difficult for senior managers to address content. It would be akin to using different financial accounting and reporting systems for different brands. It doesn't turn the spotlight on key strategic elements, and as such, it doesn't facilitate a healthy strategic dialogue.

- Essential elements are missing from the creative brief. It does not contain one or more of the essential elements needed to appropriately direct creative development. (More on this later in the chapter.)

- It includes elements that are non-essential to the task at hand for developing high-impact communications. What's wrong with this? Pure and simple, it dilutes focus from time spent on what is truly important and meaningful.

- The target-customer definition is superficial, is incomplete (such as relying solely on demographics), lacks clarity (words are imprecise), is not real (as it doesn't reflect the actual customer), or is not choiceful (e.g., no segmentation or captures too many diverse segments). In practice, marketers resist making choices trying to reach everyone, which results in a key thought that either lacks focus or is generic. Regardless, it is difficult, if not impossible, to discover a legitimate and productive customer insight and to develop a strategically compelling key thought without a precise and robust target-customer profile.

- The stated reason or objective of the marketing communication is not a behavior. "Awareness" and "trial" are not communication behavior objectives, which I covered in chapter 7. Awareness is a media objective. Trial is a promotional objective. We need target customers to adopt something they have not done, or don't do, or to switch from what they are using to our offering or to use our product more often (i.e., frequency of purchasing/use). These are behaviors. They each require very different key thoughts planted in the target customers' consciousness if we are to stimulate the precise behavior.

- The behavior objective is not SMART (as in specific, measurable, achievable, relevant, and timebound). The ultimate measure of the effectiveness of the communications is whether it drives sales in the marketplace via the achievement of the communication behavior objective. We need to identify what we expect so we can measure (i.e., inspect) for it. It also serves to make clear the task of the communications.
- Something may be written in the section of the creative brief entitled "customer insights," but these cannot be called insightful. It is amazing what passes for customer insights. They are neither legitimate (i.e., a real or perceived weakness of the competition, an attitudinal barrier that needs to be overcome, or an untapped, compelling belief) nor productive (as in the brand's ability to exploit it). They tend to be rationalizations contributing to the illusion that the creative brief and the key thought are meaningful.
- The key thought is not relevant to the target customer or meaningfully differentiated from the competition. There is no point-of-difference that represents a point-of-preference versus the competition. They promise generic or category benefits.
- There are too many benefits in the key thought. This litany of benefits would include generic benefits, handling of objections, etc., which obfuscate any meaningful differentiation. Additionally, this serves as a barrier to developing a campaign idea and to cutting through to connect with the target customer.
- The key thought contains features instead of benefits. Remember, people don't buy a 1/8-inch drill bit. Instead, they buy a 1/8-inch hole or better yet a bookshelf hanging in the family room.
- The key thought is a meaningless emotional benefit. A client for a toilet paper brand stated its key thought as "get your life back." Amazing! Where were their target customers' lives? In the toilet? (By the way, where did all of our lives go that we need to get them back?)
- The creative brief is not single-minded. The strategic triangle of target customer needs, customer insight, and key thought are not cohesive. Each points in a different direction with no clear focus for communication development or assessment. So, instead of having a

dialogue around the creative work, there is endless discussion about the strategy.

- Reason-to-believe support is not factual. Or, it is not compelling. Or, it is generic. Or, it is a benefit and not a reason-to-believe. Take your pick.
- The reason-to-believe may not link to or pay off the benefit to make the key thought believable and more persuasive.
- The brand character, or personality of the brand, is about the target as opposed to a badge or relationship of the brand bundle to the target customer.
- The brand character is articulated using the same collection of adjectives that everyone uses, such as "leader, modern, caring, trustworthy, authority" (sound familiar?) or their synonyms.
- It contains creativity-sapping, idea-undermining, dogma-perpetuating, executional mandates. Has anyone held these up to thoughtful analysis? Also, with all the mandates, why would marketers need creative resources? They have a recipe to develop executions on their own. Executional mandates do not leverage creative talent. They undermine it.
- It is not prepared in collaboration with those tasked with developing the creative to execute the strategy (whether that be the agency team, sales personnel, or internal creative resources). Instead, one side develops and shares it with the other, and it gets slapped around like a ping-pong ball at a tournament. There is little meaningful strategic dialogue or understanding.
- The marketers preparing it have little experience with developing or managing marketing communications. So, they lack technical or strategic thinking skills or both.
- Their senior managers do not provide the mature, experienced supervision needed to reflect proven principles and best practices to improve the productivity of the work. Adult supervision is absent.
- There is no real appreciation for the importance of the creative brief. It is merely a process starter. So, not much thought (but an inordinate amount of time) goes into it before the agency is given the green light to proceed with creative development. When creative development begins, the meter starts running. It eats up funding and morale.

It stacks up significant opportunity losses that are real, which few marketers, or their organizations, are measuring or acknowledging.

- Those senior client managers responsible for approving the communications, and those creative team managers responsible for delivering it, do not acknowledge their agreement to the creative brief with their signature. Their acknowledgment is essential to gaining commitment to execute against the creative brief.

- The agency does not push back against what they feel is not appropriate (e.g., too many benefits in the key thought). They (meekly?) accept the client's lack of direction. They talk about the client's failings in their own offices but do little to address them directly with the client for fear of putting the relationship in jeopardy.

- The agency or creative resource personnel do not treat the client brief seriously. Instead of engaging in a meaningful strategic dialogue, they accept the client brief and rely on creating their own internal agency creative brief. Now there are two (or dueling) briefs. Therefore, there are two sets of direction: yours (the client's) and theirs (the agency's), instead of one (ours).

- There is no standard for assessing the creative brief. It's all about opinion as opposed to objectifying subjective judgment based upon sound principles and best practices.

What can go wrong will go wrong if we do not apply all our knowledge and skill to managing the development of the creative brief. It's no wonder our communications suck. Our creative briefs suck, big time.

RX FOR DEVELOPING SMART CREATIVE BRIEFS: THE ESSENTIAL CREATIVE BRIEF

Obviously, we do not want our communications to suck. Who goes to work saying, "I want to do suck work today?" No one I know and probably no one you know either. We want our work to shine. However, there are a host of factors that get in the way of being able to do our best work; instead, these factors contribute to doing work that sucks.

We can't pass the blame. We can't make excuses. That will not produce excellence. Instead, we have to take responsibility for our actions and strive to do the right things in the right way. Here are some directions for you to consider adopting so you may produce creative briefs that will contribute to the development of high-impact marketing communications:

1. ***Start at the beginning.*** I've identified some 25 factors that undermine our ability to create excellence and to contribute to the development of a creative brief that sucks. Start by reviewing this listing with an eye towards which of these are sabotaging your ability to develop a productive creative brief. Better yet, share these with your team (creative resource team included!) to pinpoint those you need to remedy, but don't try to do it all in one go.

   Perhaps, you might want to start by working collaboratively with your creative resource team. Get on the same page regarding how communications work. Then, identify what elements to include in "our" essential creative brief, and what items to omit because they are not critical to developing high-impact brand communications. Proceed to address those factors that you believe will have the most significant impact on improving the productivity of your creative brief.

2. ***Consider the BDNI Essential Creative Brief.*** This consists of the following elements:
   - Brand Idea: I covered this in chapter 3. It is the "why" or purpose of your brand.
   - Assignment: This gets at what you are asking your agency or creative resource team to do. Is it to create a social media campaign, advertising campaign, what?
   - Target Customer Profile (as identified in chapter 6): This could be either a direct lift from your brand positioning strategy or a subset of it.
   - Communication Behavior Objective: What behavior do you want to trigger? You will use this to assess and measure the effectiveness of your brand communications (see chapter 7).

- Customer-Insight (see chapter 8): This will lead you to the key thought. It must be both legitimate and productive.
- Key Thought: This is what you must get into the minds of your target customer, your POD (or better yet, your POP) benefit or sales proposition, to get them to achieve your desired behavior objective.
- Reasons-to-Believe: This is the support for the key thought. Its purpose is to aid credibility.
- Brand Character: This is the personality of your brand. It should be lifted directly from your brand positioning strategy statement.
- Legal and Regulatory Mandates (only!): We want to comply with legal and regulatory dictums. We don't want to handcuff our creative team and lose the opportunity for the development of a big idea with "executional mandates."
- Signature of approval from the client responsible for approving the brand communications and the agency manager responsible for delivering it.

That's it! You need nothing more.

THE CAMPAIGN IDEA

I've learned that people will forget what you said, people will forget what you did, but people will never forget how you made them feel.
Maya Angelou

The campaign idea is the single most important element in engaging the customer. It *dramatizes* the key thought *in compelling customer language*. The key thought is the belief or benefit that the marketing team has determined is needed to influence the target customers' attitudes in such a way that it triggers achievement of the communication behavior objective. The key thought is strategy talk. The campaign idea is customer talk.

The campaign idea consists of three parts that work together to deliver the strategy in a single-minded communication. It serves to bring the strategic promise to life for the target customer in such a way that she feels compelled to act in a predetermined manner of your choosing (e.g., switch, adopt, etc.) to achieve the brand's business objectives (of sales, market share, and profit). The three parts are the following:

- *The Naked Idea:* This is the creative concept that informs each execution.
- *Key Copy Words:* These are a translation of the key thought into customer language.
- *Core Dramatization:* This is the visual or audial component that leads the target customer to realize the key thought.

All three parts work together to create synergy in delivering the key thought in a single-minded communication.

The MasterCard "Priceless" campaign, which ran from 1997 to 2015, is an excellent example of a successful campaign idea. It fueled exceptional growth for more than 15 years. This campaign idea has been executed in more than 100 countries, through thousands of executions, in a wide variety of media.

- *The Naked Idea:* Juxtaposition of all the things you can purchase with MasterCard linked with the one priceless moment that money can't buy.
- *Key Copy Words:* Original: "Some things in life are priceless; for everything else, there's MasterCard." Current: "That's MasterCard. That's Priceless."
- *Core Dramatization:* The priceless moment that is made possible from what was purchased using MasterCard.

The campaign idea is the "center of the plate" for all your marketing communications. It is what provides your customers with the nourishment and satisfaction they need to choose your offering. It gets target customers to *feel* your key thought, and thereby, realize your promise. The purpose of all other elements in the execution of the message is merely to serve-up the campaign idea in a way that showcases it. The campaign idea is also the backbone of not one execution, or one medium, but an entire campaign that can serve to drive brand growth for many years through a host of media vehicles.

Development of the campaign idea is the responsibility of your creative resource partners (typically your agency). It is not the responsibility of the marketer to develop the campaign idea. Instead, marketers need to be able to see, appreciate, and champion the adoption of the campaign idea.

WHY YOUR COMMUNICATIONS SUCK: CAMPAIGN IDEA

It is essential to appreciate the value of the campaign idea, and how failing to have one, or an appropriate one, or a compelling one, can undermine successful target customer engagement in, and impact of, your message. Communications suck for any (one or more) of the following when dealing with the campaign idea:

- The communications don't deliver the key thought. In simple language, it is not on strategy.
- It's the same pedestrian, expected delivery (like an overused life situation, or featuring a beauty shot of the product, or a smiling face, etc.) that is no different from your competition.
- Even if it is different from the competition, it is merely telling, as opposed to dramatizing.
- It does not contain a campaign idea.
- If it does contain a campaign idea, and it is on strategy, it lacks one of the three essential parts.
- Your communications don't contain key copy words.
- Your communications use a tagline as opposed to key copy words. A tagline is a kiss-off. Key copy words drive marketing communications. The entire execution revolves around, and can be summed up by, the key copy words.
- The key copy words are strategy, not customer-talk.

- The key copy words are ambiguous. The target customer does not understand them. They don't deliver the strategic key thought.
- The key copy words are missing the brand name. Therefore, they don't link the benefit found in the key thought to the brand.
- The key copy words lack drama.
- The key copy words appear as though the client wrote them.
- The client wrote the key copy words.
- There is no naked idea (i.e., creative concept).
- The naked idea is for an ad (i.e., a one-off), not a campaign. (A campaign is more than one in a row.)
- It is tactical - used for one medium, for one execution, for one year.
- It doesn't surprise, engage or motivate the target customer.
- Again, what dramatization? (In other words, it is predictable or bland.)
- Its life is choked-out by executional mandates (dictated in the creative brief).
- It is burdened by the weight of additional objectives or messages foisted upon the agency by the client during the creative review.
- It does not connect with the target customer on an emotional level. (The only emotional connection is the clients' self-satisfaction that they got what they wanted, and the agency's sense of relief that they are finally done working with the client!
- All three parts do not work together, to create synergy, in delivering a single-minded message.
- The key copy words deliver one benefit, while the visualization delivers the second benefit. (Both must provide both.)

If your communications don't contain a campaign idea, it is unlikely that the communications will be successful, no less produce high-impact communications. On the other hand, if you do have a campaign idea, it will enhance the likelihood that you will have effective communications. However, it is no guarantee. It will depend upon the quality of the idea in delivering the key thought in an emotive way to motivate behavior.

RX FOR SMART CAMPAIGN IDEAS

Okay, what can we do so we don't put out communications that suck? Let's make sure our marketing communications contain a provocative, compelling campaign idea.

1. ***Learn to identify the campaign idea.*** If the agency doesn't articulate it when they share their creative work, we need to be able to see it. Learn how to identify it and get practice. Start with successful campaigns - those credited with building the business, have thrived over time, and have been executed in a variety of mediums, since these are likely to contain a campaign idea. Analyze each to identify and articulate the three parts of the campaign idea. You can use the MasterCard example as your model. Some campaigns you might also consider are Allstate "Mayhem," the personification of Mac versus PC, and Cialis. Check them out on YouTube and discuss your analysis with someone else on the brand marketing team or your agency counterparts to get their reading on the creative product.

2. ***Make it clear to your agency that you need campaign ideas (if you are working on a campaign, as opposed to pooling-out one that is already working for the brand).*** Gift this book to your agency partner. If you are a member of the agency team, gift this book to your client. If you want to delve deeper, get a copy of *CREATING BRAND LOYALTY: The Management of Power Positioning and Really Great Advertising*, which my business partner Mike Maloney and I co-authored. Get on the same page regarding the campaign idea, its components, its value, and your objective to develop a winning campaign idea that will lead to the development of high-impact communications.

3. ***Don't settle.*** Demand brand communications that contain a campaign idea. If your marketing communications don't have a campaign idea, DO NOT go forward with it. Demand the best from your agency and creative resource team. But then, we are unlikely to get their best if we

are not giving our best. Go back and ensure that you are committed to executing against a strategically sound and single-minded essential creative brief, and that you can recognize a campaign idea.

4. *Use your imagination.* Marketers are not accustomed to employing campaign ideas. (If they were, then fewer communications would suck, and more would be in the elite class of high-impact communications.) We cannot expect to see all the reasons-to-believe, features and copy, frame-by-frame, the entire website, the social media play, etc. Instead, we have to appreciate where the genes of the idea could take us. (Good genes typically translate to good health; in this case, I'm referring to brand health.) That takes imagination on our part. If the prospects appear promising, then yes, we can go the next step to get a better feel for how the campaign idea might be executed.

Make sure your communications contain a campaign idea. If it does, then it is less likely that your marketing communications will suck. In fact, it is more likely that they will be successful, high-impact communications.

EXECUTION

Strategy is war games. Execution is war itself.
Leo Kiely, former President, Coors Brewing Company

You may ask, "What's there to cover in execution? Didn't we address it with the campaign idea?" Most certainly, the campaign idea is the "center of the plate" of the execution of your marketing communications. It is what provides your customers with the nourishment and satisfaction they need to choose your offering. The purpose of all other elements in the execution of the message is merely to serve up the campaign idea in a way that showcases and ensures that the target customer absorbs and realizes it.

The role of the execution is to:

- Arrest the target customer
- Engage the target to stay with the message
- Share the campaign idea most favorably
- Create strong brand linkage such that the target customer remembers the brand and its strategic message

Execution plays a supporting role in presenting the campaign idea.

ARREST THE TARGET CUSTOMER

We're bombarded with more than 2500 commercial messages per day. However, few get through to us, and fewer stimulate us to act on behalf of the messenger. Lack of a relevant, meaningfully differentiated strategic message, and the absence of a campaign idea, leads to executions that are similar. They're like wallpaper. They are out there, but we don't notice them. Beauty care communications carry the requisite models airbrushed to perfection. Pharmaceutical communications feature couples walking hand-in-hand on the beach, with their faithful Golden Retriever racing ahead or romping through fields, tail wagging, beside them. Medical device and diagnostic communications gratuitously feature a photo of the surgeon or the product itself.

Oh sure, there are some variations on these themes, but in the end, one execution is indistinguishable from another. Advertisers employ the same executional look and feel as their competitors. How can one possibly hope to break through the clutter and gain the attention of the target customer this way? The answer is, YOU CAN'T! The first task of the execution is to arrest the target customer. Stop them from going to the bathroom during the commercial break, or turning the page of that journal ad, or tuning-out the messenger on a face-to-face sales call, or not clicking to learn more about an advertised product or to place an order. So, your opening scene, line or headline has to be a grabber. It has to stand out.

ENGAGE THE TARGET CUSTOMER

Let's imagine we have arrested the target customer. Our communication has caused them to stop. Next, engagement comes in and takes over. Engagement is about getting the target customer to stick with you after you have captured her attention. The practice of turning up the audio so that it is louder than the programming is not engaging (nor is it arresting). It's **SHOUTING!** As such, it's likely to drive target customers to run for cover (to the bathroom, kitchen, or another room). At the very least, if your target customer is alive, she will turn down the volume or mute it and probably mutter some negative comment directed at your communication, and product.

No one likes to be shouted at. The communication needs to connect and involve the target customer. Connecting is about establishing a link with the target customer that ties to your offering and to what you are promising. Involving your target customer is about getting her to participate in your message. Scott Adams, the creator of the Dilbert comic strip, believes it's important to get the audience to connect the dots. In other words, let them get involved in absorbing and discovering your messaging. He feels that the smarter the audience, the more you can trust them to connect the dots. It helps them make the messaging their own and internalize it.

Many marketers confuse "entertaining" with "engaging." Entertainment is only one way to engage. Nor is humor a sure-fire way to engage. These are merely alternate ways to engaging the target customer. Don't go into the communication development process with preconceived notions as to what execution approach you need, and don't let tonality define your execution. The approach you take to execution needs to flow from the campaign idea (and reflect your brand positioning strategy).

EXECUTIONAL FORMAT

The execution needs to showcase the campaign idea. When you go into a steak restaurant and order their New York Ribeye steak (my favorite), it's your center-of-the-plate. It's your campaign idea. The jumbo baked potato with sour cream, and the accompanying sautéed broccolini serve to complement the steak. That's the role of the executional format: to complement, dress up, and make the center-of-the-plate even more attractive and fulfilling.

Many global brands will choose announcer voiceover because they believe it is more efficient. They shoot the commercial and then change the voiceover based upon the language spoken in a given country where it is aired.

The efficiency of this is merely an illusion; in reality, this announcer voice-over format rarely supports an idea. Moreover, indirect communication is less arresting, engaging and less memorable because there is no drama.

Direct voice, as in the "presenter" format, is typically more effective. Of course, it depends upon the appropriateness and charisma of the presenter. By the way, my intention is not to tell you what format to use, but to awaken you to the role of the execution in showcasing the campaign idea, which carries your strategic communication in a way that connects with your target customer, helping them realize and appreciate your message.

There are other proven principles in communicating with video, such as audio-visual synch. This is about the words and pictures going together.

When it comes to text (e.g., magazine, journal ads, advertorials, viz-aids, etc.), the headline, sub-head, visual and body copy comprise the execution. Even the font contributes to the execution. A common error is to focus on brand identification (i.e., the logo and/or packaging) above and beyond the messaging. Another is to take a frame out of the video communication to use in a text format (such as a print ad). Yet another is to use reverse-out print (white fonts scratching through a swath of color), which often makes it very difficult to read.

Another error is to make the reader work to get through the communication by too-cute placement of the elements mentioned above. Target customers will allow themselves to be engaged, but they will refuse to let you make them work. They just won't do it. Additionally, so much of what passes for text communications is pedestrian and predictable.

One practice that enhances the effectiveness of print is to include a "creative twist." A creative twist is a provocative element designed to engage the target customer relevantly in presenting the campaign idea. The title of this chapter, "Brand Communications That Suck," is intended to be provocative. At least one part of your print needs to be twisted; otherwise, the communication will bore your target customer. If more than one element is twisted, then the communication will very likely confuse the target customer. What you twist depends upon whether the communication is lengthy (such as a chapter) or short (such as a postcard). In the instance of this chapter, which captures many facets of communication, the only part to twist is the title!

Don't get locked into a specific medium, or execution format for that medium. Think of your communication as advancing the campaign idea. Follow proven principles and best practices to connect with the intended target customer.

BRAND LINKAGE

It's critical that the communications link to the brand and its message, if the marketer intends to drive sales to her brand versus the competition. When communications for products in a category lack a campaign idea, tell a similar story, and use identical executional formats, the target customer will typically associate it with their most often used brand (usually the category leader). If you think about it, your communications may be reinforcing sales of your leading competitor. That really sucks!

Once again, there are some proven principles and best practices that we need to adopt if we are to create strong brand linkage. Among the most important are to do the following:

- Make your brand integral to the story you tell
- Make the brand, not the advertising, the hero
- Link the brand with the key thought
- Tell a story in a way that only your brand could tell it

It's also essential to stay single-minded in your communication. Resist the urge, and pressure from others, to add more to your messaging. Less is more. More merely serves to obfuscate the message, burden the communication, and undermine brand linkage. Oh, they may remember the brand, but they're not likely to remember your message. And, if they do remember your message, it's unlikely they will feel compelled to act on it.

RX FOR SMART EXECUTION

Execution is another area where our communications can fail our brand. However, it doesn't have to be that way. We can make execution productive in arresting and engaging our target customer, showcasing the campaign idea and establishing strong brand linkage. Here are some actions for your consideration:

1. ***Start with a campaign idea.*** Okay, we're taking a step back to the previous section of this chapter. But this is critical to successful communications. Remember, the campaign idea is the center-of-the-plate of the execution. Don't just start with a campaign idea; make it a BIG, juicy idea.

2. ***Showcase the campaign idea.*** This is one of the key roles of the execution. Therefore, wrap the campaign idea in the story. People love good stories. They spark our interest and engage us. However, make the story integral to the brand and its idea.

3. ***Make it your brand's story.*** Strive to make it a story that only your brand can tell, and tell it in a way that only your brand can tell it. Tell it in such a way that if another brand tried to tell the same story, or tell it in the same way, it would ring false. This will serve to establish linkage to your brand.

4. ***Don't be predictable.*** This is a build on the previous point. I prefer to encourage you to be *unique.* Something that is unique stands-out, but many marketers, and their risk-averse organizations, are fearful of standing out. So, instead of suggesting something you are not likely to do, I'm suggesting that you refrain from doing what your competitors are doing. (That's not so difficult, is it?) If they are using a "presenter" executional format, find another way to tell your story. If they are picturing smiling consumers or patients, or their product, find another way! Otherwise, you are contributing to hanging wallpaper. We do not want our communications to be wallpaper, because it will not get noticed and if it's not noticed, target customers cannot act on it.

5. ***Get "twisted."*** Breaking out of the pack is not enough. It's important to stop and engage the target customer. Seek communications with a creative twist to help it emerge from the clutter, engage the target customer, and incite them to act in selecting your brand.

6. ***Learn, and develop yourself, so you may be better equipped to create leadership communications.*** To paraphrase the legendary adman, Bill Bernbach, your communications are not effective unless they sell. (He said, "It's not creative unless it sells.") High-impact communications do more than sell. They sell big time. High-impact communications stimulate the achievement of *stretch business objectives* by changing target customer attitudes in a way that incites the achievement of strategic behaviors. If you are genuinely interested in developing high-impact communications, reading this book, along with *CREATING BRAND LOYALTY* and *COMPETITIVE POSITIONING* by yours truly and Mike Maloney, is a good start to learning more. But you have to put into practice what you've learned.

PROCESS

Process is a well-thought-out sequence of carefully designed actions intended to enhance the likelihood of producing a predictable outcome.

The final piece deals with process, a frequently over-looked element of managing the development of communications. Process is a well-thought-out sequence of carefully designed actions intended to enhance the likelihood of producing a predictable outcome. However, the standard operating process for the development of communications is mindless. Little, if any, thought is given to it. The standard operating process consists of doing the same things and in the same way that they have always been done. But doing the same things in the same way seems to be producing the same undesirable outcome: communications that suck! Instead of recognizing the role that process plays in influencing the poor quality of their outcomes and, in turn, fixing it, clients blame their agencies for poor performance. Agencies blame their clients for being blind to recognizing and appreciating their creative genius.

Here are process errors marketers and their agencies need to avoid:

- *Not mapping out, or keeping to, an appropriate timeline.* It takes time to develop high-impact brand communications. Your communication professionals know best about this subject. There's a timeframe for strategy development, research, creative development, assessment and direction, more research, production, market performance analysis, etc. We need to avoid late starts to the timeline, overrunning the time designated for any of the action steps, NOT providing the creative resource team with ample time for development, and NOT providing sufficient time to determine if the communications work to achieve the communication behavior objective with the target customer.

- *Dueling creative briefs.* This is when there are two briefs, not one, but two directing the work: the client's creative brief and the agency's brief. If there are two briefs, then there are two sets of directions and very rarely (to the point of being non-existent) are they in agreement. Without single-minded direction, it is virtually impossible to produce communications that will serve the expectations of both client and agency.

- *The absence of a firm commitment to the creative brief.* The CB (creative brief) does not contain signatures from the senior client manager responsible for approving the creative product and the senior agency manager responsible for delivering it. They need to acknowledge their commitment to the direction in the CB by signing it. The lack of commitment, evidenced by the absence of their signatures, will likely lead to false starts and the need to work out the strategy while undertaking creative development, as opposed to focusing on delivering big ideas against it.

- ***The absence of validation.*** "Garbage in, garbage out." Opinions are often accepted as facts. What we think is the customer insight is not a legitimate and productive insight. What we believe is a relevant and meaningfully differentiated point-of-difference benefit (leading to point-of-preference) is neither. The creative brief is a piece of fiction that reflects the conventional wisdom as opposed to facts.

  We need to validate through some form of marketing research. This is not to suggest that marketing research has the answer or that we should not use judgment based upon our knowledge and experience. Instead, this is about ensuring that we gain valuable input from customers to inform our judgment and help us iterate our way to success.

- ***Execution precedes idea generation.*** Once we turn the agency loose to begin creative development, they undertake development of executions (i.e., print or digital comps, storyboards, whatever the assignment calls for). However, before we entertain "execution," we need to focus on and address ideas. More specifically, the campaign idea is the thing that should precede the development of execution materials, which are costly, time-consuming, premature, and undermine the opportunity for collaboration.

- ***The absence of clear standards for each step in the process.*** Not only do we need a time standard, but we also need to have performance standards that represent "go" or "no go" points along the way. In other words, if we don't have a firm commitment to achieve the key thought and all that is identified in the essential creative brief, then we don't begin creative development. If we don't have campaign ideas, then we don't commence with execution development.

- ***Inexperienced marketers managing the process.*** It takes a skillful marketing manager to successfully direct and manage the development of high-impact communications. Marketers driving the process and approving the work (which includes senior managers) should know how to properly assess creative work and provide appropriate direction. They need to be good coaches. If we aren't skilled in assessing and coaching, then we cannot expect to consistently produce favorable outcomes. Unfortunately, many managers participating in the process believe they have the skills when, in reality, they apparently do not. After all, as the saying goes, "the proof is in the pudding."

- *Allowing people who can't say yes to the creative product to say no.* Creative resource teams are often subjected to presenting creative product to junior level marketers who do not have the authority to say "yes" to it, but they can say "no," miring the agency in endless revisions that bog down the development process and undermine idea development.

- *Too many layers of approval.* Agencies typically are forced to run the gauntlet of sharing their work with numerous levels of management. This adds considerable time, often without adding value. In practice, each layer, and the resultant revisions, reduce the effectiveness of the creative work. One way of dealing with this is to drop the levels that can't say yes, or cannot influence approval of the creative work.

- *Not seeking options.* Options are a very good thing to have. Options ensure that we are considering alternate ways to connect with our target customer. Options provide us with a basis for gaining a deeper understanding and appreciation for what will, and will not, work to stimulate target customer behavior. Options provide us with more opportunities to win.

- *The absence of validation.* I'm repeating myself here, purposefully so! Validation needs to take the form of creating a dialogue with target customers and adapting the creative work as appropriate. The exchange with target customers paves the road for iterating our way to success.

- *Selling versus involving senior management.* Senior managers do not want to be sold. Instead, senior managers want to share their experiences and insights and see them reflected in the work. Therefore, we need to involve senior managers from the start and keep them engaged throughout the process. If we don't allow senior managers to collaborate with us, we will be forced to undertake more revisions, extending development time and making it more arduous physically and emotionally. Besides, those senior managers (who are skillful in managing communications) can add value to the work that we would not want to miss.

- *Client and agency work independent of each other.* We are a team. Both the client and agency can add substantial value, leading to the development of highly effective communications. However, we are more likely to be successful if we collaborate. This means that we develop the creative brief together. It also means that we get involved in the idea phase, not developing ideas but assessing them early in the process, as opposed to coming in to evaluate (thumbs-up or thumbs-down) execution.

- *The absence of marketplace validation.* Here, we appear at a different point in the process. Are the communications working in the marketplace to achieve the communication behavior objective? We won't know unless we analyze and measure results against our expectations where it counts: in the marketplace.

- *Changing campaigns too soon.* We get tired of our work long before our target customer does. Alternatively, we may succumb to pressure from the sales force, particularly if there is a new competitive entry in the marketplace or if they are having difficulty in achieving their quota. If we don't validate, we won't know if we should or should not change our brand communication campaign and begin the process anew.

RX FOR A SMART COMMUNICATIONS DEVELOPMENT PROCESS

We need a *quality process* for managing the development of a *quality outcome*. The quality outcome we seek is not just to avoid developing marketing communications that suck, but instead, to develop communications that will achieve our communication behavior objective to drive incremental line-of-sight sales growth. We need to fix a broken process to improve our likelihood of developing high-impact communications. Here are some suggestions for your consideration:

1. *Review the communication development process with your communication (internal and/or external agency resource) teams.* Make sure that you have a process, that it is a quality process, and that everyone understands who will participate, along with their roles and responsibilities. Your development process should provide appropriate (as determined by the agency) steps for creating impactful campaign ideas and include milestones with clear performance criteria for proceeding to the next activity.

2. *Include a "tissue meeting" step in the process.* A tissue meeting is where the agency shares campaign ideas, not executions, with the client in a very rough form. Remember, the campaign idea is the most critical element of the execution. It is a key ingredient in high-impact communications. The tissue meeting is an extra step in the process, but it is a step that will save time and help you achieve better ideas. Agencies share tissues internally. We need to get them to share these tissues with us so we may collaborate in selecting ideas and providing direction that will lead to more compelling messaging.

3. *Collaborate.* How we work or don't work together impacts the outcome. We need to change the old way of managing the communication development process to get away from evaluating the agency's work (which tends to promote criticism and contributes to the development

of an adversarial relationship) to collaborating in the development of the creative work. We not only need to collaborate with the agency but also with our senior management.

4. ***Stick to the process.*** Nothing works if you are not working at it! Adhere to the process steps, timing and criteria for each step. Make sticking with the process a priority. This means stay involved and engaged physically and mentally.

Let's not merely avoid communications that suck, which in itself is a big deal, but let's create high-impact communications that will achieve stretch business objectives, driving brand sales growth beyond our wildest expectations.

CHAPTER 10

OVERSTATING YOUR CAPABILITIES AND UNDERESTIMATING THE COMPETITION

Plan for success but anticipate and prepare for failure.

These two critical errors go hand-in-hand: overstating your brand and organization's capabilities and underestimating the competition. One might merely chalk-up these overlapping errors to corporate hubris, particularly in large, established companies. This may be true to a point. However, I firmly believe it's mostly a function of ignorance, lack of foresight and sound planning, and intelligent, coordinated execution. Whew, that's an eyeful!

UNDERESTIMATING THE COMPETITION

Let's take SWOTs, which virtually every marketing organization uses. SWOT is an acronym for Strengths, Weaknesses, Opportunities, and Threats. You'll find the SWOT in virtually every marketing plan. However, SWOTS tend to be a work of fiction. Few marketers know how to do them well, as attested by my experience working with clients and examining their SWOTs. There's a host of things that are incorrect, which reflect underestimating the competition and overstating the brand's and organization's capabilities. These include:

- **Mis-categorization:** Namely, strengths and weaknesses relate to the specific brand and company whereas opportunities and threats refer to competitive issues and other external factors that impact the market. It's important to categorize these correctly to promote clear, analytical thinking and provide a sound basis for decision making.

- **Fiction versus Facts:** They are rarely "fact-based." Instead, SWOT lists biased fiction that overwhelmingly favors the home team.

- **Contradictory:** A strength may also be identified as a weakness! So, what is it?

- **Competitive hearsay:** This factor traces not only to the lack of facts but also alleged competitive actions, typically garnered from sales force reporting. A common refrain, mainly when a brand is failing to meet sales goals and losing market share, is that competitors are engaging in "unfair practices." However, these are rarely borne out by facts. And, if they are, the marketer needs to decide what she is going to do about them.

- **Non-discriminating:** They are infrequently prioritized by importance, as per potential impact, and virtually never weighted for likelihood. However, the conclusion is nearly always the same, competition is inferior, and everything points to a rosy future for the marketer's "superior" product. If there is anything else that can be universally agreed, it is that competition is playing unfairly and capitalizing on their cheaper pricing.

This listing of common SWOT errors doesn't even take into consideration that there is no translation into meaningful critical success factors! Instead, the development of the SWOT is, more often than not, merely a chest-beating exercise in extolling how great we are with a concurrent understated, speculative watch-out for competitors taking liberties in the market with un-savory practices and deep discounting. The "watch out" is a CYA (cover your a!*) action in the event the brand does not reach its sales goals.

Then there's *benchmarking*. Few marketers engage in this practice and when they do it is limited to the physical versus "whole product." Guess who wins on this one? Once again, competitors lose according to the initiator of the benchmarking exercise, and everyone in the organization involved with the brand drinks this up. There is no factoring based upon customer input, other than anecdotal from the sales force about their customers. Intangibles, such as terms, support programs, etc., are rarely compared and when they are, they usually show-up as about equal. In other words, no advantage. Yet somehow, the evaluator's brand beats the competition.

Benchmarking needs to even go beyond a whole-product investigation. It should also include an *audit* of marketing factors, marketing mix elements and organizational capabilities such as distribution or access, share of voice as measured by "feet on the street," GRPs (gross rating points for measured media), the impact of messaging (as revealed by market research testing), clinical studies underway, etc. We know that the best whole product may not win if not adequately supported in the right way (e.g., with appropriate positioning strategy, messaging, clinical studies and so forth). So, these additional factors need to be included and examined in an audit.

Despite having these tools, SWOT, benchmarking and the marketing audit, to get a fix on how our brand offering stacks-up versus competition in the present and short-term future, marketers tend to overlook or misuse them. In so many cases, marketers will pervert their use by pushing their biases and treating them as facts.

Additionally, marketers tend to discount competitive actions, even when they appear to be working. If competitors launch a new or improved product or release findings from a new clinical study, marketers will rationalize them away (with the help of members from other disciplines that make-up the brand team). They will even go so far as to declare that competitors cannot sustain their current marketing efforts, or that they cannot fool target customers with their inferior quality products or outrageous claims.

OVERSTATING THE BRAND'S AND ORGANIZATION'S CAPABILITIES

One would think that overestimating the brand's and organization's capabilities and underestimating the competition are solely the product of misusing the SWOT and benchmarking exercises. (Audits are rarely conducted. It's as if the marketer's brand is the only one in the marketplace.) As Ron Popeil, the legendary pitchman would say, "But wait there's more!"

It seems that the majority of *financial forecasts are grossly optimistic,* particularly regarding top-line revenues. While all research points to a promising market for the new product, the finance team establishes the financial forecast based upon what's needed to satisfy stock analysts and stockholders. In other words, they tend to distort reality overstating the organization's capabilities to deliver on the forecast. There's little checking with what competitive products, with similar innovation, have been able to achieve. Nor is there a historical review of what the company's product launches, again with similar levels of innovation, have realized. Also, if these investigations suggest a lower financial forecast, then they too are rationalized away. It's the same old story that "we are better than that!" Really?

We've witnessed time and again *the organization failing to coordinate the execution* of an overarching marketing plan, particularly when it comes to commercializing a new product. While all the disciplines (functional areas such as payor access, sales force, retail, manufacturing, promotion, advertising, etc.) are aware of the marketing plan and are expected to execute in concert with it, there is an absence of planning by these disciplines to achieve the objectives established for them that are needed to realize the overall brand marketing plan. It's like all the sections in an orchestra playing without the score and not looking up to follow the direction of the conductor.

This failure to coordinate execution is compounded by the *absence of milestones* for critical success factors, such as the level of access, awareness among target customers, intent to prescribe-purchase-use, etc. These are lead-indicators that contribute to and explain sales performance. Moreover, where these are present, they *may not be measured and captured in a "dashboard"* to display progress on a just-in-time basis to allow for timely, previously identified and proven remedial actions.

Without measuring, that is *inspecting what you expect,* the organization has no way of getting to the heart of brand performance in the marketplace and avoid making the same mistakes in the future.

SUMMARY OF CONTRIBUTING FACTORS

There are many reasons contributing to overstating the brand's and organization's capabilities and underestimating the competition. Many of these apply to both mistakes as they overlap. These appear in the following table:

Underestimating Competition	Overstating Brand/Organization
• Poorly developed and misleading SWOT • No, or inaccurate, benchmarking • No, or skimpy, audit of comparative marketing mix elements • Biases substituted for facts • Hearsay elevated to facts without corroborating market evidence • Lack of objectivity leading to discounting the impact or promise inherent in competitive actions • Superior powers of rationalizing competitors away • Pressure to conform to groupthink	• Grossly optimistic financial forecast based upon the need to please financial analysts and stockholders, and support investment in the asset • The absence of planning by contributing disciplines/functional areas that align with the brand marketing plan • Lack of coordinated execution consistent with plans • An absence of concrete milestones for each contributing factor (with an emphasis on lead indicators) to the forecast • Limited analysis of historical performance for both the organization and its competitors • The absence of measurement of lead indicators and use of a dashboard to report and take remedial action • Biases, biases, biases

Oh yes, let's not forget *corporate hubris.*

So, what's a marketer to do to avoid these critical marketing errors beyond...

- Fixing SWOTs
- Conducting objective benchmarking
- Undertaking a comparative audit of marketing mix elements
- Validating forecasts
- Commencing planning with each of the contributing functional areas
- Establishing milestones with lead indicators, and
- Incorporating a dashboard to monitor progress?

RX FOR OVERSTATING YOUR CAPABILITIES AND UNDERESTIMATING COMPETITION

PREPARE FOR FAILURE

Back in my military aviation days, close to 50 years ago, I was taught to "plan for success but anticipate and prepare for failure." This maxim is based on Murphy's Law: "Anything that can go wrong will go wrong." So, I was trained and stayed alert for things to go wrong such as engine failure on take-off and landing—two highly critical events as they are difficult to recover from if not caught early. Moreover, if not caught early and handled immediately, it could lead to the aircraft crashing and exploding into a ball of fire (with the pilot and crew in the plane). Spiraling into the ground (or in aviation parlance "to auger in") can ruin your entire day, and life.

Marketers, particularly in preparation for launching new products, do not consider Murphy's Law. They blithely ignore or are unwilling to admit the many things that might go wrong. Predictably, they are surprised when things do go wrong. In practice they actually miss what is going wrong when it goes wrong until it is too late, or not at all, only to be impacted by the crash. They fail to achieve their revenue and market share targets due to factors that might have been foreseen and avoided.

Anticipating and planning for failure is essential if it is to be avoided, and it must be quickly remedied before it spins out of control.

THE PREMORTEM

The way to prepare for failure is to identify those places where the brand is likely to fail and where the impact is meaningful. I like to use and recommend the *premortem* in our consulting practice. We're all familiar with the postmortem. It occurs following death to ascertain the causes. In the premortem, the marketing team identifies where failure may occur before it strikes and damages, or destroys, the brand. On take-off, it could be engine failure, fire or a bird strike that cripples one or more engines.

Consider Chesley "Sully" Sullenberger's successful landing of US Airways Flight 1549 in the Hudson River following the loss of both engines due to a bird strike. Thanks to his and his crews' actions, all 155 souls on board were saved. For the marketer, it could be failure to gain a specified level of access, sufficient manufacturing supply, quality issues, competitive oppositioning, etc.

- *Start the premortem by identifying all the things that might go wrong.* With your team, visualize everything from pre-launch through year-one, or from last quarter of the current year and into the next planned year, that could go wrong. It is also wise to study past launches to identify what, if anything, went wrong with them. These are typically not rare occurrences but will more than likely point out weaknesses within the organization that need to be addressed if we are to avoid repeating them. Otherwise, in the words of the New York Yankee great and Baseball Hall of Fame catcher Yogi Berra, it's "déjà vu all over again."

- *Weigh the likelihood of occurring and potential impact of each.* One may use a simple 3-point scale where: "3" means it is *very likely* to happen and have *a significant impact*; "2" is *somewhat likely* to happen and *modest impact*; and "1" is *not very likely* to happen and *no perceptible impact*. If something is rated a 1 or 2 for likelihood but a 3 for impact, then one better prepare for it. The likelihood that Canadian geese would collide with Flight 1549 was not very likely to happen, but if so, the impact could prove disastrous. If an item measures 3 for likelihood and impact, then get all appropriate hands-on-deck to prepare for this one!

    A helpful way to identify those that warrant a 3 for impact is to identify "what keeps you up at night?" Is it failing to get FDA approval for the label you are seeking? Is it that the sales force call pattern is not aligned with the target customer segment you need to win? Is it the looming specter of receiving a black-box warning from the FDA? What!?!

- *Next, identify potential actions you might take in the event an impact item occurs and choose the most appropriate one.* By the way, the response (not reaction) could be recommending or alerting management of, a reduction in forecasted revenue.

Using Captain Sully's incident as an example, here's how it might look (note, in this instance, there isn't one action but many "sequential" actions, and procedures, that he and his crew had to take):

Prepare for Failure What could go wrong?	Likelihood – Occurrence	Likelihood – Impact	Avoid/Remedy Failure Action(s)
Bird strike on take-off with engine failure(s)	"1"	"3"	1. Fly the aircraft (many aircrafts have crashed when the pilots tended to the emergency but ignored flying the aircraft) 2. Identify the situation correctly (what do I have here – what's working and what's not?) 3. Take decisive action (based upon the appraisal of facts coupled with *proven* practices) 4. Talk (i.e., notify and prepare crew and passengers for action)

In a business enterprise, reporting may precede taking-action, as approval may be needed. However, when reporting to senior management, the marketer should recommend specific actions and the basis for the recommendation. Don't make it your proposal alone but gain the experience and insights of those most familiar with the subject under investigation (e.g., sales, manufacturing, regulatory, etc.). Unlike the Flight 1549 incident, the marketer is planning how to respond to a potential occurrence, not reacting in the moment.

THE OODA LOOP

Another approach to augment the premortem is the OODA loop. OODA is an acronym for observe, orient, decide and act. It was developed by John Richard Boyd, an Air Force fighter pilot and military strategist. Observe what ills have struck other brands in your company and those of the competition. Orient is about understanding the implications for these occurrences and maneuvering into position to deal with the situation. Decide to pursue a specific action to remedy or avoid the situation. Act is to follow-through with execution. OODA can be reduced to OA: observe to act, when one has the experience and the foresight to prepare for what might go bump in the night.

The premortem and OODA loop are sound practices for avoiding the mistakes of overstating your capabilities and underestimating the competition; they also help you to be prepared to respond to challenges in a way to keep your brand marketing on track.

THE ENEMY IS US

The cartoonist Walt Kelly borrowed the phrase, "We have met the enemy, and he is us" for use in his popular Pogo syndicated cartoon strip. It means that we are responsible for harming ourselves, often more so than the so-called external "enemy," the competition, which is certainly true when we overstate our organization's capabilities and underestimate our competitors. We are our own worst enemy when we do not prepare for the possibility of failure.

The enemy is us

A good practice is to acknowledge and entertain the notion of our brand and organization as the enemy and attack it to reveal weaknesses that need to be shored up. It will also help serve to focus on the generation of ideas to make our marketing more productive.

WAR-GAMING: CONTINGENCY PLANNING

Some of the clients we serve (namely the large, conservative pharmaceutical companies) don't allow the term *war-gaming*, as it suggests being predatory to their legal counsel. Other names include contingency planning and scenario planning, or even competitive scenario planning. Choose whatever terms are suitable in your organization; it doesn't really matter to me. What matters is that you take your competition seriously and anticipate what they might and could do if they possessed knowledge of our marketing plans – strategies and execution (including clinical studies, segmentation, etc.).

The objective is to walk in the shoes of your key competitors and think like them in responding to your brand's and organization's plans. In other words, marketers and their functional, supportive cast should assume the role of the competition. The proposed framework is to:

1. Identify the many ways that competitors might thwart the marketer's brand plans and gain the upper hand in the marketplace with target customers. Do this for all constituencies. For example, in pharmaceutical and medical device companies one should consider the HCP (Health Care Practitioner), patient, payor, non-clinical target, retail pharmacy and, perhaps, caregivers among others. In the FMCG sector this would address consumers, distributors and retailers.

5. Once the marketer has a listing of competitive actions, then she and the team need to identify the likelihood of each occurring and the adverse impact on the brand plan should the competitive actions occur.

6. The final step would be to brainstorm actions that deflect, neutralize or turn the competitors' actions against them.

As a marketing team thinketh so shall it act. It is important that we drop our insular, overinflated view of the market and our brand's place in it and take the perspective of the competition (namely, what you would do if you were the competition). The enemy is our brand and organization, and the objective is for us, taking the role of our competitors, to defeat it!

A CASE HISTORY

My time at Coca-Cola USA revealed the benefits of waking in the shoes of your competitors—specifically, role-playing one or more significant competitors. We had completed preliminary marketing plans and attempted to probe for weaknesses. Additionally, I wanted to encourage out-of-the-box thinking of BIG ideas capable of generating incremental sales. Unfortunately, the broad functional team could not envision any weaknesses, or what we might do differently or more of that might improve the impact of our marketing. After all, we were Coca-Cola, a perfect beverage with the most powerful bottlers, the most effective marketing, and most resources. (Does this ring familiar? If not, go back and reread the Prologue.). According to the team, we were impregnable, until I asked them to assume the role and perspective of the competition.

One group from the team volunteered to take on the role of the PepsiCo organization and Pepsi-Cola brand, another 7-Up, and yet another Dr. Pepper. If we were engaging in this same exercise today, we would include other beverage categories such as bottled waters, sports drinks, and single-serve coffee brands, as these have been eating into the carbonated soft-drink category (CSD) and Coca-Cola USA's CSD growth. At the time, our goal was (and probably remains) to increase Coca-Cola's share not just of CSD but of stomach for liquids (i.e., take usage occasions from coffee, milk, water, etc.).

As each group took on the role of a competitor, they began to see differently and found ways to advance attacks on all things Coca-Cola. When everyone was satisfied and proud of their accomplishments, we identified the top competitive actions that could hurt the brand. We then followed with brainstorming actions for brand Coke (and other Coca-Cola USA brands) that would not only thwart these competitive actions but would have a significant incremental impact on growing our brand. We found a way with war-gaming to avoid underestimating the competition and making our marketing more productive.

ACTION PLAN

There are many actions one might take in war-gaming/contingency planning/ competitive scenario planning. Here are some worthy of your consideration:

1. *Be the Competition.*
   - **Competitive Review:** Review competitive activity over the past few years, with particular emphasis on key events in the most recent past. Key events are occurrences versus trends that have a significant impact, such as the introduction of a new product, campaign, publishing clinical study results, access with payors, winning a tender or getting exclusive distribution, and so forth. Address pricing, positioning, messaging, promotion – their use of marketing mix elements, how and to what extent they are using them. This review will provide a sobering appraisal and insights into how the competition goes to market.
   - **Pressure-Test Your Brand:** Review and adapt previous work such as your SWOT, benchmarking, and marketing research, as seen from your competitor's perspective, to identify vulnerabilities, pressure testing and adapting, as appropriate, the brand positioning strategy, messaging, segmentation and target customer focus. Given how competition views us how might they position themselves, and what can/should we do about it?
   - **Wreck-Havoc:** Within the role of specific competitors, identify/ brainstorm specific strategies and initiatives you might take as your competitor to protect their brand and best ours. Don't just stop at one pass but make multiple runs on what you, in your role playing the competitor, might do. Think big, bold and bad. Wreck-havoc!
   - **Choose for Impact 1:** Make choices based on the likelihood of doing and the impact on besting your brand. Approach this from two angles: 1) competitors' histories; and 2) their taking extraordinary, but plausible, measures to prevent your brand from taking hold in the marketplace and/or progressing.

2. *Be Your Best.*

- **Self-Offense:** The adage "the best defense is a good offense" is the focus here. Brainstorm to identify specific solutions/actions your brand and organization could/should undertake to thwart, counter and/or remedy the most likely and significant competitive actions identified above in "Choose for Impact 1." As George Washington wrote, *"Offensive operations, often times, is the surest, if not the only (in some cases) means of defense."* Let your offense be your defense to stymy competitive action or cause their action to be ineffective and, perhaps, even damage perceptions of them. If we use our team to think out-of-the-box when posing as our competitors, we need everyone to be equally creative in thinking out-of-the-box to come up with high-impact solutions for our brand.

- **Choose for Impact 2:** We can't do everything! There are just not enough resources in any and all organizations (not even Apple or Google). So, we must be selective. This is about making the difficult choices to establish priorities by distinguishing the "essential high-impact" activities from the "nice to do, but non-essential" activities based upon perceived (better yet, proven) impact on sales and market share.

  Indeed, there are many exercises an experienced, strategy-minded facilitator can employ to maximize results within each activity. Also, it is essential that the facilitator be able to challenge where appropriate to make sure that the team is not falling-back on overstating their brand's and organization's capabilities and, underestimating the competition.

OPPOSITIONING

Oppositioning is the way competition is most likely to come at your brand (and organization), particularly where the sales force is the primary vehicle for messaging. Specifically, your competitors are going to do your job for you. Namely, they will position your brand. However, it will be in the most unflattering terms, revealing or creating perceptions of weakness and vulnerability, that they will exploit to their full advantage. They'll use oppositioning to take your brand down, even before it is launched, and bolster their brands. What we're talking about here is their creating and controlling the dialogue in such a way as to negate your brand's positioning and messaging to elevate themselves in the minds of target customers.

We're currently working with a pharmaceutical client that is about one year away from launch. They will be the first in a new therapeutic area. The competitor is approximately one-year behind our client. However, the competitor is already talking about our client's emerging product, attempting to disparage its efficacy and undermine its viability. The competition is trying to block the adoption of our client's product, so they may swoop in and seize the market.

Whether engaged as part of war-gaming or an entirely separate exercise put yourself in your competitors' frame of mind and find ways to opposition your own entry. Look for potential vulnerabilities and pounce on it. Then you can deal with countering the oppositioning. It helps to include sales personnel in all of these exercises as they bring a unique perspective and deep understanding of the target customer and competition.

CLOSE

Anticipating and preparing for failure will enhance your likelihood for succeeding, if nothing more than providing well thought out responses rather than reacting inappropriately or too late. Failure can come from overestimating our capabilities (internal) and/or underestimating our competition (external). Either way, the results won't be pretty so *plan for success but anticipate and prepare for failure.*

CHAPTER 11

LACK OF IDEAS IS THE MARK OF A DULL BRAND

He is not only dull himself; he is the cause of dullness in others.
Samuel Johnson

A BIG idea is one that generates a significant impact in the marketplace.
Richard Czerniawski

If your brand does not contain a BIG idea, it will pass like a
ship in a moonless, overcast night, with its lights out.
Richard Czerniawski

YOUR BRAND IS DULL

Far too many brands are, well, dull. As a result, they do not attract, engage or create loyalty with their intended target customers.

The way to break out of dullness is to create BIG, juicy ideas. Ideas make the world go around. They inspire, provoke, engage, refresh, motivate and activate potential target customers to purchase, prescribe, use, recommend and prefer your brand. Importantly, they drive incremental line-of-sight sales and fuel a healthy ROI. If there are no ideas, you will fail to generate strong growth and a positive ROI, if any at all. A paucity of ideas marks a lackluster and rather dull brand, one headed for obscurity as more creative competitors nibble away at, or leap ahead of, your brand.

Let's be clear; the use of digital devices for marketing is not an idea. It's a vehicle or marketing mix element. Use of social media is not an idea. It too is a marketing mix element. The idea is what you do with digital, social media or, for that matter, any marketing mix element and device that generates a favorable sales impact and ROI in the market.

When BDNI began instructing marketers more than 25 years ago regarding how they could make their marketing matter more, one of the participants kept raising the question, "When are we getting to the BIG idea?" Back then I believed it was a judgment of relative value as in one idea proves to be more fruitful than another. There are so-called ideas, and then there are really big, like in huge, ideas. But I've come to learn that's part of it. There's more to it, much more. Chances are that if you are hunting for ideas (and you should be!) you're searching for a BIG idea. After all, nobody wants little ideas. Even small brands and companies want and need BIG ideas.

WHY IS IT IMPORTANT?

A BIG idea can make the difference between success, mediocrity, and failure. It's that important! As I've repeatedly proclaimed, we live in an "age of abundance and sameness." There is a plethora of products in virtually every category that do the same things in the same ways and produce comparable results. Most of us cannot win by employing cheaper pricing than our competition. Moreover, that's a downward spiral into oblivion. Nor can we afford to win by out-muscling our competitors (such as putting more feet on the street, or pumping-up our marketing budgets). In fact, it is highly likely that your company has been "streamlining," cutting people and/or marketing support funding to make bottom-line profit targets. And, superior execution is a dream realized by so very few brands and companies.

So, we need to differentiate our offering from our competition. One fundamental yet significant way we do this is with the development of a BIG idea. Generating and executing a BIG idea gives us more bang for our marketing support dollars. It is about driving incremental sales and a highly favorable ROI. It's about being able to leapfrog your current position and the competition. It's about driving brand preference and winning and maintaining customers.

Accordingly, pursuing a BIG idea should be a priority. However, generating the proverbial "BIG idea" is easier said than done. Why? Because many marketers, and their organizations, don't know what a BIG idea is, even if it's smacking them in the face. They haven't established criteria for it. What's more, they lack the ability to recognize one, particularly if it comes from someone or someplace else (NIH, "not invented here," syndrome) and/or it's so different from anything they, or competitors, have ever done. As such, they are more likely to kill a nascent BIG idea than embrace it.

WHAT'S A BIG IDEA?

Let's start by defining what's a BIG idea. Well, the word "BIG" is defined as *something of great power; something that is significantly or surprisingly great.* That's BIG! "Idea," to my way of thinking, could be described as *a realization of a possible way of doing something that successfully solves a problem or exploits an opportunity.* Pulling it all together we may define it as follows:

The BIG idea is a way of doing something that
arrests, engages, and compels the behavior of customers (consumers, healthcare practitioners, patients, etc.), and other constituencies (such as management, the sales force, retailers, and so forth), to achieve stretch business objectives.

While it may ride on societal trends,
it capitalizes on a legitimate and productive customer insight.
As such, it fits the brand perfectly, and if any other brand tried to do it it would be false (or not work as effectively).

It is distinctive, getting customers to see the brand in a new,
and highly favorable light.

It not only drives brand preference but also may even drive
competition to distraction.

It is capable of enduring a long time across many mediums and executions.

It is more, much more than advertising (or a clever advertising slogan)
or engaging in social media!

If you prefer, we can distill the aforementioned full explanation to the following headline:

A BIG idea is one that generates a significant impact in the marketplace.

CLASSIFYING BIG IDEAS

There's too much emphasis on chasing after the BIG "ad" (as in advertising) Idea, or a way to take advantage of the so-called new media and social media. These are, at best, tactical. It's not to say that these aren't important; instead, there are other, highly productive places to look. What follows is my classification of BIG ideas. You may note some overlap from one classification to another. I believe it's because BIG ideas, regardless of the type, spill out and influence other elements.

BIG Idea Classification

Idea Type	Key Driver	Example(s)
Brand	Brand Positioning	AXE, Dove, Cialis
Product	Technology/ Intangible	iPad; EES Realize Behavior Modification
Marketing	Marketing any of the "Ps" that join them all	Amazon.com; Apple Retail Stores; Gatorade; Crest ADA Endorsement
(Advertising/ Communication) Campaign	Advertising	MasterCard "Priceless"; Lipitor "Lower Numbers You're Looking For"
Ad	Execution	MasterCard "Home Office."
Tactic	Marketing Activity	Zithromax "Z-Pak"; Prilosec/ Nexium – The "Purple Pill."

- **Brand idea:** As discussed in chapter 3, Mis-Positioning (Brand) Positioning, this is the theme for the subsequent development of a "competitive" brand positioning strategy that differentiates it from its competitors in a relevant way for its target customers. Everything the brand does is consistent with the brand idea, including the campaign idea (see below), which is the center of the plate for their advertising (or, if you prefer, a different term, "marketing communications").

  The AXE brand is an example of a BIG brand idea that while no longer being used by Unilever remains in play in the market in the minds of many of its target customers. You know it: *guys can become "chick-magnets" if they use AXE products.* Now we don't believe we'd become chick-magnets (not anymore, that's for sure!), but (pre) adolescent males, their target customer, think differently. They choose AXE as opposed to competitive products. Why? Is it because AXE has some unique formulation that gets them cleaner, or prevents perspiration and odor better? Hardly. AXE, regardless of the product line, has basically the same ingredients as its competition (and works in the same fundamental ways, etc.). The answer is the brand idea! Moreover, everything, absolutely everything, that the AXE brand has done in its marketing (brand communication campaign, tactics, and so forth) has been about supporting the brand idea that their consumers can become chick-magnets.

- **Product idea:** The product idea can be either for a new product or a product enhancement. It comprises product tangibles and intangibles. The key is that it leads to customer preference for the product offering versus competition.

  Apple Corp's iPod is an example (if you can remember back that far) of a product idea that revolutionized how we purchase and listen to music. It replaced Sony Walkman and arrested and reversed growth of the market for CDs. It led, in turn, to the iMusic store. Technology and design elements helped it leapfrog competitors. Then there's the iPhone, and then the iPad …

  Ethicon Endo Surgery (EES) is an example of adding an intangible service to enhance its product offering. Specifically, EES added a behavior modification program to its bariatric surgery product to assist patients in not just losing weight but helping them keep it off. It's an "intangible" that adds value to the company's offering, differentiating it from competition to help drive brand preference and sales.

- **Marketing idea:** This is a new way of marketing the brand. Remember the 4-P's of marketing? That's right – product, price, promotion, and placement. (There are more, and the most important "P" is positioning!) Change any of these from the accepted practices, and you could be on to a marketing idea. The idea translates into a complete marketing campaign to promote the brand to customers.

  Amazon.com represents a marketing idea – sell books (and now, other stuff) directly to customers versus through bookstores. Apple Retail Stores is another example. Both deal with placement (or distribution) that provides distinct advantages to customers versus conventional retail outlets.

  Apple retail stores support Apple brands. There's a dedicated sales team of Apple evangelists, the Genius Bar to assist with problems, and training specialists to help customers get the most out of their Apple brands.

  Another example might be Gatorade's development and use of endorsements from all the major professional athletic associations. It's been a BIG marketing idea for a campaign that has permeated how it goes to market in everything it does. Is it consistent with its brand idea? Sure. It reinforces that Gatorade is the essential athletic equipment of champions that can make you a winner! It has made Gatorade a winner.

  Crest Toothpaste securing the endorsement of the ADA (American Dental Association) back in the mid-1950s is a classic example. No brand had ever received the ADA endorsement. Crest proved its worth with clinical studies that demonstrated it reduced cavities by more than 80%. The ADA endorsement became the focus of the brand's advertising. It was highlighted on its packaging. The endorsement also became the basis for marketing the brand to dental professionals. It served as the impetus for all of the Crest brand's marketing efforts. It was indeed a marketing idea that propelled the brand to the leadership position in the toothpaste cavity that spanned some 50 years.

- **Advertising/communication campaign idea:** The campaign idea dramatizes the *key thought* (that which the customer must realize for your brand to stimulate a specific target customer behavior that is favorable to your brand), identified in the creative brief, in provocative customer language in the brand's advertising (or, again, if you prefer, brand communications). As explained in the last chapter it consists of the naked idea, which is the creative concept that defines each execution regardless of the medium; key copy words, a sort of post-it note that links the brand name and benefit; and core dramatization to strike a responsive chord in the hearts of target customers. All three work harmoniously to deliver a single-minded message (the key thought) in a single-minded way that will connect with target customers on a gut, or emotional, level. The campaign idea is the center of the plate for advertising or, more broadly stated, brand marketing communications.

  To repeat an earlier example, the MasterCard "Priceless" campaign epitomizes a BIG campaign idea. The campaign turned MasterCard from an also-ran to a leading competitor. It did it all behind a campaign idea, no change to the product, or its distribution system. There have been well over 500 television spots and thousands of print ads (including the use of digital media!) fueled by the "Priceless" campaign.

  Lipitor launched via a DTC (direct-to-consumer) campaign. The brand, which has since gone generic, took the lead from its branded competitors (Pravachol and Zocor) and grew to about 15-billion dollars worldwide. The naked idea: Patients share with a loved one that they failed to achieve the doctor's goal and, as such, the MD prescribed Lipitor. The key copy words: "Lipitor. The Lower Numbers You're Looking For." The core dramatization: "Sharing optimism with a loved one." This campaign achieved its behavior objective of switching. They followed-up another campaign (Lipitor. For Less Cho*les*terol."), which was designed to grow the market by encouraging patients to seek cholesterol testing and, if they have high cholesterol, to adopt Lipitor (more specifically ask their MD to prescribe it). By the way, it did work to grow the market, and Lipitor's business.

- **Ad(vertising) idea:** This is the idea for a *specific execution*, regardless of whether it is TV, print or digital. (Perhaps, a better way to classify the various media is video and text - among which we have a plethora of vehicles, or tools, at our disposal.) Each of the TV commercials and print ads has an ad idea. The ad idea has the same components as a campaign idea, but it is for a specific execution.

  Let's go back to the MasterCard example, because each of its ads contains an ad idea, that perfectly executes the campaign idea. For example, one of the earlier television spots, initially produced in Singapore, contrasts all the home office equipment purchased with a MasterCard with that one priceless moment of being able to work from home, where the purchaser could be with and enjoy his family. That's the naked idea for a specific execution within the campaign. What makes the MasterCard campaign "priceless" is how every one of the ads contains a compelling ad idea that stands on its own and yet works to support the campaign to build the business.

  Concerning the second Lipitor campaign "Lipitor. For Less Cho*les*terol.," one ad showed a fit and distinguished grey-haired gentleman at the community pool being ogled by female sunbathers as he approaches the diving board. The ad boasts of his physical fitness – does 50 pushups, 100 sit-ups, etc. However, in the middle of his dive, his high cholesterol number appears, and he does a belly-flop splashing everyone around him, much to the chagrin of his female admirers. That's a specific ad idea to support the campaign idea of "people with all the right dimensions for weight, fitness, and so forth, whom one would not expect to have a cholesterol problem, take a pratfall when the ad reveals their high cholesterol numbers."

  Many brands don't pursue campaign ideas. Marketers claim they don't have the budget to support a campaign, or so they think. They use advertising to launch a new product or line extension via an individual TV spot, video, print ad or other messaging. (That's one approach to marketing, one I firmly believe is suboptimal. Even if you use advertising just in support of new products, product improvements or line extensions, you should use it to pay-off a campaign idea to reinforce the brand positioning and build brand equity.) Regardless, there's just no excuse to employ advertising that does not have an idea. To improve your ability to drive incremental sales and generate a positive ROI all advertising should contain, at a minimum, an ad idea.

- **Tactic idea:** This is an idea for a marketing element (other than advertising) such as what you will do (as in execution) at medical conventions or PR (public relations) or your third- quarter consumer promotion. The marketing tactic idea should be consistent with the brand, marketing and campaign idea. It is a sibling to the ad idea. It's an idea for the execution for a specific tactic in one of the other marketing mix elements at your disposal.

  Axe Antiperspirant Dry created a 1-hour TV program for MTV, the *Gamekillers*, to introduce the product line to guys interested in hooking up with girls. Gamekillers are people whose sole mission in life is to keep a guy from hooking up with a girl. They defined gamekillers as people like the one-upper, the mother hen, and the mess (the worst "wingman" of all time), among other insufferable types. Each gamekiller, they claim, is based upon archetypes from real life.

  The show features a real guy going on a date with the "object of his desire" (hey, I didn't make up this stuff nor did I participate in the development of the brand idea and positioning strategy for AXE) only to face gamekillers who are trying to ruin his game (as perspiration can). Despite the gamekillers, the guy must keep his cool, the messaging for the product benefit, to get the girl and "all the 'jiggly' stuff that goes with it" (the consumer benefit). If he doesn't keep his cool, then he doesn't get the girl.

  The program offered tips on beating gamekillers. It generated a lot of buzz and millions of free impressions that communicated the product and consumer benefit of using AXE Antiperspirant Dry. "Keep your cool. Axe Dry." Note that the tactic idea is consistent with the brand idea, which became the basis of the advertising campaign idea. (Also, note that if employed today, this theme would rightly draw ample fire from the #metoo movement!)

The Zithromax "Z-Pak" is a packaging idea that we should all be familiar with. It reinforces the brand's selling proposition "5 days and you're done." Patients needing an antibiotic often ask their doctor to prescribe a Z-Pak based upon its convenience and ease of use coupled with its perceived efficacy.

Prilosec and, in turn, Nexium from AstraZeneca (AZ) colored its pills purple to help differentiate this PPI (proton pump inhibitor) from its competitors for HCPs treating GERD and consumer-patients suffering from it. Patients know each product as "the purple pill." Perhaps, you might classify this as a product idea, but to me, it is more of a branding element and tactic. Regardless, it worked well for AZ twice – Prilosec and then, when it went generic, it was employed for Nexium.

BARRIERS TO GETTING TO (BIG) IDEAS

While managers in most companies may claim that they want and need BIG ideas they, and their organizations, often thwart their development. Getting to the BIG idea is akin to walking through a minefield, where hidden barriers can spring-up to destroy our ability to introduce new ideas into the marketplace. Being aware of where the obstacles lie may help us to successfully confront and manage them so that we may snatch victory from the jaws of defeat and achieve success. Here are some of the frequently encountered barriers, which we need to find a way to resolve before we can get to the BIG idea:

- **Busyness:** As effectiveness diminishes in this age of abundance and sameness, marketers are being challenged with doing yet more things. We've never been so busy: addressing scores of emails; sitting through numerous, endless, mind-numbing meetings; conducting multiple revisions and presentations on the same subject, where little, if any, value is added; addressing random questions and objections from the sales force; addressing product quality issues; and so forth. With all this on our plate, who among us has time to think? Who has time to dream? Who has time to create? Accordingly, we need to make time, or it won't get done!

- **Culture:** It's one thing to extol the value of ideas, but it is an entirely different matter to encourage and embrace them. What happens when you proffer an idea in your organization? Do managers build upon it? Do they generate additional ideas? Or, do they continually choose the expected over the unexpected? It's in the culture. Management needs to demand ideas. If they don't then we need to find a way to get them to buy into considering and adopting ideas.

- **Orthodoxy:** This is about buying into the conventional wisdom and the rise of dogma. It's *doing what your competitors do in the way they do it* based upon the belief that this is what drives sales. If competitors use celebrities in their advertising, then we must use celebrities to support our brands. If competitors participate in medical congresses, then we must join in the same congresses. We believe that not only must we engage in these same things as our competitors but that *we must also do it in the same way they do or the way we've always done it* (including arming our sales personnel with 16-page viz-aids that neither get presented nor are read). Worshiping at the altar of orthodoxy may also be claimed by the litany of executional "considerations" (which are really "mandates") we use when providing direction to resource teams (such as the advertising agency) or using these so-called considerations to measure the value of the work.

- **NIH:** This is an acronym for *not-invented-here* syndrome. We do not need to be the font of all the ideas. Instead, we must be sensitive and responsive to the ideas generated by others since ideas can come from anyone and any place, at any time. Moreover, NIH suggests that we may be of the disposition to look for what is wrong as opposed to what might work (perhaps, with some thoughtful and meaningful adaptations).

- **Fear:** New ideas can be frightening. They represent an unknown. After all, no one has done it or is doing it that way. If we champion the novel, we are seen as, well, "different." It makes us feel that others (particularly our senior managers) may not perceive us as "one of them." That's frightening!

What's more, the idea may fail. And, if our name is attached to the idea, it could be career ending (at least with your current organization). So, when confronted with a new idea we react by saying "NO!" because it is safer to say no than it is to say yes to new ideas.

- **Target fixation:** This is a term whose origin is military aviation. It means being so fixated on the target that one is oblivious to what is going on around him and, inadvertently, flies into the target. Focusing on one marketing mix element, one tactic, one medium (such as "what can we do with mobile phones to market our product?") could result in target fixation and cause us to overlook tremendous opportunities such as a BIG brand, marketing or campaign idea.

- **The absence of a quality process:** There are really two thoughts here. One is about *making the generation of ideas an ongoing process, not an episodic event.* The worse time for seeking to generate a BIG idea is when we desperately need one or we are on a very tight timeframe. The pressure can prove to be overwhelming. Moreover, the time constraint will lead the organization to settle or do something that has not been checked for productivity prior to execution in the marketplace. We need to *build a pipeline of proven ideas.* The second thought is about *not having a quality process for generating and assessing ideas,* essential to leading us to choose those that are strategically appropriate and productive in stimulating desired customer behaviors and building the business.

- **Focus on idea fragments versus complete ideas:** Idea generation sessions, or our individual creative thinking, generally lead to *idea fragments* as opposed to *complete ideas.* In other words, the details of the concept are missing. While idea fragments may inspire us (and there is nothing wrong with that), it is merely the first step. We need the details to get to a complete idea. We do not need the details for *all* the idea fragments we generate, merely for those that meet pre-established criteria. (By the way, being genuinely excited about the potential for an idea is a valuable criterion for moving forward.) Without a complete design, we are unable to give full wings to the idea and any attempt to assess it (e.g., with a concept) will likely lead to false results.

- **An absence of standards:** So, why do we think we have a BIG idea? Do we have pre-established criteria and measurements? Are the criteria linked to results? It's not about merely liking an idea because, for example, it's creative. Remember, the late, great David Ogilvy, a lion in the history and development of advertising, stated, "It's not creative unless it sells." Therefore, we need to establish standards for ideas (as we should set standards for all our initiatives) and inspect that our ideas exceed or, at a minimum, meet them.

HOW TO RECOGNIZE A BIG IDEA

The late David Ogilvy also advised that "Unless your advertising contains a big idea, it will pass like a ship in the night." I want to take this one step further and relate it to ideas. *If your brand does not contain a BIG idea, it will pass like a ship in a moonless, overcast night, with its lights out.* In other words, customers will neither notice the brand nor be moved by it.

Mr. Ogilvy also said, "It is horribly difficult to recognize a good idea. I shudder to think how many I rejected." This is coming from someone who was in the idea business. This is an individual who was incredibly creative in his own right. What chance then do left-brained, MBA marketers have to recognize whether they have a potential BIG idea? Well, here are seven questions, the first three of which Mr. Ogilvy asked himself whenever he assessed advertising, the others I've amended or added for recognizing a BIG idea:

1. *Did it make me gasp when I first saw it?*
2. *Do I wish I had thought of it myself?*
3. *Is it unique?*

4. *Does it fit the brand idea to perfection such that it will contribute to building brand equity?*
5. *Does it address a critical business issue such as overcoming a problem or exploiting an opportunity?*
6. *Will it motivate a change in customer behavior (consistent with our marketing objectives) and lead to more rapid sales growth?*
7. *Will it endure as a campaign or contribute to energizing a campaign?*

How to Assess Ideas

Recognizing a BIG idea is subjective. While the aforementioned questions may help us identify potentially BIG ideas from, hopefully, a plethora of idea fragments, we need to quantify their value. This quantification requires us to gain feedback from customers regarding their merit, as measured by the likelihood of motivating the behavior (e.g., switching, adoption) we seek from these customers. Marketing research personnel can assist you in conducting the appropriate customer research in addressing this issue. However, there are steps we need to take before and after marketing research too. Here are five-steps following the generation of ideas (regardless of the method used to create them):

- The first step is to *transform idea fragments into complete ideas,* for those ideas that generate affirmative answers to the seven questions noted in the section mentioned earlier and meet internal screening criteria. The complete idea contains a target customer definition, customer insight, benefit and details (which could be reason-why support, product features, how the product, compound or service works, among others – depending upon whether the idea is for a positioning strategy, product or tactic).
- The second step is to *rescreen the complete ideas to ensure each continues to pass your internal screening criteria.* It is beneficial to get team members (from different functional areas) to *rate and rank each idea.*
- The third step is to *develop a concept that translates the complete idea into a format that customers can understand, appreciate, and respond to appropriately and reliably.* The stimulus material can take the form of a prototype, white card concept, etc. The idea itself informs the format.

206

(For example, a product idea may better lend itself to a prototype, particularly if it is novel. On the other hand, an idea for positioning strategy may benefit from a white card concept.)

- The fourth step is to *undertake marketing research* to gain customer feedback. Marketing research will aid in decision-making and may even lead to adaptations to help make the idea more productive.

- The final step is *in-market testing* of the execution. We should validate the marketing research and measure real-world results to *determine the impact on incremental sales and return-on-investment* that we may expect from executing it on a broader scale.

RX FOR GETTING TO THE BIG IDEA

In this age of abundance and sameness, BIG ideas can make the difference in gaining a competitive advantage, creating brand loyalty, reinvigorating the brand (and even, the organization), and fueling more rapid growth to achieve *stretch* business objectives. Here's how you can get there:

1. ***Break down barriers.*** Identify the obstacles you face in getting to the BIG idea. Then figure out what you need to remove them. For example, if your management is reluctant to adopt new ideas, obtain the marketing research support you need to bring them onboard. (Peter Larson, one of my former managers at J&J, called it "buying insurance.") Make it easy for them to accept and buy into doing something different or in a different way.

2. ***Make idea generation a priority and an on-going process.*** One of the marketer's many responsibilities is to build the brand. Yet we spend so much of our time doing those urgent, non-important tasks, crowding-out time for those non-urgent, critically important tasks such as developing new ideas capable of growing the business. Make time for this critically important task and get it on your calendar. Make an appointment with yourself and your extended brand team to spend

time ideating. We might consider devoting the first Friday of every quarter for idea generation.

3. ***Think BIG.*** Yes, we want to ideate regarding ways to overcome barriers and ways to capitalize on perceived opportunities. But we should think BIG as in ideating around the brand idea and the development of a marketing idea.

4. ***Demand the unexpected.*** Don't even think about doing the same things, in the same ways that you, or your organization, always do them. For that matter nor should you do the same things, in the same ways, as your competitors do. That's a waste of money. At best it neutralizes competition. However, it keeps you from realizing incremental sales and boosting ROI. Dare to be different. Go ahead, think and act differently.

5. ***Develop complete ideas.*** It's important to take those idea fragments that pass internal screening criteria to the next level – complete ideas. This will contribute to the further development of the idea, and provide a basis for yet additional, more reliable screening.

6. ***Set standards.*** It's not just about having ideas but developing BIG ideas. While I've offered a definition of a BIG idea and identified objectives, establish and set standards for your brand and organization. This will provide a basis for investing your limited resources (and we ALL face limited resources) against ideas that are likely to deliver incremental sales and a very attractive return-on-investment.

7. ***Develop an idea pipeline.*** We all recognize the value of building a rich new product pipeline in generating future growth. It's a mark of a healthy company. Likewise, an idea pipeline will serve to fuel future brand growth. It's a mark of a healthy brand.

8. ***Measure the impact of all ideas.*** We should strive to measure incremental line-of-sight sales and ROI on all the ideas in our pipeline. This will

enable us to predict with greater accuracy and reliability the financial impact on the brand from executing them. It will also serve to enable us to manage the achievement of the brand's business objectives of sales, market share, and profit.

9. *Incentivize for impact of idea generation.* Put together a program for recognizing business building ideas, and those people that created them, that have generated significant sales impact. An incentive program doesn't have to be anything expensive. It could be an annual awards ceremony, a luncheon, a company-wide (or brand team) email, anything that recognizes the individual and her idea and contribution to the business. Do what it takes to demonstrate that you value the ideas and their generators for making a difference. We should also consider incentivizing adoption of a marketing idea developed in another geography or sector that has been proven to work. However, ensure it works for your brand in your geography before executing it on a broad scale basis.

10. *It has got to sell!* Remember, as David Ogilvy stated, "It's not creative unless it sells." The BIG idea doesn't have to be creative, as in being artsy. It just has to be appropriate, different and, importantly, work! It has to connect with customers at the gut level if it is going to grow preference and drive incremental sales and a positive ROI.

Get excited about creating BIG ideas as their adoption will turn around a dull brand to make it exciting to target customers, other external constituencies, and your management team.

CHAPTER 12

EMINENCE-BASED VERSUS EVIDENCE-BASED MARKETING

Eminence-based marketing is dumb marketing.
Richard Czerniawski

The definition of insanity is doing the same thing, in the same way, over and over again, and expecting different results.
Albert Einstein

EMINENCE-BASED MEDICINE

In the early days of medicine, and as late as the last century during which many current marketers entered this world, eminence ruled practice. Eminence-based medicine is where *patient treatment is derived from the opinions of perceived experts owing to a specialty or their prominence in their field.* It is just about where every field begins.

The practice of eminence-based medicine led to rather bizarre and radical treatments such as performing lobotomies on patients who have mental illness. Alternatively, bleeding patients with leeches to rid them of excess "humours" believed to cause disease. Mothers would treat babies suffering from teething with formulations that contained alcohol, and morphine! Let us not forget trepanation, which amounted to drilling holes in the heads of patients to treat seizures and migraines. Yes, that will help those migraines and any thoughts the sufferer had to fly away!

How did these practices become SOC (standard-of-care)? It certainly wasn't through careful study, the kind required by the FDA (Food and Drug Administration). Instead, these practices came about by following someone of perceived eminent status based upon where he (it was always a "he" back then) received his medical degree, what hospital he was associated, social status, specialty, experiments he (Dr. Frankenstein, I presume) initiated and conducted, among other factors including number of years of practice. There was no evidence to support the aforementioned dangerous practices. In fact, there's been plenty of evidence, along with good common sense (duh), to overturn them.

From Eminence-Based to Evidence-Based Medicine

It was also a common practice to surgically remove an inflamed appendix (appendicitis) before it ruptured. Not bizarre but, perhaps, a bit invasive and severe. If you had appendicitis, you could count on undergoing the scalpel even though the majority of cases could be alleviated with the use of antibiotics. What has changed that practice? The Cochrane Organization (formerly the Cochrane Collaboration), an independent group that organizes research findings to facilitate evidence-based choices, uncovered this outcome. Now if you have appendicitis an antibiotic regiment is considered and, if it isn't, you should be asking your MD to consider it! It's a case of evidence over eminence.

Evidence-based medicine is using findings from clinical studies available in the medical literature, or undertaking studies to evaluate a hypothesis, to identify the most appropriate or best treatment option based upon outcomes, not opinions. It's not about taking action based upon the reputation of any individual, or current practices, but what has proven to work in achieving and improving outcomes. It is science-based, not opinion-based. It is what has contributed, among other things, to extending our quantity and quality of life expectancy. It is what is, prayerfully, helping us avoid practices that not only do not work but can cause irreparable harm, as many of those past eminence-based practices did.

EMINENCE-BASED MARKETING

Unfortunately, there's still too much of what passes for marketing today that's eminence- over evidence-based. Eminence is a function of senior people directing and approving initiatives for which they have no evidence, only unexamined, misinterpreted and/or highly biased experience. They have nothing but an opinion. It isn't the value of their view, but the value of their authority derived from her/his position or eloquence with which they speak that carries the day and drives others to follow. Add to this the practice of doing things the way they've always been done. This practice, too, is eminence-based marketing, leading to a blind obedience to follow from those up and down the organization. And, if a marketer questions the eminence-based opinion or practice, then she may be harshly judged as not understanding the business or being one of us (as mentioned in the previous chapter).

Eminence-based marketing is dumb marketing. There's no factual, proven support. It leads to faulty decision making. It's "garbage in, garbage out." It is indeed not the mark of a high-performance organization. In fact, it underscores an ignorant enterprise, one that despite successes is falling short on impact, efficiency and proper utilization of resources. It has no link to optimizing marketing success in creating brand loyalty.

Imagine, your target goal is to achieve a market share of X (whether it be 15, 25, 35% or more) by Y-time. Beyond receiving your weekly (or daily) sales results, and a share report from a custom or syndicated data source, *do you know what it takes and if you'll achieve the target sales and market share goals?* No, then yours is an eminence-based organization or brand.

Don't get me wrong; this is a difficult question to answer. It's one that *gets to the heart of your understanding of what drives the business and explains the performance of your brand and, importantly, your ability to manage it effectively.* If you are unable to answer this question, then you are asking the organization to gamble precious resources on key strategies and initiatives because you are unable to identify that they will work and to what extent. If you want to place a bet, head-out to Vegas. The enterprise is not the place for gambling. You have a fiduciary responsibility to shareholders and a moral obligation to both employees and customers to not gamble with their investments, careers, and lives. To avoid gambling and ensure consistent, predictable levels of success we need to build high-performance organizations and brands, and the way to do it is through the practice of evidence-based marketing at both the brand and organization level.

EVIDENCE-BASED MARKETING

Working with many companies, from a wide range of sectors, throughout the world, I've encountered the same practice. It's not a good one either. Instead, it's lousy. The practice I'm referring to is that marketers are going from business objectives (sales, market share and profit goals) directly to tactics. There are no performance goals for all that goes between the business objectives and those tactics. Instead, we have a performance gap that we need to fill.

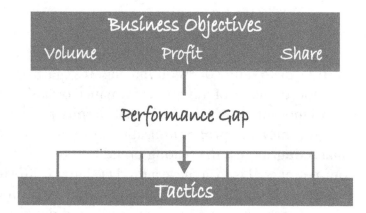

There are no objective criteria for selecting or assessing these tactics either. It's like doing the same things in the same ways we have always been doing them. If we have been growing at x%, then we should continue to achieve x% growth. Well, are you? If you are, it's probably fortuitous if you are not addressing the performance gap. We cannot rely on luck, nor hope if we are going to achieve high-impact marketing on a predictable basis. If you are not meeting these goals, then perhaps these marketers and their leaders are insane. Albert Einstein stated, "The definition of insanity is doing the same thing, in the same way, over and over again, and expecting different results."

I certainly do not believe you are insane. Nor do I think your leadership is insane such that they would keep spending to support tactics for which they do not know the incremental impact and ROI (return on investment) or produce a poor ROI. Has your working budget been cut? That's evidence of sanity if those tactics or strategies have not demonstrated incremental sales or a positive ROI. I doubt management is cutting funding from programs or tactics that clearly show a boost in incremental sales and healthy ROI. Now, that would be insane!

GOING FROM EMINENCE-BASED TO EVIDENCE-BASED MARKETING

What's missing? What do we need to have to bridge the performance gap? What do we need to create a high-performance brand and organization that we can count upon to deliver predictable results? We need to go from eminence-based to evidence-based marketing. Specifically, we need SMART target customer behavior objectives, identification of and allocation of resources against the key business drivers, SMART objectives for each of the key business drivers and strategies to achieve your objectives and, finally, BIG idea tactics that compel the desired customer behaviors.

This look something like this:

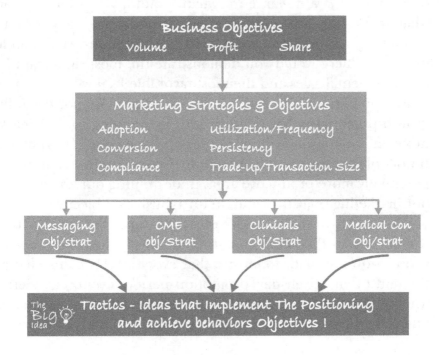

215

More on each:

- **Marketing Objective** – This is the specific target customer behavior(s) we expect and need to achieve to deliver against the business objectives of sales, market share, and profit. Marketing objectives include adoption (i.e., first time using a category of products), switching (from a competitor's offering to your brand), frequency of purchase, compliance, et cetera. We've covered behavior objectives in "Chapter 7: 'Bad' Behaviors."

  Terminology is critically important here. Understand that business objectives are not the same as marketing objectives. And, marketing objectives are not visionary or qualitative statements. They are quantifiable behaviors pure and simple! If you achieve these marketing objectives, then you will deliver on the brand's or organization's business objectives.

- **Key Business Drivers (KBD)** – This relates to the most productive marketing mix elements. If you only had one unit of funding (regardless of whether it is a dollar, euro, yuan, pound, yen, whatever) against what marketing mix element (e.g., advertising, trade promotion, continuing medical education, medical congresses, etc.) should you invest it? Where would you demonstrate the most significant impact on incremental sales and the most favorable ROI with that monetary unit? Don't know? Too bad. Limited funding does not mean limited growth potential. What limits growth is spending against marketing mix elements for which there is little impact and our ROI is not optimal. It not only limits growth from that spending but diverts funding from potentially more productive areas undermining our ability to achieve our marketing objectives and, in turn, business objectives.

  We need to develop SMART objectives for each of the KBDs. These should link to the achievement of the marketing objectives. Again, you can do the math to ensure that everything is connected and at the end of any given day, promotion period, event, etc., determine whether you have contributed to delivering against the marketing and business objectives. An example of a product sampling promotion objective might be to sample X% of households during the 4th-quarter to achieve Y% switching. An objective for CME (Continuing Medical Education) might be to train and qualify Y% of surgeons to perform a specific procedure within the first two months of launch. An example of a media sales' call objective might be to reach Z% of customers N-times during a specific 13-week schedule.

The strategies are the specific routes you are going to take to achieve these KBD objectives. For example, the sampling strategy might be to provide salable samples to the trade (i.e., this is where the retail trade sells the samples to their customers through their outlets).

- **BIG Idea Tactics** – This "animates" the strategy in that it brings it to life to encourage achievement of the KBD behavior objectives. It's about creating execution that compels customers to act as you wish for them to behave. An example of a BIG idea tactic might be NutraSweet's intro sampling of gumballs to consumers or BOTOX parties to generate leads for potential patients.

  A couple of points to note. The tactics must have SMART behavior objectives. So you ask, we've already undertaken that for the KBD (i.e., the marketing mix element)? Yes and no! You may have more than one objective for a given marketing mix element and/or you may need more than one tactic to achieve the KBD marketing mix element objective. For example, the KBD consumer promotion strategy may be to focus on trial and repeat purchasing. In this case you will need a tactic for each one and each will have a different SMART behavior objective (e.g., switching or adoption for the former and frequency of purchasing for the latter).

RX FOR SMART EVIDENCE-BASED MARKETING

Let's be accountable. Bridge the performance gap with your evidence-based marketing.

1. *Fix your nomenclature.* Business objectives are sales, market share and profit goals. Marketing objectives are customer behaviors. End of story.

Don't let high priced consultants contrive new words or definitions for these terms. Nor do you need to make up new terms for these that are proprietary to your company. Neither advances thinking. Obfuscation of meaning through poor terminology leads to fuzzy thinking. And, we need to be very clear with our thinking.

2. ***Include marketing objectives in your planning.*** Determine which behaviors your brand needs to achieve to deliver the business objectives. Nearly every brand has more than one marketing objective. However, a given KBD or tactic will not address all of them. For example, let's assume we have two marketing objectives. The first is to generate switching and the second is increasing frequency of usage or, for you healthcare marketers, improving compliance. In this instance, you might use your mass brand communications campaign to address the switching behavior objective. You may then use promotion to increase the frequency of purchasing and compliance.

3. ***Get SMART with your marketing objectives.*** I've mentioned SMART behavior objectives throughout this book. I need the numbers, and they must be Specific, Measurable, Achievable, Relevant to achieving the business objectives and Timebound. Then do the math to ensure that the achievement of these objectives will prove to the business objectives.

4. ***Undertake zero-based budgeting.*** Identify key business drivers and prioritize funding allocation against these more productive priorities that hold promise for the most significant incremental sales growth and favorable ROI.

5. ***Develop SMART objectives for each of the key business drivers and strategies to achieve these objectives.*** Achievement of the objectives for each KBD will add up to the marketing objectives which, in turn, will lead to the achievement of the business objectives. If they don't then "Houston, we have a problem." This practice will reveal whether our business objectives are potentially too high or, perhaps, that we are not sufficiently aggressive with our marketing or that the business objectives should be taken higher.

6. ***Once again, do the math.*** Check to ensure that achieving the objectives for each of the key business rivers will lead to realizing the marketing objectives and, in turn, the brand's business objectives.

7. ***Generate BIG idea tactics.*** Don't settle for anything less than truly BIG idea tactics. BIG ideas serve to leverage the productivity of key business drivers. BIG idea tactics serve as accelerators to growth.

8. ***Test and iterate your way to success.*** All tactics need to be tested against your objectives for it. This practice will lead you to use your marketing support funding wisely. If it meets expectations, then it becomes a candidate for taking it broadscale. If it doesn't then you don't launch it as it will neither give you the incremental sales impact nor favorable ROI that you desire and need.

9. ***Inspect what you expect.*** Measure the results of each tactic against your expectations. Importantly, get to the root cause of any variances in performance versus goals. Use your learning to guide future brand activity.

Get SMART. Let's make a real difference with our marketing. Let's go from eminence-based to evidence-based marketing. Bridge the performance gap to deliver line-of-sight high-impact results predictably in establishing a high-performance brand and organization.

ADDITIONAL PRACTICES FOR SMART MARKETING

Here are additional personal and organization practices to employ in your quest to promote smart marketing and advance your pursuit of true marketing excellence or, at the very least, make your marketing (and you) matter more.

CHAPTER 13

BE THE BRAND PRESIDENT

---

*Just change your business card to read "brand manager" from marketing
manager, product manager or whatever, to change your thinking and
approach to marketing, and move into the role of
being the president of your brand.*
Richard Czerniawski

WHAT'S IN A TITLE?

Will Shakespeare writes in *Romeo and Juliet*, "What is in a name? That
which we call a rose by any other word would smell as sweet." Our
client marketers would undoubtedly agree as it relates to titles for marketers,
with little regard for how their title impacts thinking and function. They
use different titles depending largely on company heritage and how they
perceive the role of marketing. Some are marketing managers, others are
product managers or Directors, and yet others are brand managers. These
are often considered the same, like Juliet's rose, but I'd argue they are, in
practice, very different.

- The marketing manager is typically wrapped-up in supporting the
  sales force and/or engaged in project management.
- The product manager or director (I prefer the director label since
  it sounds like a higher level in the hierarchy and, therefore, would
  suggest a higher level of compensation) focuses on the physical
  product.

- The brand manager's focus in on the management of the brand, that constellation of values going beyond the mere physical product that establishes the bond we develop with target customers based upon their experiences (which we build into our offering) with it.

It's been more than 45 years since I joined Procter & Gamble (P&G) following service in the U.S. Navy and grad school, where I earned an MBA. At P&G, we strove to be brand Managers. We were responsible for the *general (marketing) management* of the brand. While my MBA concentration was in finance, I joined P&G because they promised to help me become, as brand manager, president of one of their many brands. Since I intended to become a financial analyst, I figured that becoming a brand manager would be excellent training for the financial world. If I could learn how to be president of a brand, then I figured I would be better equipped to become a leading financial analyst.

BRAND MANAGEMENT: THE STRATEGIC ADVANTAGE

P&G created the brand management system to gain a strategic advantage. That advantage was the focus they gave to creating and managing brands. It would be difficult for any one person to develop and maximize their management of all their company's many brands equally effectively. (The company recently reduced a listing of 200 brands worldwide, more than 70 having annual sales of $100 million or more, and 22 blockbuster brands whose sales exceed $1 billion annually, given the difficulty of focusing on them equally despite their brand management system.) Focusing all of one's attention and energies on the development of one brand, not product, was expected to boost understanding and competitiveness, and garner better results in the marketplace, as evidenced by increasing market share and gaining (and sustaining growing) market or segment leadership.

I encourage all our clients who do not have the title of brand manager to convert to it. I also advise them, tongue in cheek, not to ask the permission of their HR Department since its managers will probably take two years to review and study it (with input from a committee of several or more people), only to deny it in the end. Just change your business card to read "brand manager" from marketing manager, product manager or whatever, to change your thinking and approach to marketing, and to move into the role of being the president of your brand. (You might try "brand president" if you can get away with it without more senior managers crashing down on you.)

At Procter & Gamble, the brand manager, serving as president of the brand, was at the center of the wheel. All support groups, including the sales force, pulled in the same direction as charted by the brand manager and her plans for the brand. Now don't get me wrong, the brand manager did not have carte blanche. She had an active and powerful board of directors who needed to buy into plans and proposals for resources, based upon securing a competitive advantage and attaining specific, agreed-upon business objectives of sales and market share. (We were not responsible for profit at P&G. It was a function of delivering on sales and market share targets and staying within budget.) Moreover, the brand manager had to gain the cooperation of the support groups through agreement borne of thoughtful analysis and collaboration (not consensus!). Everything had to be evidence-based, or it didn't fly.

This wheel represents the (P&G) brand management model:

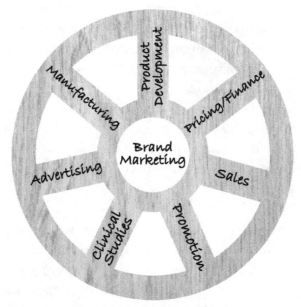

Brand Management Model

THE ROLE OF THE BRAND PRESIDENT

How do brand managers differ from marketing managers and product managers? They start by thinking like brand presidents and assume that role. Regardless of what the HR job description might hold, living up to this title leads to a very different mindset and focus. Here are just a few of the key differences:

1. *Brand presidents have the big picture and take the long view.* They appreciate the value of a brand over a mere physical product and strive to create one built around positive customer experiences that will bind target customers to the brand. They think competitively and search out ways to create a distinctive, meaningful brand idea and positioning strategy. They see where the market is going and race to make it happen sooner by leading the way with innovation whether it be improvements to the physical product to satisfy previously unmet needs, development of a compelling campaign and other major innovations. They know what their brand is capable of achieving and develop a plan to realize its full potential. They build their plan on selective segmentation, a firm knowledge of their customers' needs and desires, competitors' positioning and marketing, the discovery of legitimate and productive customer insights, and recognition of company capabilities and brand potential within the business enterprise, among others. Moreover, they recognize the importance of the entire organization (i.e., all their support groups such as R&D, sales, et al.) in achieving the brand's potential. They manage their business (e.g., development of brand equity, product pipeline, and so forth) as opposed to letting the daily demands of the business manage them.

2. *They create impact.* It's not about the number of projects undertaken and completed but doing what really matters. It's going from spinning one's wheels pursuing and crossing-off the urgent, non-critical tasks to focus on those non-urgent, critically important ones. What is critically important? Those that will have an impact, as defined by

growing *incremental* sales and market share. If the category is growing at X%, then they identify and champion activities that will exceed that growth. It's subscribing to the Pareto principle where about that 20% of strategies and actions will yield 80% of the results. What two or three strategies or initiatives might you undertake that will have a significant impact on growing incremental sales?

3. ***They're responsible stewards of the brand.*** Brand presidents recognize that they're entrusted with the management of a valuable company asset, and they need and want to make the most of that trust. They think incremental sales and ROI. Like the parable of the landowner who entrusts each of three servants with a bag of gold coins to deploy wisely, he seeks the greatest bang for the buck (or whatever currency they're dealing with). Therefore, they do not undertake anything for which they do not know the impact, and ROI. To ignore this would be to gamble with company resources and they do not gamble! Instead, they invest in building the brand, its reputation, and sales. By the way, ROI is not just influenced by the marketing mix elements you choose but by ideas. So, they seek out BIG, juicy ideas. Then they test and analyze before rolling-out their ideas and continue to measure the results in the marketplace to gain valuable feedback for future decision making.

4. ***They serve.*** They recognize the key to success is better serving customers than their competition. So, they develop a deep understanding of the customer and make serving them not just their priority but that of the entire organization. They ask not only whether an activity will help to embed their brand's positioning strategy but whether it serves the interest of customers. They also serve their support teams by ensuring they get the resources needed (which could include sufficient time!) to get the job done properly. Recall the line out of the 1996 movie *Jerry Maguire*, where Jerry (played by Tom Cruise), a sports agent, tells his client, a professional football player (played by Cuba Gooding), "Help me help you." Ask and serve! And, go beyond just asking "what can we do with what we have?" Find out what's needed to do that will

grow the business and, then, be a champion in advocating for the resources to make it happen.

5. ***They build winning teams.*** They collaborate, communicate, and orchestrate. Moreover, like the leader of an orchestra, they gain the input of support groups in both strategy development and execution. They collaborate not merely for buy-in but to include and get the best input from everyone. In this manner, they gain support from team members. Then, they communicate, over and over again, to keep everyone on the same page and ensure execution fulfills intent. They coordinate the concentration of forces to promote optimal implementation in the marketplace. Success, in turns, draws talent to the team.

TWO ADDITIONAL THOUGHTS WORTH NOTING

1. Back in 1972, when I joined P&G, it was the second leading developer of company presidents, trailing only the Harvard B-School. (So I was told.) Accordingly, the business world valued the general management training and role that I had. I believe it is just as important, if not more important, today given that we compete in an "age of abundance and sameness" when it comes to products and services.

2. The brand management model is valuable irrespective of sector. It doesn't matter the specific spokes. Substitute medical congresses for promotion or key opinion leaders for media vehicles or digital for traditional media, whatever. The main point is that one manager has the responsibility of building the brand with the contributions from support team members.

THOUGHT LEADERSHIP

Let's face it. Even with the title of brand manager, no one in the organization is going to grant you the role of president of the brand. You have to earn it the old-fashioned way by exhibiting what at BDNI we refer to as "thought leadership," followed by delivering on target business objectives.

Thought – Having a definitive point of view resulting from experience, knowledge of the brand environment – its heritage, competition, customers, the marketplace – testing and valid analysis

Leadership – Choosing to champion proven strategies and actions that will have an impact in the marketplace in contributing to building growth and brand equity

So, pulling it together, we may define thought leadership as *"having a definitive point of view resulting from experience, knowledge of the brand environment—its heritage, competition, customers, the marketplace—testing and valid analysis, and choosing to champion those proven strategies and actions that will have an impact in the marketplace in contributing to building growth and brand equity."*

Everyone has an opinion. However, a POV is the conclusion flowing from the marriage of findings, deep-seated knowledge, and insights, to turn that knowledge into impact. If the marketer can't back-up his POV, he won't be trusted to manage the brand. Leadership requires you to unhesitatingly share your POV. Don't just express it; you must eagerly champion it in a way that is convincing and compelling.

Thought leadership earns you a place at the table with the BIG and IMPORTANT decision makers! As one of my former managers, Peter Larson, would tell me: "Senior management doesn't buy your plans. What they buy is confidence in you." The way we instill confidence is through thought leadership. This thought leadership could be the result of a solo effort but is likely to be more effective, convincing and compelling if done collaboratively. In other words, one must gain the agreement of relevant support groups (that make-up the extended brand team) that what the brand manager is proposing is valid and will advance brand development and growth. That is, the proposed strategies and actions make sense and have been proven to work for all team members. Pure and simple!

GETTING TO A POSITION OF THOUGHT LEADERSHIP AND A SEAT AT THE TABLE AS BRAND PRESIDENT

Here are many of the things that will enable you to achieve a position of thought leadership required for assuming the role of brand president:

- Change your title, change your thinking. Change the title on your business card brand manager (if you want to go all the way, make it brand president). Act like the brand president. Acting will lead to thinking like the brand president.

- Get competitive. It's not competing to merely participate in the marketplace but seek to gain a competitive advantage at all times and exceed the company's expectations for your brand. You've been entrusted with this asset now it's up to you to make the most of it.

- Get below the surface to get a deep understanding of the marketplace, competition, customers, your brand and company capabilities. Understanding leads to knowledge, and knowledge is more than reciting facts. It's translating those facts into action that create impact.

- Get beyond the product you sell and think about the more satisfying customer experience you deliver to create and market "brands." This will be the basis for developing a long-standing relationship with target customers.

- Capture the intended, winning customer experience in the development of a unique brand idea and positioning strategy. Focusing on the intended experience takes you beyond giving stuff to providing meaning to target customers.

- While you need to achieve short-term goals maintain a focus on the long-term and speed its arrival through your strategies and actions (e.g., product development, new campaigns, among other works). Incorporating the long view will give you a lead on competition and enable you to create the brand's future as you help drive the market's future.

- Creatively segment the market and make choices to pursue those segments where you want and can win with your brand. These choices include those customers you will seek to serve and invest against as well as those you will not.

- Encourage the development of BIG, juicy ideas. Ideas make the world go around! They will motivate customers to specific behavior objectives (e.g., switching) and excite both support teams and your senior managers.
- Seek impact! Identify the two or three most significant actions (like BIG ideas) that you will undertake this year to accelerate brand growth above and beyond category growth.
- Discover legitimate and productive customer insights to better serve customers than your competition. Don't settle for unsights – those accepted customer beliefs (which at one time may have been legitimate insights), facts or generic needs. Make sure your brand, not product but the brand, can pay-off legitimate insights. Remember, it is not an insight if it does not lead to relevant, meaningful differentiation and impact.
- Understand the causal factors for brand performance versus goals. Importantly, understand those indicated actions to achieve your brand's goals. If you don't know the what, why and how, then how can senior managers possibly view you as a thought leader?
- Test, TEST, **TEST** to ensure that you are investing in proven strategies and actions that will not only generate incremental sales but also deliver a highly favorable ROI.
- Inspect what you expect. In other words, measure results versus expectations to gain invaluable feedback that can lead to better decisions in the future and productive adaptations. This is non-negotiable. It will advance you from gambling and squandering resources to investing for impact and a favorable ROI.
- Collaborate, COLLABORATE, **COLLABORATE** with your support groups (internal and external) to capture the collective wisdom of your team. Also, collaborate up the line. Gain the benefit of your senior managers' experiences and insights.
- Communicate, COMMUNICATE, **COMMUNICATE** to unify and keep everyone focused on the same page so that you achieve optimal execution. Repetition is good! Repetition is good! Repetition is good!
- Always seek to serve others, particularly your target customers, rather than yourself. This includes serving your team.
- Take time to celebrate the wins with the team and acknowledge their contributions to those wins!

- Then get back to finding new ways to win! Success can breed inertia and inertia opens the door for competition.

Remember, the organization is not going to anoint you with the role of brand president. You've got to earn it through thought leadership and practices. How do you stack up as a candidate for the position of brand president? Identify the top 2 to 3 things you need to do to make your role and marketing matter more and get started on them. Now!

CHAPTER 14

THE KAIZEN WAY TO SMARTER MARKETING!

改善

We returned from conducting a brand positioning strategy workshop in Japan for a new pharmaceutical product to be launched there. No, I haven't learned to speak Japanese, at least not yet. My primary language remains "marketing!" However, while in Japan, I was reminded of how Japan Inc. came to conquer the US automotive industry through kaizen. The characters above stand for kaizen in Japanese. Regardless of whether one speaks or reads the language it may serve one well to know the word "kaizen" and its meaning and put it into practice to make your marketing smart.

According to Wikipedia, the Japanese word means "change for the better." However, in English, for businesses who have adopted the Toyota Way (Toyota is noted for adopting and spearheading the practices of kaizen to achieve significant success), it has come to mean "continuous improvement." As Robert Maurer, Ph.D., author of *The Spirit of Kaizen: Creating Lasting Excellence One Small Step at a Time,* quotes Lao-tzu to Brett McKay in an *Art of Manliness* podcast, "A journey of a thousand miles begins with a single step." This single step is the 1% improvement that leads to producing big results.

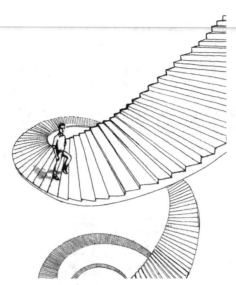

A journey of a thousand miles begins with a single step. **Lao-tzu**

Over the many years that Mike and I have been writing and publishing *DISPATCHES*, my *Marketing Matters* blogs, and through the pages of this book, I've provided you with thousands of actions for your consideration to make your marketing smart, one step at a time. As Robert Maurer says, making small improvements can lead to profound change and success. In this spirit, I'll share just one small thing that you can implement immediately to enhance your marketing and effectiveness as a manager, the 5 Cs checklist.

THE CHECKLIST MANIFESTO

As a former naval aviator in an age long ago (most likely before you, my devoted reader, were born), I learned the importance of religiously using checklists to ensure proper handling of my aircraft and avert potential disaster. Aviation has long used checklists to cut down on accidents. Atul Gawande, surgeon and author, picked up on the successful use of checklists in the world of aviation to deal with complexity and its consequences to apply it to, of all things, the world of surgery. He claims the use of a simple checklist he developed in collaboration with others, "reduced deaths and complications by more than one-third in eight hospitals around the world." His book,

The Checklist Manifesto, reveals the potential benefits of checklists in bringing about "striking improvements well beyond medicine," and, I would add, aviation.

Laval St. Germain, an airline pilot and adventurer, in another *Art of Manliness* podcast, "Life Lessons from an Adventurer," shared his habit of making and using checklists. He claims they've helped him with everything. He used checklists to help him conquer Mt. Everest without oxygen. He also employed them in his preparation and adventure in rowing solo across the Atlantic in 51 days. He even developed and applied a checklist to help his family and himself to overcome the tragic loss of his son in a canoeing accident. The use of checklists helps provide valuable direction and keep everyone on track for success.

ONE SMALL STEP ON YOUR JOURNEY TO MARKETING MANAGEMENT EFFECTIVENESS

While I, along with Mike, have developed checklists for assessing a creative brief, agency submissions and, even, coaching among many others, the one small step I am focusing on here is the 5 Cs checklist. I introduced it in "Chapter 3: Mis-Positioning (Brand) Positioning." You can use the 5 Cs checklist to assess and review your brand positioning and brand communication strategies, as well as your strategic thinking and proposals and that of others. I'm expounding upon it here. It addresses the question, "Is your work …"

1. **Clear:** Is the work or what others are saying clear? We take the word "clear" one step further to mean "incapable of being misunderstood." This requires considerable polishing as you check out with others whether or not your work and words are understood. One of the things to guard against is using fat words. These are imprecise and make it difficult for everyone to be on the same page. For example, a word often used in pharmaceutical marketing is "efficacy." Beyond suggesting something works, does it mean speed, quality, completeness, duration of relief, some combination, or something entirely different?

2. **Complete:** This means you've addressed all required fields. For example, when we review the target customer profile for the brand positioning strategy statement or creative brief does it include demographics, psychographics, patient-condition for healthcare brands or occasion-need state for consumer brands or patient-condition/procedure for medical device brands, and current usage & dissatisfactions. If not, it is not complete. Also, completeness includes being robust. Often, I'll hear managers criticize something for being too wordy. It's true we should not have one word too many or one word too few than necessary. We need the precise number of words to describe something and complete our thought. However, when you hear someone speaking who is filling in beyond the written word (appearing in a document or on a slide) to help you to understand it then you have a real inkling that the written word is incomplete!

3. **Competitive:** We need to drive preference for our brands versus the competition. Before you jump ahead and say, "We are not allowed to mention the competition," let me say that I'm not asking you to do so. One may be explicitly or implicitly competitive. If you cannot be explicitly competitive (i.e., name and compare your brand versus competitors), you must be implicitly competitive. Otherwise, one is not driving target customer preference that leads to using, prescribing, recommending or coming back to your brand. If you are satisfying dissatisfactions that the selected target customer is experiencing with competitive brands, then you are competitive.

4. **Cohesive:** "Cohesive" means that there is alignment with all parts of your positioning strategy, creative brief, etc. I could have used the word "alignment" but then we wouldn't have 5 Cs and would be sacrificing simplicity and memorability. An example of cohesiveness is the link between current usage and dissatisfactions in the target customer profile with the key thought (typically the point-of-difference or, better yet, point-of-preference benefit) in the creative brief. These have to match! Imagine you tell someone you're thirsty (a dissatisfaction that identifies a need) and, according to you, need water. If that someone

offers you something else, like a Snickers bar, then he did not align with your dissatisfaction and resultant need. It is not cohesive. Two other places to look for cohesiveness: the key thought must also link to the brand idea (the theme of the positioning strategy – your purpose); and the reasons-to-believe must link to the key thought.

5. **Choiceful:** Ah, this is about being single-minded. Senior managers in nearly every client company that we work with will extol value and encourage their marketers to make choices. I agree whole-heartedly. Unfortunately, these same managers fail to confront their marketers who are not being single-minded and, many times, add additional ideas. Choicefulness is not to suggest that you cannot have more than one benefit. If you are marketing a product that is a combination of analgesic and sleep-aid, then it needs to deliver pain relief and a soporific to help the target customer get to and stay asleep. Instead, what I'm referring to when I urge you to be single-minded is not having multiple themes or ideas. More is less. When we add yet another idea, we reduce the likelihood of success geometrically.

Give the 5 Cs checklist a try. Take out your current brand positioning strategy (If you don't have one, what are you waiting for? Get to work on it!), or creative brief, and use the 5 Cs checklist to identify areas for improving its productivity. By the way, this will work on assessing the effectiveness of your work and coaching others! It's a 1% solution that promises excellent yield.

Kaizen on!

CHAPTER 15

COACHING TO WIN

Coach, noun, *a vehicle for transporting people to a place*
they could not easily reach by themselves

Our job, as brand marketers, particularly for those of us who take ownership of the role of president of the brand, is to get our resource team members to execute consistent with the brand idea and develop *high-impact* ideas and executions. High-impact actions enable us to achieve a specified target customer behavior and realize "stretch" business objectives and build brand equity. When we talk about "stretch" business objectives, we are referring to strategies and actions that do not merely contribute to sales growth (although that would be a nice start) but turbo-charge it. So, for example, if the brand has been growing at 8%, the activity would contribute to helping triple the growth rate to 24%. Brand equity is the value the customer bestows upon our brand offering. It is the result of connecting target customers to the brand idea on an emotional level, leading to forging a special relationship with the brand. The effect is to command loyalty, despite attempted competitive inroads via discount pricing, new products, improvements, and so forth.

It takes skillful coaching to help get your resource team members to reach beyond their normative, *good* work to develop *excellent* work. "Good is the enemy of great." Moreover, if it is not great, it is not marketing excellence. Coaching is not about settling. "Good" is settling. That sucks as it does little to help make our marketing matter more. Coaching is about bringing out everyone's best.

239

Coaching not about evaluating, which is pointing out what is wrong with the work. Instead, coaching is about *add-valuating* (a term my business partner, Mike Maloney, coined), not evaluating, the work, which consists of properly assessing and then commenting on the needed direction to make the work more productive. The goal is to achieve, at a minimum, the SMART behavior objective for the specific marketing mix element and activity, or, better yet, stretch objectives.

There's a significant difference between coaching and evaluating! The act of evaluation identifies what someone judges is incorrect. It does not provide direction. It merely states, "this is incorrect." It could lead to feelings of personal attack and lack of recognition of what is correct. On the other hand, coaching points the way to improving the quality of the work. It does not criticize the work but lets the recipient of the coaching understand what needs to be done (i.e., the direction to take) to make it more productive.

To illustrate, imagine the CMO stops by your office and says, "I need you to come into my office immediately. I want to tell you why you're not getting promoted here!" That's evaluating. She is going to tell you everything you are doing wrong. It's scary. It also will put you on the defensive. As a result of her evaluating your performance, you are likely to shut down, protest or counter with the whys and wherefores. The practice of evaluating is far from being productive or helping others to be more productive.

On the other hand, imagine the CMO stops by your offices and says, "I need you to come into my office immediately. I want to tell you what you need to do to get promoted here!" The CMO is the same. The situation is the same. So is the tone, volume and intensity of the summons. Yet, there's a significant difference between the two statements. While the first, featured in the preceding paragraph, is evaluating, this second approach is one of coaching. There's also a significant difference in your response. While you rue the first, you are eager to hear and are receptive to coaching in the second.

A great coach can make the difference between a championship and also-ran season, or even a winning and losing season. When I think of great coaches the names Vince Lombardi and Phil Jackson spring to mind. (Today, it's Bill Belichick of the New England Patriots and Mike Krzyzewski of the Duke Blue Devil's Men's basketball team. Who is it in the time of your reading this book?)

Vince Lombardi represents old school coaching at its best. His football teams were winners, if not championship, teams. His Green Bay Packers were a shining example, winning three successive and five total Super Bowl championships in seven years. The Super Bowl trophy, for the best team in professional football, is named for him. Vince Lombardi got the best out of every one of his players, on every play. He demanded it. He drilled for excellence over and over until a given play was unstoppable, even when the opposing team knew it was coming.

Phil Jackson is the winningest coach in the history of professional basketball. He won 11 NBA (National Basketball Association) championships. He got his big-ego players, among them Michael Jordan, Dennis Rodman, and Scotty Pippen, to get along and play together, as a team, not as a collection of superstars.

These winning coaches were ardent students of the game. They could both soberly assess performance and knew how to direct their players to achieve levels of performance that these players could not easily reach without their coaching.

To be an effective coach, to achieve high-impact results from ideas and their execution, one needs to be able to assess skillfully and then provide relevant direction in an appropriate way to the proposed work produced by the specific resource team or one of its members. You cannot comment effectively (i.e., appropriately provide relevant direction) unless you *know what you think* about the work. Think first. Speak second. That's the way it needs to work.

The thinking part is where your assessment is critical. However, I'm not going to get deep into assessment here since it will vary somewhat by what you are assessing, including strategy, marketing mix element, and action. At the crux of assessing the work of others, and even your own, are the following four questions:

1. Is it consistent with the brand idea?
2. Is it a potentially BIG idea?
3. Will it lead to achieving the specific target customer behavior objectives identified for it?
4. Does the proposed execution maximize its potential?

If you are assessing a proposed strategy, you can use the 5 Cs checklist to assess the work. It will point the way to what needs to be done to make it clear, complete, competitive, cohesive and choiceful. Likewise, there's the Creative Brief ScoreCard, which will assist you in objectifying your subjective judgment as to the quality of the work that has gone into the creative brief.

If you are eager to learn more, check out the BDNI blogs *DISPATCHES* and *Marketing Matters* at www.bdn-intl.com You'll find the Creative Brief ScoreCard there along with other helpful checklists to assist in your assessment of work.

COMMENTING WITH SKILLFUL MEANS TO DIRECT YOUR RESOURCE TEAMS

We comment to direct our resource teams. Ah, this is the coaching part, delivering our assessment and providing direction. Coaching is a "skill" that is essential to develop if we are to make our marketing matter more in creating high-impact brand strategies and initiatives. However, few marketers possess the ability to comment with skillful means. (*Skillful means* is a Buddhist term. It means doing something, or commenting, in a way that improves the situation without causing collateral damage.) Here are some best practices for your consideration:

1. *Focus your assessment on the work.* Your assessment should start with identifying whether or not the work is consistent with the direction you provided, or if it meets the standards established for it. Again, if you are reviewing a strategy statement, you might want to use the 5 Cs checklist as it establishes essential, worthwhile standards. If you are reviewing proposed initiatives for a specific marketing mix element (e.g., advertising) check that it contains an idea (in the case of advertising, a campaign idea) that reflects the brand idea and is consistent with the direction you provided.

2. *Comment with skillful means.* Don't speak until you know what you think! Think before speaking is good advice in all walks of life, but it is difficult for all of us, including me. However, it is absolutely essential

if we are going to make sense with our coaching and earn the respect of the members of our resource teams. Once you are clear about how you feel about the work (based upon a disciplined assessment, such as the use of the 5 Cs checklist), here's how to comment with skillful means:

- **Start with an overview:** The overview lets the team or individual know where you stand regarding the quality of the work. This is your conclusion about the work product. It could be that your overview is that the work is ready to proceed to the next step, or that while it is close, it requires some additional work, or that we need to go back to the drawing board because it requires significant work.

- **Provide productive direction:** Don't talk about what you see that you don't like. That's evaluating. Instead, talk about what you need to see for the work to be more productive. That's coaching with skillful means. For example, in reviewing advertising, instead of saying, "The keywords don't communicate the key thought," say, "I need for the keywords to capture the key thought in customer language." Be specific with your direction but not prescriptive! Point the member of your team in the direction he needs to go and let him figure out how to get there. Avoid fat language, which is open to many varied interpretations.

- **Summarize next steps:** Let the individual or team know what you expect them to do next. Use this opportunity to crystallize the next steps to ensure understanding of what actions they are to take. Next-steps direction could include revising the proposed idea or developing a new one, adapting the work, demonstrating where the team may go with future iterations, etc.

3. *Learn to coach effectively.* Coaching is a skill. Like all skills, it needs to be developed experientially, through practice and feedback (the coach being coached). Coach Vince Lombardi is attributed as saying,

"Practice does not make perfect. Perfect practice makes perfect." So, we need to practice and get appropriate feedback from a skilled coach to enable us to take our practice and performance to the next level. If you are interested in developing your coaching skills (assessing and commenting) and improving the productivity of your work and that of others, make coaching a daily practice. Many opportunities arise each and every day, in all walks of life, for you to coach rather than evaluate. Make the most of them.

Coaching, rather than evaluating, will help make the work and your marketing matter more.

CHAPTER 16

SACRIFICE TO ACHIEVE MORE

I'm as proud of many of the things we haven't done as the things I have done.
Steve Jobs

Let's face it, we can't do everything we want. Sacrifices are a reality. Constraints such as budgets, time, attention, personnel resources and organizational commitment confront all brands and businesses. These constraints necessitate decision-making. Sacrifice is about *deciding* what *not* to do from among alternative opportunities. It's about choosing wisely to achieve more.

Some of the key strategic areas that require sacrifice include:

1. *Portfolio Management:* Our clients typically manage a plethora of brands, many competing in the same category or therapeutic area. Moreover, many have brands with multiple product lines and/or product offerings. The reality is that we cannot support all of them equally, nor would it make sense to do so. They possess different degrees of attractiveness as defined by strategic value, marketplace potential, targets served, income streams, profit margins, and so forth. Given a company budget of X-dollars, what brand should you first back? What specific product line or product within the brand? Item?

2. *Brand Positioning Strategy:* All marketers would agree with the statement "a brand, or business, can't be all things to all people." Agree, yes; practice, no! Marketers frequently violate this basic principle when developing brand positioning and advertising strategies. These violations may be driven by demands to make the numbers (as in sales, market share and profit), by lack of appreciation for the strategic and business value of alternate target constituencies and segments, by an inability to discern and/or crystallize the benefit proposition, etc. Among choices I address here are targeting and benefit selection:

- **Targeting:** Start by identifying the constituency that is most important to the brand. If you market a pharmaceutical product, you will need to choose from among health care practitioners, consumer-patients and any other constituencies you deem important to establishing your positioning. If it's a consumer product, it could be the purchaser, gatekeeper, user or, perhaps, retailer. Once a constituency has been selected, we choose from alternate target customer segments. In the words of Simon Sinek, an executive coach, our "goal is not to sell to everyone who needs what we have but to people who believe what we believe." What constituency and target customer segment within it is essential to establishing your brand? They will give you the biggest bang for your buck and the most significant return on marketing expenditures.

- **Benefit:** An all-too-common practice is to attempt to communicate everything about the product or brand. When we fail to be single-minded, we dilute, instead of strengthen, our value. Marketers throw in cost-of-entry benefits, or benefit promises that serve to counter potential customer objections, or benefits that are not relevant to achieving the communication behavior objective, as opposed to clearly focusing against a benefit promise derived from discovering a legitimate and productive customer insight that will lead to the achievement of your SMART communication behavior objective.

3. *Marketing Objective:* We must be clear on objectives before proceeding to marketing mix elements and tactics, particularly the marketing objective. The marketing objective is about customer behaviors. It ties directly to your business objectives. Basically, it comes down to choosing between "selling to people who are currently not purchasing your brand" or "selling more to current customers." When selling to non-purchasers, we must choose between adoption (i.e., getting people who are not category or segment purchasers into the category) or switching (i.e., converting competitive brand users to your brand). Selling more to current customers requires choosing from among the following: increasing transaction size, trading up customers to a new product in your line, increasing purchase frequency (i.e., compliance to pharmaceutical marketers) and getting customers to purchase longer (i.e., persistency or repeat purchasing, depending upon your sector).

You can determine the most appropriate marketing objective by computing the contribution of each to achieving your business objectives. For example, if you accomplish the behavior objective of switching 5% of competitive brand users, what will that mean to sales? What if you increase purchase frequency from 3.1 times per year to 4.0 times? Compute each to determine which will have the most significant impact on achieving the brand's business objectives. Factor in achievability. Then, decide what choice is best for your brand.

Can we have more than one marketing objective? Yes, most brands have more than one. However, you will need to use other marketing mix elements to achieve different objectives. For example, if the marketing objectives are to switch competitive users to your brand and increase frequency of purchasing among current customers, we might use advertising to achieve the former objective and promotion or a personalized media vehicle to achieve the latter.

4. *Marketing Mix Elements and Tactics:* There are many ways to promote and support a brand. We can choose from among product developments (e.g., product improvements and line extensions), advertising, public relations, trade and/or consumer promotions, clinical studies for new

indications, medical congresses, KOL development, etc. However, we can't make this selection until we first identify the key brand and business drivers. What returns do we earn (in market share, sales and profit growth) when we choose to invest in developing new indications versus participating in a medical congress or airing a television commercial? We should not be making marketing mix elements or specific program initiative decisions without first learning, through thoughtful analysis, the relative impact and return for each.

Make sacrificing a discipline. Here are some essential practices that can help you do smart marketing:

1. *Put everything to the 1-unit-of-currency (dollar, euro, yuan, whatever it may be) test.* Answer this: "If you only had one unit of currency to support your brand, where would you invest it?" What brand, line or product would you support? Whom would you market it to? What button(s) would you push? And, what would you promise? It's all about getting the biggest bang (i.e., highest sales impact and return-on-investment) for your money.

2. *Choose not to try and do everything.* This is a sure way to failure. Weigh the impact and return from your many opportunities. When we choose to invest in one brand, product line, constituency, target group, benefit promise, marketing objective, marketing mix element and tactic, we are making a clear choice not to invest in (or fully support) another. That's a sacrifice we have to make.

3. *Achieve critical mass with available resources.* If we can't achieve threshold support, we will be unable to achieve our goals. Critical mass is driven by the magnitude of goals, competitive position, and commitment. It's about more than where we put 1 unit of currency. It's also about where we put the second and third units. We shouldn't look to other opportunities until we have critical mass with the most promising one to make it work.

< = >
Less is more!

Adopt the discipline of sacrifice to achieve more. It's smart marketing.

Chapter 17

BEST PRACTICES FOR MARKETING TRAINING

conundrum (con-un-drum) *n.* an intricate and difficult problem

There needs to be a series of programs, each inter-related
and building upon the others.
Richard Czerniawski

Don't just train; mobilize for success!
Richard Czerniawski

Business managers today face a conundrum. As one manager put it, it's like "a Gordian knot"—a problem for which it is difficult to find a solution. The problem is that marketers are expected to grow sales, market share and profit while resources for marketing support are being slashed. This dichotomy is indeed our conundrum.

To solve it, we need to grow our capabilities. I use the word *capabilities* instead of *competencies* since the latter suggests that if you don't possess them, you are incompetent. I would hate to think any marketer is incompetent, wouldn't you?

Companies throughout the world recognize this need to grow individual and company capabilities to compete more effectively with, or without, less financial and/or people resources. This is why "marketing excellence" programs have sprung-up within many organizations. However, as pointed out in articles on my blogs, *DISPATCHES* and *Marketing Matters*, marketing excellence is nothing more than getting marketers to some norm of competency for many organizations. Whatever the norm, it is far from excellent.

The architects of organizational training need to approach this conundrum from different angles. The first thing to do is to identify clear goals. A key question to ask is, if the business needs to increase X% and resources are not growing as quickly, or if they are flat or even down Y%, then what percent do we need to grow the capabilities of our marketers and organization? If we don't grow individual and organizational capabilities, the likelihood of achieving our financial growth goals will become more like wishful thinking than predictable outcomes. Neither wishful thinking nor hope is an effective strategy. Establishing goals is a best practice for all functions within an organization, marketing included. Additionally, developing your people adds to the long-term value of the organization.

With these goals in mind, training needs to be developed and conducted to move people and the organization to climb up the capability ladder. But not all training programs are going to be equal. Like marketing efforts, the training programs of some organizations are non-productive while the training programs of others are highly productive. What's the difference? Here is what I've discovered to be the best practices for marketing training:

1. *Train for the mission.* It is amazing that organizations will take months and sometimes years to discover what competencies marketers need to be more effective. Doesn't the leadership know enough about marketing to know the role of its marketers and therefore what they need to be capable of doing? In the first place, the focus should not be on competencies. It should be on achieving the *mission.* A best practice for marketing training starts with training managers for their mission. This is no different from the military or sports teams. They train for their mission, whether it is on the field of battle or play. The mission of marketers is to build brands. Organizations that utilize best practices understand their mission to develop a *brand positioning strategy* and to manage *power positioning* that leads to creating brand loyalty, and they train for this.

    They understand the mission to develop *high-impact advertising* that establishes a relevant, meaningfully differentiated promise and that delivers it in a compelling campaign idea to achieve stretch business objectives.

They train for the mission to *discover legitimate and productive customer insights* that lead to a competitive positioning, repositioning or prositioning (i.e., proactive positioning evolution) strategy, new products and/or services and high-impact communications that drive customer preference.

They train their marketers to develop *marketing plans* that marry brand and business planning to generate predictable results.

They train their managers to *coach,* as opposed to evaluate, their resource teams to make planned activities more productive.

These are some of the essential missions for which they train their managers. As these organizations train their managers for the mission, the appropriate competencies are brought into play in an integrated manner and developed, not for their own end but to achieve the mission.

2. *Institutionalize the training into the operations of the organization.* Training for the mission assists in institutionalizing the practices, tools, and processes. While this is a good start, it is not enough. If the training program merely focuses on individual marketers, then it has done nothing more than build on the capabilities of select managers. It has not grown the capabilities of the organization. Individual and organizational capabilities must go hand-in-hand. Otherwise, the learning and skill development of the individual will not be fully utilized and leveraged by the organization.

Some managers will apply what they learn but the majority will not unless the organization adopts them in its operations. More than likely, many marketers will abandon the mission (such as developing a brand positioning strategy), even if they believe in it, because support for it by the organization leadership is absent (as perceived by senior leadership not demanding and reinforcing it). As a consequence, marketers will revert to performing those urgent but non-critical activities (such as email) as opposed to applying their talents to those critical but non-urgent activities, such as positioning the brand to gain a competitive advantage in the marketplace.

Best practice for institutionalizing learning demands that everyone, including senior leadership, undergoes training for the mission. Let's face it, no one in the marketing chain of command is beyond the need to be aware of, and skillful in, what is being trained if they are going to reinforce it on a daily basis in developing their managers and in accomplishing the mission, whether it be the development of a competitive brand positioning strategy or high-impact advertising.

Additionally, marketing support team members (such as advertising agency personnel, marketing research, and even product research and development) should be included in the training so all appreciate and can contribute to the achievement of the mission. Organizations rely on teamwork. All disciplines need to be pulling in the same direction if the mission is to be successful.

Finally, the principles, tools, practices, and processes are consciously adopted by the organization, becoming a part of the marketing planning, new product, and advertising development processes. For example, the positioning strategy statement and positioning matrix are incorporated into the marketing plan; the "tissue" session for the agency to share campaign ideas becomes a required step in the ad development process; the achievement of SMART marketing objectives are quantified and proven to the business objectives; etc.

Institutionalization is about putting the training into practice in daily operations.

3. ***Training is designed and conducted by expert practitioners and reinforced by marketing management leadership.*** Few people in a given organization are expert marketing practitioners with real-world successes. Fewer still have a broad view of marketing as practiced throughout the world, among different business sectors, companies and categories so they can capture and share *best practices* for achieving the mission. Fewer still can be objective and therefore willing to adopt new practices, tools, and processes that are different from how their organization currently perceives and does things. Moreover, fewer still will devote

all their time and one hundred percent of their being to training others as opposed to managing their brands. A best-training practice is to use *outside expert practitioners* (as opposed to internal managers or academic theorists); although, these organizations need to choose the expert practitioners that are best for their organization. (In the spirit of full disclosure, at BDNI, we are outside expert practitioners.)

It is not enough to just use the outside experts for training. Best-practice organizations include these experts as partners in the development of the training curriculum. The outside experts know the mission because they have successfully undertaken it. Importantly, they typically have a more realistic view of the capabilities and needs of individual marketers and the organization. Moreover, as mentioned previously, they have a view of practices that is broad, going well beyond one company, sector, category or even country. As a result, they can provide significant help with curriculum and individual program design.

Additionally, the best outside expert practitioners are ones who deliver *principle-based* instruction. They focus on principles and skill development as opposed to preaching dogma, which typically results from internal managers establishing company versus principle-based training programs. The "principles" organizations teach internally is usually dogma regarding how they do things. It undermines building critical thinking skills, and instead, it focuses on small-minded execution, which is devoid of sound strategic thinking.

However, best practices for marketing training also includes the utilization of the marketing management leadership within the company. It's not whether we should not use internal management resources for training but how they will be employed. Best practices call for leveraging senior managers, not for formal training but for the critically important, informal, day-to-day reinforcement of the principles, practices, tools, and processes essential to achieving the mission. As such, everyone aids and abets in the training to reinforce the formal training, building individual and organizational capabilities.

4. *It's a curriculum, not a one-time event.* Marketing managers and their organizations have many development needs. Organizations cannot address their multitude of needs with one program or one event. That is totally unrealistic. Even doctors and surgeons undergo "*continuing medical education*" to stay abreast of the latest information and to hone their skills. Professional athletes undergo training and practices before, throughout and following their seasons. There needs to be a series of programs, each inter-related and building upon the others.

   Additionally, best practices employ "familiar task transfer," where the learning and skill development in one mission carries over into another. For example, how we select and define the target customer for the brand positioning strategy is utilized in the same way to select and profile the target customer for any of our marketing mix elements, such as advertising. It includes the same elements, even though the advertising target customer could be a subset of the positioning target.

   Another example is to create relevant and meaningful differentiation in our brand positioning strategy, communication strategy and messaging. This recognizes the need for two fundamental practices: repetition and progression. Best practice is to have many practice occasions to be able to achieve the requisite skill levels. When we reach the desired skill level, it is essential to progress to the next level of expertise. Development, whether it is to be individual or organizational, is a process of iteration and progression.

5. *Develop skills versus merely imparting information.* Marketers have to be able to "*just do it.*" Organizations must be able to achieve the skill involved in accomplishing the mission. It's one thing to explain segmentation and to know, intellectually, what it is. However, it is an entirely different matter to have the requisite skills to be able to conduct market segmentation and to select a strategically appropriate target customer. To develop those necessary marketing skills, managers need to undergo experientially based training programs, where they learn not from lecture but from doing and receiving feedback on their work. It is in doing where real understanding takes place and skill development begins to take hold.

Managers also need sound coaching that provides them with appropriate feedback from expert practitioners so they may adapt their work while developing requisite skills.

6. *Measure, analyze, record and share learning from marketing activities to create a high-impact, performance-driven organization.* This separates the great from the good. Unfortunately, the vast majority of training programs overlook this essential practice. Great training organizations are learning organizations. They establish expectations for all activities and then inspect for what they expect.

But, it doesn't end there. There's the critical need to analyze the results, seeking understanding for actual performance versus expectations, and to memorialize the learning. The learning is shared throughout the organization. In this way, marketers create a learning culture and organization. Managers are thereby able to go beyond formal training programs and informal training to make every activity a learning laboratory for themselves and for the organization.

That's best-training practices for marketing! It takes the employment of best practices to enable us, and our organizations, to do smart marketing and to achieve the best results. It takes best practices to help us solve our conundrum. It takes best practices to go from doing dumb training to smart training to achieve smart marketing.

CHAPTER 18

COMMITTING TO MARKETING EXCELLENCE

The search for excellence is a never-ending quest
because once achieved, we need to take our performance to
yet a higher level.
Richard Czerniawski

As I write this, the New Year is just a few months away. How quickly the year has gone by. Many of us will be making resolutions for the new year. Undoubtedly, if we do, our resolutions will include what we hope to achieve in our work life. After all, we are all marketing professionals. One of the resolutions I hope you will make is to commit to achieving marketing excellence for yourself and your organization through instituting those proven principles, best practices and quality processes that define smart marketing.

In the previous chapter, I expressed my concern with the vast majority of marketing excellence programs and initiatives. As mentioned, these programs have typically been about getting marketers to perform up to some norm. However, the norm is not excellence. It's far from it. The norm is merely average performance. Excellence is about superior or outstanding performance. The search for excellence is a never-ending quest because once achieved, we need to take our performance to yet a higher level.

Dr. Atul Gawande, surgeon and author of *BETTER: A Surgeon's Notes on Performance*, explores variations in performance of health care practitioners and their organizations. Specifically, in his book, he relates significant differences in the performance of specialized centers for the treatment of cystic fibrosis. Those of us interested in achieving excellence, whether it is in marketing or in some other area, can learn from his discoveries.

Cystic fibrosis is a genetic disease that strikes children. The disease is recessive—both parents must be carriers and pass on the defective gene. A mutant protein interferes with the cell's ability to manage chloride in the body. The result is a thickening of secretions throughout the body. The thickening of secretions leads to blocking the flow of digestive enzymes in the pancreas. This, in turn, results in the child's inability to absorb food and grow strong. More critical, however, mucous fills, thickens and hardens in the small airways of the child's lungs. This significantly diminishes lung capacity and progresses until the lungs no longer function.

Dr. Gawande reports that 117 specialized treatment centers for cystic fibrosis, all having undergone and passed stringent certification, produce vastly different outcomes. Success, in this case, is not just another number; it means a real difference in keeping patients alive and thriving longer. Dr. Warren Warwick, a pediatrician, and his organization, Fairview-University Children's Hospital, is the positive deviant (or, as Malcolm Gladwell would call it, the "outlier"). He is keeping his patients alive and thriving for longer—significantly longer. No matter how well the other centers progress, his center keeps getting better. It outperforms the rest by a wide margin.

What makes Dr. Warwick and Fairview-University Children's Hospital achieve excellence in treating cystic fibrosis? His approach is *uncompromising*. He sets the bar exceedingly high and gets everyone (himself, the organization and his patients) to stretch for it. No exceptions. No excuses. If a patient's lung capacity diminishes from 109% to 90%, Dr. Warwick seeks to determine the cause and remedy it. While 90% may appear excellent to most healthcare providers, he is not satisfied. He wants more for his patients, and he will work with his patients to achieve it.

Dr. Warwick explains to Dr. Gawande that what may appear to be an insignificant difference daily can be profound when one reconsiders it within the context of a year. He states that someone with CF (cystic fibrosis) has a daily risk of getting a bad lung illness of only 0.5%, which appears rather insignificant. That someone receiving treatment has a 0.05% daily risk of illness. In other words, the patient has a 99.5% chance of staying well without treatment or 99.95% if she is undergoing treatment. Does that seem to be a big difference to you? I rather doubt it. I would wager that the vast majority of people would conclude that these are both excellent and virtually the same, particularly where the treatment is rather onerous (which it is with CF). But not Dr. Warwick. When viewed from the perspective of a year, it's the difference between a 16% chance of the patient getting through the year without getting sick or an 83% chance. Now that's something we can all agree is significant, especially if you are the patient, or one who is committed to keeping a child well or one who is seeking to achieve excellence.

	Daily Risk (%)		Annual (%)
	Getting Illness	Staying Well	Staying Well
CF	0.5	99.5	16
CF Plus Treatment	0.05	99.95	83

Significant progress has been made in the treatment of cystic fibrosis, thanks to the pioneering efforts of Dr. Warwick and his predecessor in this area, Dr. Leroy Mathews. According to Dr. Gawande, the average life expectancy of a CF patient back in 1957 was only 3 years of age. Today, a patient with cystic fibrosis has a life expectancy into their forties. CF patients can expect to live even longer under the care of Dr. Warwick. To him, averages mean nothing. He is a doctor on a mission, not just to treat but also to heal. He doesn't just measure patient performance; he adapts and innovates treatment protocol to extend and enhance the quality of his patients' lives.

Resolve to achieve marketing excellence by avoiding critical marketing errors and dumb marketing. Instead, adopt smart marketing practices. If you do, you are committing to being, like Dr. Warwick, a positive deviant or outlier.

RX FOR ACHIEVING MARKETING EXCELLENCE

Here are some final suggestions for achieving marketing excellence, both on a personal level and for your organization:

1. *Set the bar high, and don't compromise.* Being average doesn't amount to much. Sure, most people fall into the norm. But, you are committing to excellence, and the norm, or standard, is not the same thing. As Leo Burnett, the founder of the advertising agency that bears his name, stated, "When you reach for the stars, you may not quite get one, but you won't come up with a handful of mud either."

   The second part is to be unyielding in your quest. Do not compromise. Staying well on a given day of 99.5% is not enough for Dr. Warwick. He can do better and so can we. Accept no excuses. Make excellence happen.

2. *Measure everything and understand what the results mean.* Quantify what you expect or hope to achieve. Then, measure the results. If no such measurements exist, then go out and innovate in getting relevant measures. Importantly, get beyond the numbers to understand the reasons for variances, both positive and negative.

   Even if you believe you cannot quantify or get the measurements you need, find a way to "objectify your subjective judgment." Stick with best practices, processes, and principles. Find a way to score whether you and your organization are following them. For example, I have developed a creative brief scorecard to measure the potential effectiveness of a given creative brief. (If you are interested in receiving it, email me and I will forward it to you, or go to www.bdn-intl.com to find and download it.) It helps serve to indicate where and what work is needed to make the creative brief strategically appropriate and technically sound.

3. *Adapt and innovate.* Use your creativity to adapt plans and work to meet your expectations. A key difference will be your ability to innovate, to

go where others have not gone, or even dreamed possible, in achieving excellence. For example, Dr. Warwick created a mechanized chest-thumping vest for patients to wear. Thanks to his innovation, some 45,000 patients today can comply and persist with essential therapy to keep their lungs free of breath-suffocating mucous.

4. ***Work hard to execute flawlessly.*** Don't forget execution. Pay attention to each and every detail to ensure your implementation is perfect. Sometimes, the difference between excellence and the norm is superior execution.

5. ***Read BETTER: A Surgeon's Notes on Performance.*** Be an active reader and look for additional practices found throughout Dr. Gawande's book on improving performance.

Contrary to Charlie Munger's quote, avoiding doing dumb is not enough to win in the marketplace. Yes, it's a good place to start. However, if we are to realize the true potential of our assets, we need to be clear on what constitutes marketing excellence. We need to be committed to it and live it in everything we do in better serving target customers and building compelling brands.

WHERE / WHY MARKETING DOES MATTER

Start with the end in mind.

What you perceive you can achieve, or so I've been told.
Richard Czerniawski

There now exists a land where marketing matters. Oh, managers just don't say it matters; they know it matters because they drive line-of-sight incremental sales and market share growth. They build vibrant, healthy brands that enjoy the highest level of customer loyalty and performance ratings, from among the plethora of products that crowd their category. And, these marketers are recognized and rewarded for it. What goes on in this land where marketing matters?

The marketing department is led and comprised of career marketers. They are drawn to marketing with a strong sense of purpose. Being labeled a "marketer" is part of their identity. It is not something unseemly or anything to be ashamed of. In fact, they're proud of it. They market to serve and benefit their chosen target customers. When they fail to create a customer, they're troubled that they missed their mark in providing prospective customers with something of real value in uniquely satisfying their physical and emotional needs.

No, they don't believe they are second-class citizens or inferior to other functions within the company. Instead, they believe what Dr. Peter Drucker said: the purpose of the enterprise is to create customers, and marketing, along with innovation, is the essential and critical function for making this happen. They believe that marketing is at the center of all things in creating and maintaining customers and in growing healthy, enduring brands.

In this land, senior-most management recognizes and appreciates the role of marketing. They know in their hearts and minds that smart marketing is the way to be successful in this "age of abundance and sameness." Marketing is the chosen path to leverage corporate assets and to fuel the enterprise. So, the marketing function is fully utilized and challenged to do and matter even more.

Accordingly, marketers assume the role of brand presidents. It isn't that they started at the top. They started at the bottom of marketing, as brand assistants, where they began to learn the science of marketing. They toiled in the proverbial kitchen where they began cleaning pots and pans. They sweated for many years, working their way up the ladder to cook, then to sous chef, and finally to executive chef.

However, they know their role as brand president is an attitude in how they approach their position coupled with a way of managing the business. Their actual title may read manager, but the title on their business card doesn't really matter to them. They reach beyond to operate as brand president. It is how they perceive and undertake their role in serving customers. They occupy the proverbial hub of the wheel, and they provide direction to each of the spokes, the functions that support the brand, so the wheel runs true.

They know that their notion of being the brand president doesn't afford them carte blanche in managing their brands. They answer to a powerful board of directors—namely, everyone in their line to whom they report. While they have accountability for results, they do not have authority over the individual functional teams such as sales, manufacturing, etc. Therefore, they know they need to exhibit thought leadership if they are to be entrusted with managing their brand enterprise and getting all functional areas in the company to support the brand in creating a strong bond with customers through value-added experiences.

So, they reject eminence-based marketing, and instead, they embrace evidence-based marketing. There are no sacred cows. They question the way things have always been done by the company, category, and their competitors. Importantly, they learn from conducting adaptive experiments. They inspect for what they expect in everything they undertake. When they take a seat at the board table or sit down with the leadership of other functional areas, they come prepared with hard evidence, basing their conclusions and recommendations on facts. Their work is not a solo endeavor but enlists the efforts of these other functions in a highly collaborative endeavor, including conducting and analyzing the research itself.

Marketers are in search of relevant, meaningful differentiation in this land where marketing matters. They recognize that products are like eggs. They do the same things in the same ways and produce the same general results. How they serve up their eggs makes the difference in driving target customer preference and winning in the marketplace. So, they develop a competitive positioning for their brands. They recognize that positioning is the most important "P" in marketing. Each of their brands has a brand idea, and a supportive brand positioning strategy, that differentiates their offerings from competitive entities. Their positioning goes beyond what they say in their marketing communications. They reflect it in everything they do to transform mere products, compounds or services into brands.

They don't try to serve everyone who needs what they offer. Instead, these marketers target those prospective customers who believe what they believe. This is their first step in segmentation and target-customer selection. They know whom they intend to serve, their bull's-eye target customer of one. They also know whom they don't plan to expend energy in serving with their limited, precious resources. So, they don't dilute their efforts trying to be all things to all people. Instead, they target, so they can better serve their target customers rather than their competition. In this way, they make the most effective and efficient use of resources and can achieve higher growth acceleration rates, yielding more sales and profit, which they reinvest in their brands to create a virtuous cycle.

By the way, in this land, everyone understands that a brand is more than a product and that a product is more than the tangible aspects of the physical entity. They know there is much more in the whole product, which includes intangibles that have a tangible impact on success in establishing a connection with customers. So, they focus on creating the whole product to help create differentiation. The whole product includes intangibles, those things outside the box, such as the way they go about doing business with generous terms and added-value services.

Their focus goes beyond the product to the experience that they deliver to customers. They appreciate that they must get beyond products, whether it be the physical or the whole product, as fast followers may neutralize these. So, they seek to create a rewarding experience for their target customers that leads to forming a special bond between the customer and the brand, immunizing the brand from competitive inroads.

While they are acutely aware of tenders and deep price discounting by competitors, they are not troubled by them. Despite their premium pricing, their brands represent a value to their target customers. That's because their whole product is more desirable, the experience more rewarding and the brand idea more compelling. It is not merely the opinion of these marketers; they have evidence from conducting appropriate research, whether it be consumer, clinical, B2B, or some other form.

These marketers dig for legitimate and productive customer insights for their chosen target customer segment. They not only appreciate the value of customer insights, but they know the difference between unsights and insights. They use potential insights in ALL aspects of their marketing (e.g., brand idea, messaging, etc.) to generate BIG, juicy ideas because they know ideas make the world go around. However, they test their ideas to ensure they make a sizeable impact on sales and market share and produce an attractive ROI before they roll them out in the market.

In this land, the marketers have their eyes on the future and pull the organization along to bring it forward sooner and to get there before their competition. However, their goal is not to be first but to be right first. In this manner, they avoid issues of poor quality and out of stocks, which would hurt the reputation of their brands. Instead, they deliver a rewarding experience to their target customers that gives rise to creating evangelists and contributes to creating a virtuous cycle.

Messaging is strategically sound and compelling. It's proven to generate incremental sales and a positive ROI. It's no accident! That's because these marketers direct their messaging against achieving a SMART behavior objective for a chosen target customer. They know which behavior objective drives incremental revenue the most. They use legitimate and productive customer insight to develop their strategic messaging and to test it before undertaking creative development. Moreover, their creative brief is single-minded and technically sound. They deliver their brand's message with a BIG, juicy campaign idea that connects with target customers on an emotional level to achieve the target behavior objective.

In this land, the marketers are never satisfied. They'll take a moment to celebrate their wins. However, they are quick to return to work to make their brands more desirable and more attractive, and to make everything they do more productive. They neither overestimate their capabilities nor underestimate their competition. They address the failings of their brand and organization.

Additionally, they prepare for success but plan for failure. In this land, they undertake war games in an attempt to anticipate what competition might do and to identify measures to deflect, neutralize and defeat those competitive actions. They are prepared to respond intelligently as opposed to react blindly and badly. Moreover, they employ kaizen to squeeze a 1% improvement, day by day, in the product and everything the brand does in their relationship with customers, both current and prospective. They use checklists to assess the work supporting the brand and to inspect for what they expect.

These marketers, in this land, are idea people. Not that they are the font of all ideas; instead, they seek and encourage the generation of many ideas. They appreciate that ideas can make the difference between good and great performance campaign idea. As mentioned previously, they test these ideas to determine their ability to drive incremental sales and to compel preference.

In this land, marketing planning is taken seriously. Senior management actively participates, as they appreciate it is their map to creating brand loyalty and to achieving target business objectives of sales, market share, and profit. They are not mere judges of the plan but active collaborators. They put away their devices during marketing plan reviews to engage in a productive exchange. It is not a presentation meeting but a dialogue.

Everyone participating in marketing planning appreciates the importance of target-customer behavior objectives and their relationship to business objectives, key marketing objectives, objectives for marketing mix elements and tactics, etc. Moreover, they demand SMART objectives every step of the way. In this land, senior management sees the connection among the levels of target objectives. They follow the SMART objectives to confirm that the plan will achieve their business goals. All marketing plans contain the same essential elements, formats, and nomenclature. This homogeneity fosters clear thinking and a spirited dialogue regarding objectives, strategies, and actions.

In this land, marketers undergo training, not for training sake but to mobilize them in getting real work done on their brands that will make their marketing matter more. Training is designed and conducted by outside experts who have a broad view of training practices. There's no internal chest thumping that promotes conventional wisdom nor eminence-based marketing. It consists of workshops that address specific missions, such as developing high-impact communications or a "marketing by behavior objectives" marketing plan.

Accordingly, everyone attends these workshops, including the senior management who is responsible for approving marketing's work products, regardless of whether it is addressing the creative brief or the marketing plan, or developing high-impact brand communications. Everyone is on the same page, which means that proven principles, best practices, and quality processes are reinforced by those senior managers who've participated in the workshops. Their participation serves to help avoid critical marketing errors and to lead the progression of the marketing organization to marketing excellence. Not only are individual capabilities enhanced but so are those of the entire enterprise.

Coaching, not evaluation, is the way individuals and the organization develop in their unending quest to leverage talent, to achieve full potential, and to make the work products more productive. Coaching not only brings out the best work, transporting marketers to a place they could not reach on their own, but it transforms the coach into a thought leader and a more effective manager.

In this land, management understands the impact of marketing. It is not blind faith. It is true faith backed by evidence.

THE END (OR IS IT JUST THE BEGINNING?)

Well, we've come to the end of the book. Congratulations! However, there's more work to be done. I want to share one final story about what it takes and means to be a black belt.

I know what it takes, because I have multiple black belts. To be precise, I've earned four black belts in taekwondo and an additional four in hapkido. Does that make me an expert in each art? Hardly. It means I know a little more about what I don't know and cannot do. It means I have an opportunity to go deeper and really learn the meaning of these arts.

My acknowledgment is not a mark of humility. It is a recognition of fact. Earning a black belt is not the end; it is merely the beginning. The story goes that we begin with a white belt. It signifies that we are clearly at the start. As we go to work in the dojang (Korean word for a dojo, the place where we train and practice our martial arts), our white belt becomes soiled. It goes from white to gray. The more we train, the darker our belt becomes. There comes a time, many years and thousands of hours later, when our belt becomes black. We have achieved the rank of black belt.

Something curious occurs. As we continue to train, the black begins to chip off and fade away from our belt. It goes from black to gray, growing ever lighter with each day of training. There comes a time, many years and thousands of hours later, when our black belt returns to white. This transformation from black belt to white signifies a return to the beginner's mind, where we know how to learn and all things are possible.

Here's wishing you well in advancing to black belt and back to white in making your marketing matter even more.

THANK YOU!

Thank you for reading *AVOIDING CRITICAL MARKETING ERRORS: How to Go from Dumb to Smart Marketing*. I hope you found it informative and thought provoking. I also hope it has shined a light on what you can do to bring your marketing to the next level in your quest to achieve genuine marketing excellence.

If you'd like to keep up on proven principles, best practices and quality processes to make your marketing matter more, I'd encourage you to go to www.bdn-intl.com and subscribe to *DISPATCHES* and *Marketing Matters*—two blogs that I write (the former with Mike Maloney) on all things marketing. They're free and I've found that marketers who read them get promoted faster. (OK, I'm joking about "getting promoted faster." However, reading them sure wouldn't hurt your prospects for promotion.) Both *DISPATCHES* and *Marketing Matters* are written in real time. In other words, while what I share is timeless, the examples are current and up to the minute.

If you'd like to go deeper, consider a workshop. This isn't training for training sake but mobilizing to get real work done. In other words, we'll work on your brand(s) with your brand team(s). Or, if you need a speaker who can inspire your marketing team to improve their performance, I'd be pleased to assist you. If you are interested, contact me (see below) for more information.

Now, I've a favor to ask—well, actually two. I believe that if I get one useful thing out of a book, it is well worth my investment in money and time. I hope you took away many useful things from my book. If you did, I would so appreciate it if you'd provide a review and star rating that reflects your opinion.

Secondly, if you feel this book has been helpful then, perhaps, you'll recommend it to your other marketers, your brand teammates, senior management and, even, purchase it for your department.

Finally, I feel we, marketers, are family. I'd enjoy hearing from you and your experiences. You can reach me as follows:

Website: www.bdn-intl.com
Email: richardcz@bdn-intl.com
Phone: 847-312-8822

Again, thank you and Godspeed in your journey in marketing and in life.

Peace and best wishes,

Richard Czerniawski

SUGGESTED READING

O h, there's so much to learn and yet so little time. However, if you don't take the time, you'll find yourself falling behind. All it takes is to get one idea from a book that can make a difference in your life and marketing. That makes the price of the book a bargain to my way of thinking. Below you'll find some of my suggestions for your consideration.

Let's start with two books I coauthored with my business partner, Mike Maloney. These books don't' tell the reader "what" to think but, instead, focus on "how" to think about marketing. Plus, these books are loaded with tools, practical advice and real-world examples.

- *CREATING BRAND LOYALTY: The Management of Power Positioning and Really Great Advertising.* Richard D. Czerniawski and Michael W. Maloney (AMACOM, 1999). This book has been called "the definitive guide," "the bible," among other labels, for developing really great advertising—as in achieving stretch business objectives.

- *COMPETITIVE POSITIONING: Best Practices for Creating Brand Loyalty.* Richard D. Czerniawski and Michael W. Maloney (Hudson House, 2010). Positioning is the mother of all marketing—the Alpha and

Omega. This book is the Alpha and Omega for creating a competitive and enduring positioning strategy to build a healthy brand.

Then there are those books that I found illuminating and inspiring:

- *Poor Charlie's Almanack: The Wit and Wisdom of Charles T. Munger.* Charles T. Munger (Author), Peter D. Kaufman (Editor) (Donning, 2005). Mr. Munger is Warren Buffet's quick-witted, sharp-spoken partner. It's well worth your investment in the cost of the book and the time to read and re-read it. One of his quotes about avoiding doing dumb, inspired the underlying theme and sub-title for my book, *AVOIDING CRITICAL MARKETING ERRORS: How to Go from Dumb to Smart Marketing.*

- *BETTER: A Surgeon's Notes on Performance.* Atul Gawande (Picador, 2007). While written by a surgeon, this goes well beyond surgery with principles that will help anyone interested in doing better to achieve better performance.

- *THE CHECKLIST MANIFESTO: How to Get Things Right.* Atul Gawande (Metropolitan Books, 2009). Another book from the surgeon and author on the use of checklists to help avoid failure.

- *Different: Escaping the Competitive Herd.* Youngeme Moon (Crown Business, 2010). Refreshing. Hopefully, it will help you see things differently and encourage you to ditch conformity.

- *ZAG: The #1 Strategy of High-Performance Brands.* Marty Neumeier (New Riders, 2007). Mr. Neumeier calls for "radical differentiation." I love his analogy of playing "rock, paper, scissors" to the evolution of companies.

- *The Marketing Imagination.* Theodore Levitt. (The Free Press, 1983). C' mon, Professor Levitt is a legend!

- *SELLING THE INVISIBLE: A Field Guide to Modern Marketing.* Harry Beckwith (Warner Books, Inc., 1997). So simple, yet so profound.

- *Difference: The One-Page Method for Reimagining Your Business and Reinventing Your Marketing.* Bernadette Jiwa. (The Story of Telling Press, 2014). It's not just about being different but creating a difference that matters.

- *THIS IS MARKETING: You Can't Be Seen Until You Learn to See.* Seth Godin (Portfolio/Penguin, 2018). This is Seth Godin! Reading and listening to Mr. Godin, you are blessed with wisdom, authenticity and conscience. By the way, he's the author of scores of excellent books on marketing.

- *Start with Why.* Simon Sinek (Penguin, 2011). It will inspire you to discover your, and your brand's, "Why." Check him out on YouTube. I've seen his talk on "Why" scores of times.

- *Ogilvy on Advertising.* David Ogilvy (Prion Books Ltd., New Ed edition 2007). Here's wisdom on advertising from the man dubbed "The Father of Advertising."

- *Advertising Pure and Simple.* Hank Seiden (AMACOM, 1990). A true professional, a great creative director and a very dear human being. I'm privileged to have known and worked with him. He makes advertising all so pure and simple.

- *Differentiate or Die: Survival in Our Era of Killer Competition.* Jack Trout with Steve Rivkin (Wiley, 2010). Jack Trout, along with Al Reis, have been key influencers in competitive marketing thinking. You might also want to read the *22 Immutable Laws of Marketing* and *Positioning: The Battle for Your Mind*—both of which were written by Messrs. Trout and Reis.

- *The TOM PETERS SEMINAR: Crazy Times Call for Crazy Organizations.* Tom Peters (Vintage Books, 1994). Tom Peters is brilliant and irreverent. The perfect combination for managing the modern-day chaos of the marketplace and corporate management. Don't stop with this one. Dig into: *The Circle of Innovation, The Little BIG Things; 163 Ways to Pursue Excellence, Thriving on Chaos: Handbook for A Management Revolution, Re-imagine!: Business Excellence in a Disruptive Age,* and discover more. Bust through conventional thinking!

- *THE FIFTH DISCIPLINE: The Art & Practice of The Learning Organization.* Peter M. Senge (Doubleday Currency, 1990). This book blew me away when I first read it. I've since read it three more times. It is about overcoming the learning disabilities prevalent in organizations and making learning a competitive advantage. It's as relevant today as it was when it was written nearly 30 years ago. I think it is virtually impossible to become a high-performance organization without making learning a practice.

> *Develop into a lifelong self-learner through voracious reading; cultivate curiosity and strive to become a little wiser every day.*
> **Charles T. Munger**

Read and apply your learning.

ABOUT THE AUTHOR

Richard D. Czerniawski is the founder of Brand Development Network International, Inc., a marketing resource company dedicated to empowering marketers to create brand loyalty and achieve genuine marketing excellence. Richard has held every position in brand marketing, from brand assistant to brand manager to chief marketing officer to general manager. He has even served as a director on the board of a start-up, during his more than 45-year career with brand building companies such as Procter & Gamble, Johnson & Johnson and the Coca-Cola  Company, where he has contributed to the success of well-known brands such as Folger's Coffee, REACH Toothbrush, Band-Aid Brand Adhesive Bandages, and Coca-Cola Classic—among others. He also has extensive experience and achievements across a broad spectrum of sectors including pharmaceutical and medical device and diagnostics. Moreover, his work is international in scope, providing expert consulting and training services to some of the world's largest and most successful multi-national companies and brands.

Richard is co-author of two books on marketing management: *CREATING BRAND LOYALTY: The Management of Power Positioning and Really Great Advertising*, and *COMPETITIVE POSITIONING: Best Practices for Creating Brand Loyalty*. Additionally, he is the author of hundreds of articles on marketing management for the two blogs he writes and publishes on marketing: *DISPATCHES* and *Marketing Matters*. He has lectured and conducted workshops for undergraduate and MBA programs at Notre Dame Mendoza College of Business, Northwestern Medill School of Journalism, DePaul University, Lake Forest College, and Thunderbird International School of Management.

Richard is a former naval aviator and achieved the rank of Lt. Commander. He also holds 8 black belts in martial arts. He is a 4th-dan black belt in both taekwondo and hapkido. He was a co-founder of the Moodo Martial Arts Club, where he served as the lead instructor. His additional interests include physical fitness and reading. He has recently begun studying clarinet and Brazilian Jiu-Jitsu; he has found both to be quite humbling.

Richard received an MBA and was selected to "Who's Who in American Colleges and Universities."

He has been married for 49 years. He has 3 daughters and 4 granddaughters.

Richard can be reached at (847) 312-8822 and richardcz@bdn-intl.com. For more information about Richard, and to subscribe to his blogs, go to www.bdn-intl.com.

INDEX

A

AAdvantage Loyalty Program, 69–70
accepted customer belief (ACB), 127
accountability, 81, 266
actions: brainstorming, 187, 188, 190; decisive, 184; for insights, 142–43; intended, 108, 170; planning, 189–90; potential, 184; remedial, 180; sequential, 184; significant, 231
activities: competitive, 189; essential high-impact, 190; inherited, 111; non-critical, 253
ad idea, 200–1
Adams, Scott, 166
added-value offerings, 45, 68
adjunctive behavior, 116–17
adoption behavior, 114; and conversion, 114; and switching behaviors, 112–13
advertising: campaign, 54, 64, 158, 201; campaign idea, 199–200; *vs.* power positioning, 30–31; target customer, 256
AFib, 23
age of abundance and sameness, 23, 76, 194, 202, 207, 266
Amazon, 52–53, 62, 83, 196, 198
Amazon Prime, 35–36, 52–53, 62, 89
American Airlines, 49–51, 62, 63, 68, 69; ConciergeKey, 50–51, 59, 62
AMEX (American Express), 51, 52, 58, 62–63, 137–38

Angelou, Maya, 159
Apple, 14, 35, 45, 49, 53–54, 63, 190, 196, 198
aspirational/launch positioning, 30
assessment, focusing on work, 242
AstraZeneca (AZ), 202
attitudes, 127; brand president, 266; about condition, 106; target customer, 33, 133, 159
attitudinal barrier, 130–31
authentic behaviors, 113–18, 121–23
authority, 61, 213
awareness: and access, 112; and trial, 154
AXE, 28, 197, 201

B

"bad" behaviors, 111–13
BDNI, 20, 36, 40, 104, 142, 194, 229, 242, 255
bdn-intl.com, 242
BDNI Customer Insight Tool, 135–36, 148, 158, 194
BDNI Litmus Test Tool, 144–45
behavior objectives, 109, 110–11, 119; communication, 158; essential, 113; SMART, 121–23, 215; for target customer, 134
behaviors, target customer: authentic, 113–18, 121–23; "bad," 111–13, 123; correct, 119–20; critical, 113;

E

F

CPSIA information can be obtained
at www.ICGtesting.com
Printed in the USA
LVHW102226140720
660731LV00011B/1362